Better Homes and Gardens

cook once eat twice

SLOW COOKER RECIPES

MEAL
TONIGHT
1

MEAL
TOMORROW
2

Meredith Books
Des Moines, Iowa

BETTER HOMES AND GARDENS® COOK ONCE EAT TWICE
Editor: Carrie Holcomb
Contributing Project Editor: Karen Davis
Contributing Writer: Winifred Moranville
Contributing Graphic Designer: The Design Office of Jerry J. Rank
Copy Chief: Terri Fredrickson
Publishing Operations Manager: Karen Schirm
Senior Editor, Asset & Information Management: Phillip Morgan
Edit and Design Production Coordinator: Mary Lee Gavin
Editorial Assistant: Cheryl Eckert
Book Production Managers: Pam Kvitne, Marjorie J. Schenkelberg,
   Rick von Holdt, Mark Weaver
Contributing Copy Editor: Amanda Knief
Contributing Proofreaders: Jeanette Astor, Monica Bruno, Gretchen Kauffman
Contributing Indexer: Elizabeth T. Parson
Test Kitchen Director: Lynn Blanchard
Test Kitchen Product Supervisor: Marilyn Cornelius
Test Kitchen Home Economists: Elizabeth Burt, R.D., L.D.; Juliana Hale;
   Laura Harms, R.D.; Maryellyn Krantz; Greg Luna; Jill Moberly; Dianna Nolin;
   Colleen Weeden; Lori Wilson; Charles Worthington

MEREDITH® BOOKS
Executive Director, Editorial: Gregory H. Kayko
Executive Director, Design: Matt Strelecki
Managing Editor: Amy Tincher-Durik
Senior Editor/Group Manager: Jan Miller
Senior Associate Design Director: Ken Carlson
Marketing Product Manager: Gina Rickert

Publisher and Editor in Chief: James D. Blume
Editorial Director: Linda Raglan Cunningham
Executive Director, Marketing: Steve Malone
Executive Director, New Business Development: Todd M. Davis
Executive Director, Sales: Ken Zagor
Director, Operations: George A. Susral
Director, Production: Douglas M. Johnston
Director, Marketing: Amy Nichols
Business Director: Jim Leonard

Vice President and General Manager: Douglas J. Guendel

BETTER HOMES AND GARDENS® MAGAZINE
Deputy Editor, Food and Entertaining: Nancy Hopkins

MEREDITH PUBLISHING GROUP
President: Jack Griffin
Executive Vice President: Bob Mate

MEREDITH CORPORATION
Chairman and Chief Executive Officer: William T. Kerr
President and Chief Operating Officer: Stephen M. Lacy

In Memoriam: E.T. Meredith III (1933–2003)

All of us at Meredith® Books are dedicated to providing you
with the information and ideas you need to create delicious
foods. We welcome your comments and suggestions.
Write to us at: Meredith Books, Cookbook Editorial Department,
1716 Locust St., Des Moines, IA 50309-3023.

Our seal assures you that every recipe
in *Cook Once Eat Twice* has been
tested in the Better Homes and
Gardens® Test Kitchen. This means
that each recipe is practical and
reliable, and meets our high standards
of taste appeal. We guarantee
your satisfaction with this book for
as long as you own it.

cook once eat twice

CONTENTS

cook once eat twice

cook once eat twice slow cooker recipes

WILL CHANGE THE WAY YOU THINK ABOUT LEFTOVERS. THEY'RE NO LONGER SOMETHING TO BE TOLERATED OR SHUFFLED AROUND IN THE FRIDGE UNTIL YOU FINALLY THROW THEM AWAY. THEY'RE SOMETHING TO SAVOR—THE SPRINGBOARD FOR MEALS YOU'LL LOOK FORWARD TO ALL DAY, THE NEW BEGINNINGS FOR RECIPES YOU'LL BE PROUD TO SHARE WITH FAMILY AND FRIENDS.

You make one delicious meal, then another day, with a few quick tricks and fresh ingredients transform the leftovers into an imaginative, exciting, and wholly satisfying new meal. These are more than just leftovers—the term conjures up something you eat because it's there, not because it's something you crave.

Here's how it works. Flip through the book and choose a recipe that intrigues you. How about Balsamic-Sauced Pork Roast for a weekend dinner with friends? Or Moroccan Short Ribs for a globally inspired bistro-style dinner? Craving Mexican? You'll find all kinds of choices, from Mole Chicken on Polenta to Adobo Pork Tostadas. And now that your kids have discovered that they love Buffalo Chicken Wings when dining out why not bring the favorite home, in a main-dish version made with drumsticks? Whether you're looking for something guest-worthy, weeknight-perfect, or kid-friendly, you'll find a recipe that is sure to hit the spot.

Next cook up the recipe in your trusty slow cooker—the appliance you've long appreciated for its fix-and-forget ease. Every recipe has been tested and perfected by the experts in the Better Homes and Gardens® Test Kitchen, so you know you'll get surefire results every time.

Stash a bonus batch in the refrigerator or freezer for later. When you prepare and enjoy these recipes, you'll notice something—beyond how easy they are to make and how good they are to eat. You'll see that each recipe makes two batches, one to enjoy now and one to hide away to use later. No guesswork needed—each recipe tells you how and how long to store this extra batch.

Another day, cook up something new—in minutes. Take that bonus batch and add a few creative twists and turns. Presto—dinner's ready. With a tortilla here, a pizza crust there, some pasta, cheese, or fresh-and-lively stir-ins, you're on your way to a whole new meal. That pork roast becomes Pork and Noodles—so comforting after a busy day. The Moroccan Short Ribs morph into Moroccan Pita Pizza. And the Mole Chicken on Polenta becomes lickety-split Mole Chicken Tostadas. You'll love the way one great meal leads to another again and again throughout this book.

And check out the bonus chapters: One offers easy five-ingredient slow cooker entrées; and the other features desserts and sides—exciting extras that make the meal!

cook once eat twice

meats

you've always loved
the way meaty cuts
cooked up to tender
succulence in the
slow cooker.
so little effort—
so many great rewards!
now check out how
each hearty and satisfying
recipe makes a stunning
comeback in an all-new
fabulous dinner.

1

herb-rubbed pot roast

THIS IS IT! THAT EASY BUT SPECIAL SLOW-COOKED POT ROAST RECIPE YOU'VE BEEN LOOKING FOR. SERVE IT WITH RICE OR HOT BUTTERED PASTA TOSSED WITH PARMESAN CHEESE.

PREP
20 MINUTES

COOK
11 HOURS (LOW) OR
5½ HOURS (HIGH)

MAKES
6 SERVINGS + RESERVES

1	teaspoon dried oregano, crushed
1	teaspoon dried basil, crushed
1	teaspoon fennel seeds, crushed
½	teaspoon dried thyme, crushed
2	1½- to 2-pound boneless beef chuck pot roasts
1	tablespoon olive oil
4	medium carrots, cut into 1-inch pieces
3	medium parsnips, cut into 1-inch pieces
1	large onion, sliced
⅓	cup beef broth
⅓	cup red wine or beef broth
3	tablespoons quick-cooking tapioca
2	tablespoons tomato paste
4	cloves garlic, minced
	Hot cooked rice (optional)

STEP 1 Stir together oregano, basil, 1 teaspoon black pepper, fennel seed, ½ teaspoon salt, and thyme. Set aside. Trim fat from meat. Brush oil over all sides of meat. Sprinkle herb mixture over meat; rub in with your fingers.

STEP 2 In a 5- or 6-quart slow cooker stir together carrot, parsnip, onion, broth, wine, tapioca, tomato paste, and garlic. Add meat.

STEP 3 Cover and cook on low-heat setting for 11 to 12 hours or on high-heat setting for 5½ to 6 hours.

STEP 4 Remove meat from cooker. Chop enough meat to make 2½ cups (12 ounces); store as directed below. Transfer remaining meat and all of the vegetables to a serving platter. Skim fat from juices. If desired, serve meat, vegetables, and juices with hot cooked rice.

TO STORE RESERVES Place meat in an airtight container. Seal and chill for up to 3 days. (Or freeze for up to 3 months. Thaw in refrigerator overnight before using.) Use in *Beef Enchilada Casserole*, page 9.

NUTRITION FACTS
PER SERVING
430 CAL., 8 G TOTAL FAT
(2 G SAT. FAT), 89 MG CHOL.,
346 MG SODIUM,
48 G CARBO., 6 G FIBER,
37 G PRO.

DAILY VALUES
176% VIT. A, 22% VIT. C,
8% CALCIUM, 32% IRON

EXCHANGES
2½ STARCH, ½ OTHER
CARBO., 4 LEAN MEAT

beef enchilada casserole

THIS IS A FAMILY-FRIENDLY CASSEROLE FOR A MEXICAN-FOOD-LOVING FAMILY. HINT: THE BOTTLED SALSA IS OPTIONAL, BUT USING YOUR FAVORITE BRAND OF SALSA IS A GREAT WAY TO PERSONALIZE THIS DISH TO YOUR OWN TASTES.

1	cup chopped onion (1 large)
3	cloves garlic, minced
1	tablespoon olive oil
2	10-ounce cans mild or hot enchilada sauce
	Reserved meat from Herb-Rubbed Pot Roast* (see recipe, page 8)
½	teaspoon ground cumin
¼	teaspoon ground cinnamon
1½	cups shredded Monterey Jack, Chihuahua, or cheddar cheese (6 ounces)
10	6-inch corn tortillas, cut into 1-inch-wide strips
	Dairy sour cream (optional)
	Bottled salsa (optional)

STEP 1 In a large saucepan cook onion and garlic in hot oil over medium heat until tender. Reserve ¼ cup of the enchilada sauce; set aside. Stir remaining enchilada sauce, reserved meat, the cumin, and cinnamon into saucepan. Bring to boiling; remove from heat.

STEP 2 Spoon half of the meat mixture into a greased 2-quart rectangular baking dish. Sprinkle with ½ cup of the cheese. Top with half of the tortilla strips. Spoon remaining meat mixture over tortillas. Sprinkle with ½ cup cheese. Top with remaining tortilla strips. Pour reserved ¼ cup enchilada sauce over tortillas. Cover with foil.

STEP 3 Bake, covered, in a 350°F oven about 35 minutes or until heated through. Remove foil. Sprinkle with remaining cheese. Bake, uncovered, for 5 to 7 minutes more or until cheese melts. If desired, serve with sour cream and salsa.

* There should be 2¼ cups chopped reserved meat.

PREP
30 MINUTES

BAKE
40 MINUTES

OVEN
350°F

MAKES
6 SERVINGS

NUTRITION FACTS
PER SERVING
382 CAL., 16 G TOTAL FAT (7 G SAT. FAT), 70 MG CHOL., 615 MG SODIUM, 33 G CARBO., 2 G FIBER, 26 G PRO.

DAILY VALUES
11% VIT. A, 6% VIT. C, 28% CALCIUM, 26% IRON

EXCHANGES
2 STARCH, 3 LEAN MEAT, 1 FAT

1

mushroom onion pot roast

HERE'S POT ROAST JUST THE WAY YOU LOVE IT, WITH TENDER MEAT THAT FALLS APART WITH THE NUDGE OF A FORK AND A RICHLY FLAVORED, MUSHROOM-LACED SAUCE.

PREP
30 MINUTES

COOK
10 HOURS (LOW) OR
5 HOURS (HIGH)
+ 5 MINUTES

MAKES
4 SERVINGS + RESERVES

1	3-pound boneless beef chuck pot roast
½	teaspoon salt
¼	teaspoon black pepper
2	tablespoons cooking oil
2	large onions, halved and sliced ¼ inch thick (about 4 cups)
3	cups small button mushrooms, sliced
1	10.5-ounce can condensed beef consommé
½	cup dry red wine
4	cloves garlic, minced
1	teaspoon dried thyme, crushed
2	tablespoons cornstarch
2	tablespoons cold water
2	cups hot mashed potatoes

STEP 1   Trim fat from meat. Sprinkle meat with salt and pepper. In a very large skillet brown roast on all sides in hot oil over medium heat; set aside. In a 5- or 6-quart slow cooker place onion and mushrooms. Top with meat. Stir together consommé, wine, garlic, and thyme. Pour over meat in cooker.

STEP 2   Cover and cook on low-heat setting for 10 to 12 hours or high-heat setting for 5 to 6 hours.

STEP 3   Reserve and shred one-third of the beef (about 9 ounces). Remove 1 cup of vegetables and reserve 1½ cups of cooking liquid. Store as directed below.

STEP 4   Place remaining meat on a platter; keep warm. Place remaining cooking liquid and vegetables in a medium saucepan. Stir together cornstarch and the cold water; stir into saucepan. Cook and stir over medium heat until thickened and bubbly; cook and stir 2 minutes more. Serve meat, vegetables, and sauce over hot mashed potatoes.

TO STORE RESERVES Place meat, vegetables, and cooking liquid in separate airtight containers. Seal and chill for up to 3 days. Use in French Dip Sandwich with Red Wine au Jus, page 11.

NUTRITION FACTS
PER SERVING
523 CAL., 18 G TOTAL FAT
(5 G SAT. FAT), 135 MG
CHOL., 958 MG SODIUM,
30 G CARBO., 3 G FIBER,
55 G PRO.

DAILY VALUES
5% VIT. A, 25% VIT. C,
6% CALCIUM, 38% IRON

EXCHANGES
½ VEGETABLE, 2 STARCH,
7 LEAN MEAT

french dip
sandwich with red wine au jus

WHEN IT COMES TO FRENCH DIP SANDWICHES, THE MOISTER THE BETTER! THIS VERSION GETS EXTRA OOZINESS FROM THE RESERVED MUSHROOM AND ONION MIXTURE AND SLICES OF PROVOLONE CHEESE.

4   **French-style rolls or hoagie buns, split**
     Reserved Mushroom Onion Pot Roast* (see recipe, page 10)
8   **slices provolone cheese (6 ounces)**

STEP 1   Preheat broiler. Hollow out bottoms of rolls. Divide reserved meat and vegetables among roll bottoms. Place 2 slices provolone cheese on top of each.

STEP 2   Broil 3 to 4 inches from the heat for 3 to 4 minutes or until cheese melts and sandwiches are heated through. Top sandwiches with tops of rolls.

STEP 3   Meanwhile, in a small microwave-safe bowl microwave cooking liquid on 100 percent (high) power about 1 minute or until heated through. Serve sandwiches with heated liquid for dipping.

* There should be about 1½ cups (9 ounces) shredded reserved meat, 1 cup reserved vegetables, and 1½ cups reserved cooking liquid.

START TO FINISH
20 MINUTES

MAKES
4 SERVINGS

NUTRITION FACTS
PER SERVING
718 CAL., 24 G TOTAL FAT (10 G SAT. FAT), 96 MG CHOL., 1500 MG SODIUM, 73 G CARBO., 5 G FIBER, 49 G PRO.

DAILY VALUES
8% VIT. A, 3% VIT. C, 46% CALCIUM, 40% IRON

EXCHANGES
5 STARCH, 5 LEAN MEAT, 1 FAT

moroccan-spiced beef

IS YOUR POT ROAST IN NEED OF A MAKEOVER? THE KICKY MOROCCAN SEASONINGS RAMP UP THE SLOW-COOKER STANDBY. COUSCOUS MAKES A QUICK ACCOMPANIMENT.

PREP
25 MINUTES

COOK
10 HOURS (LOW) OR
5 HOURS (HIGH)

MAKES
6 SERVINGS + RESERVES

1	3½- to 4-pound boneless beef chuck pot roast
1	tablespoon curry powder
2	teaspoons ground cumin
1½	teaspoons salt
¼	teaspoon black pepper
⅛	teaspoon cayenne pepper
2	medium onions, cut into thin wedges
2	14.5-ounce cans diced tomatoes
½	cup beef broth
3	cups hot cooked couscous

STEP 1 Trim fat from roast; set roast aside. In a small bowl stir together curry powder, cumin, salt, black pepper, and cayenne pepper; rub into roast on all sides.

STEP 2 Place the onion in a 5- or 6-quart slow cooker. Place roast on top of onion. Pour undrained tomatoes and broth over roast.

STEP 3 Cover and cook on low-heat setting for 10 to 11 hours or on high-heat setting for 5 to 5½ hours.

STEP 4 Skim fat from pan juices. Reserve half of the roast and half of the onion mixture; store as directed below. Serve remaining roast and onion mixture over couscous.

TO STORE RESERVES Shred reserved roast. Place beef and onion mixture in an airtight container. Seal and chill for up to 3 days. (Or freeze for up to 3 months. Thaw in refrigerator overnight before using.) Use in Beef and Vegetables over Rice, page 13.

NUTRITION FACTS
PER SERVING
278 CAL., 5 G TOTAL FAT (2 G SAT. FAT), 78 MG CHOL., 534 MG SODIUM, 23 G CARBO., 2 G FIBER, 32 G PRO.

DAILY VALUES
15% VIT. C, 5% CALCIUM, 23% IRON

EXCHANGES
1½ STARCH, 4 LEAN MEAT

beef & vegetables over rice

ADD A FEW WELL-CHOSEN, FLAVOR-PACKED STIR-INS TO THE RESERVED MOROCCAN-SPICED BEEF AND YOU WILL HAVE A SATISFYING STEW THAT'S FINISHED IN THE TIME IT TAKES TO COOK THE RICE.

START TO FINISH
20 MINUTES

MAKES
6 SERVINGS

Reserved Moroccan-Spiced Beef* (see recipe, page 12)

1½ cups thinly sliced carrot (3 medium)

1 tablespoon olive oil

½ cup golden raisins

⅛ cup mango chutney

2 tablespoons snipped fresh cilantro

3 cups hot cooked rice

2 tablespoons pine nuts, toasted

STEP 1 Remove any fat from surface of reserved beef mixture; discard fat. In a large skillet cook carrot in hot oil over medium heat about 4 minutes or until tender. Stir in beef mixture, raisins, and chutney; heat through. Stir in cilantro.

STEP 2 Serve beef mixture over rice. Sprinkle with pine nuts.

* There should be at least 1½ pounds shredded reserved beef mixed with about 2½ cups reserved onion mixture.

NUTRITION FACTS
PER SERVING
406 CAL., 9 G TOTAL FAT
(2 G SAT. FAT), 78 MG CHOL.,
591 MG SODIUM,
48 G CARBO., 3 G FIBER,
33 G PRO.

DAILY VALUES
70% VIT. A, 23% VIT. C,
8% CALCIUM, 32% IRON

EXCHANGES
3 STARCH, 4 LEAN MEAT

italian pot roast

ALTHOUGH BOTH ADD FLAVOR, CONSIDER CHOOSING FENNEL OVER CELERY TO ADD DELICATE SWEETNESS AND A HINT OF LICORICE.

PREP
20 MINUTES

COOK
9 HOURS (LOW) OR
4½ HOURS (HIGH)

MAKES
4 SERVINGS + RESERVES

1	3-pound boneless beef chuck pot roast
1	teaspoon garlic salt
1	teaspoon fennel seeds, crushed
½	teaspoon black pepper
2	medium fennel bulbs, trimmed, cored, and chopped, or 2 cups chopped celery (4 stalks)
1½	cups chopped carrot (3 medium)
1	cup chopped onion (1 large)
1	26-ounce jar pasta sauce
2	to 3 cups hot cooked penne pasta
	Grated Parmesan cheese (optional)

STEP 1 Trim fat from roast. In a small bowl stir together garlic salt, fennel seeds, and pepper; rub into roast on all sides.

STEP 2 In a 5- or 6-quart slow cooker stir together fennel, carrot, and onion. Place roast on top. Pour pasta sauce over roast in cooker.

STEP 3 Cover and cook on low-heat setting for 9 to 10 hours or on high-heat setting for 4¼ to 5 hours.

STEP 4 Reserve one-third of the roast and 2 cups of the sauce; store as directed below. Serve remaining roast and sauce over hot cooked pasta. If desired, sprinkle with Parmesan cheese.

TO STORE RESERVES Chop reserved roast (about 2 cups). Place beef and reserved sauce in separate airtight containers. Seal and chill for up to 3 days. Use in Beef & Olive Calzones, page 15.

NUTRITION FACTS
PER SERVING
535 CAL., 13 G TOTAL FAT
(4 G SAT. FAT), 134 MG
CHOL., 944 MG SODIUM,
47 G CARBO.,
6 G FIBER, 55 G PRO.

DAILY VALUES
76% VIT. A, 15% VIT. C,
7% CALCIUM, 42% IRON

EXCHANGES
2 STARCH, 1 OTHER CARBO.,
7 LEAN MEAT

beef & olive calzones

A COMPLETE MEAL PACKAGED IN A GOLDEN PASTRY AND
BURSTING WITH DELIGHTFUL SURPRISES MAKES FOR A TRUE
WEEKNIGHT GIFT.

	Nonstick cooking spray
1	10- to 13.8-ounce package refrigerated pizza dough
	Reserved beef and sauce from Italian Pot Roast* (see recipe, page 14)
1	cup finely shredded Italian cheese blend (4 ounces)
¼	cup sliced, pitted ripe olives

STEP 1   Line a baking sheet with foil; lightly coat foil with cooking spray.
Unroll pizza dough on prepared baking sheet. Cut dough in half crosswise
and lengthwise to make 4 rectangles; set aside.

STEP 2   In a blender or food processor puree reserved sauce. In a medium
bowl stir together ⅓ cup of the pureed sauce, the reserved beef, cheese, and
olives. Place about ½ cup beef mixture in center of each dough rectangle. For
each calzone, fold a short edge of a dough rectangle over filling to opposite
edge, stretching slightly if necessary. Seal edges with the tines of a fork.
Arrange calzones so they are evenly spaced on the baking sheet.

STEP 3   Prick tops of calzones to allow steam to escape. Bake, uncovered,
in a 400°F oven for 18 to 20 minutes or until golden. Let cool for 5 minutes
before serving. Meanwhile, in a small saucepan heat remaining pureed
sauce; serve with calzones.

* There should be about 2 cups reserved beef and 2 cups reserved sauce.

PREP
20 MINUTES

BAKE
18 MINUTES

COOL
5 MINUTES

OVEN
400°F

MAKES
4 SERVINGS

NUTRITION FACTS
PER SERVING
165 CAL., 17 G TOTAL FAT
(6 G SAT. FAT), 87 MG CHOL.,
951 MG SODIUM,
40 G CARBO., 4 G FIBER,
37 G PRO.

DAILY VALUES
39% VIT. A, 8% VIT. C,
21% CALCIUM, 29% IRON

EXCHANGES
3 STARCH, 4 LEAN MEAT,
½ FAT

beef stew in rich red wine sauce

WITH NICELY TENDER BEEF AND VEGETABLES, JUST THE RIGHT AMOUNT OF HERBS, AND A WINE-ENHANCED BROTH, STEW PERFECTION IS ACHIEVED! HINT: A CALIFORNIA PINOT NOIR IS A GOOD CHOICE FOR THIS RECIPE—AS WELL AS FOR THE WINE YOU SERVE WITH THE STEW.

PREP
25 MINUTES

COOK
8 HOURS (LOW) OR
4 HOURS (HIGH)

MAKES
4 SERVINGS + RESERVES

3	pounds beef stew meat, cut into ¾-inch cubes
2	tablespoons cooking oil
2	medium onions, cut into wedges
2	cups sliced carrot (4 medium)
2	cups sliced celery (4 stalks)
4	cloves garlic, minced
1	cup dry red wine
1	cup beef broth
3	tablespoons quick-cooking tapioca
1	teaspoon salt
1	teaspoon dried basil, crushed
1	teaspoon dried thyme, crushed
1	teaspoon dried rosemary, crushed
1	teaspoon black pepper
4	cups hot cooked mashed potatoes

STEP 1 In a very large skillet brown beef, half at a time, in hot oil over medium heat. Drain off fat. Place beef in a 5- or 6-quart slow cooker. Stir in onion, carrot, celery, garlic, wine, broth, tapioca, salt, basil, thyme, rosemary, and pepper.

STEP 2 Cover and cook on low-heat setting for 8 to 10 hours or on high-heat setting for 4 to 5 hours.

STEP 3 Reserve 4 cups stew; store as directed below. Serve remaining stew over hot cooked mashed potatoes.

TO STORE RESERVES Place stew in an airtight container. Seal and chill for up to 3 days. (Or freeze for up to 3 months. Thaw in refrigerator overnight before using.) Use in Sherried Beef Stroganoff, page 17.

NUTRITION FACTS
PER SERVING
549 CAL., 13 G TOTAL FAT
(4 G SAT. FAT),
125 MG CHOL.,
1,309 MG SODIUM,
50 G CARBO.,
5 G FIBER, 49 G PRO.

DAILY VALUES
84% VIT. A, 29% VIT. C,
11% CALCIUM, 36% IRON

EXCHANGES
1 VEGETABLE, 3 STARCH,
5 LEAN MEAT

sherried beef stroganoff

CLASSIC STROGANOFF INGREDIENTS COMBINE WITH THE BEEF
STEW YOU HAVE STASHED AWAY FOR A SECOND MEAL THAT'S
EQUALLY AS ELEGANT AS THE FIRST!

1	8-ounce carton dairy sour cream
1	tablespoon all-purpose flour
2	cups sliced fresh mushrooms
1½	cups frozen small whole onions
1	tablespoon cooking oil
	Reserved Beef Stew in Rich Red Wine Sauce* (see recipe, page 16)
¼	cup dry sherry
2	cups hot cooked egg noodles

STEP 1 In a small bowl stir together sour cream and flour; set aside. In a large skillet cook mushrooms and onions in hot oil over medium heat for 5 to 7 minutes or until onions are tender. Stir in reserved stew and sherry; heat through.

STEP 2 Stir in sour cream mixture. Cook and stir until thickened and bubbly. Cook and stir for 1 minute more. Serve over noodles.

* There should be 4 cups reserved stew.

START TO FINISH
25 MINUTES

MAKES
4 SERVINGS

NUTRITION FACTS
PER SERVING
563 CAL., 25 G TOTAL FAT
(10 G SAT. FAT), 132 MG
CHOL., 507 MG SODIUM,
38 G CARBO., 3 G FIBER,
38 G PRO.

DAILY VALUES
63% VIT. A, 6% VIT. C,
12% CALCIUM, 32% IRON

EXCHANGES
1 VEGETABLE, 2 STARCH,
4½ LEAN MEAT, 2 FAT

asian flank steak

HOISIN SAUCE—A REDDISH-BROWN BEAN SAUCE FLAVORED WITH SOY, VINEGAR, GARLIC, CHILES, AND SESAME—MAKES IT EASY TO ADD A LOT OF FLAVOR WITHOUT ADDING EXTRA INGREDIENTS. THE HINT OF ORANGE ADDS A LITTLE SOMETHING EXTRA TOO.

PREP
35 MINUTES

COOK
8 HOURS (LOW) OR
4 HOURS (HIGH)
+ 30 MINUTES

MAKES
4 SERVINGS + RESERVES

¾	cup hoisin sauce
¾	cup orange juice
¾	cup beef broth
¼	cup dry sherry or orange juice
2	tablespoons bottled minced garlic (12 cloves)
1	teaspoon ground ginger
2	tablespoons quick-cooking tapioca
1½	cups bias-sliced carrot (3 medium)
1	large onion, thinly sliced
3	pounds flank steak
1½	cups snow pea pods, trimmed
1½	cups red sweet pepper strips (2 medium)
2	cups hot cooked white or brown rice

STEP 1 In a 4- or 5-quart slow cooker stir together hoisin sauce, orange juice, beef broth, sherry, garlic, and ginger. Sprinkle with tapioca. Stir in carrot and onion. Trim fat from steak; add steak to cooker.

STEP 2 Cover and cook on low-heat setting for 8 to 9 hours or on high-heat setting for 4 to 4½ hours.

STEP 3 If using low-heat setting, turn to high-heat setting. Add pea pods and red peppers to cooker. Cover and cook for 30 minutes more.

STEP 4 Remove steak from cooker and thinly slice across the grain. Reserve 12 ounces of steak (about ⅓). Remove vegetables with slotted spoon; reserve ¾ cup. Reserve 1¾ cups of the cooking juices. Store reserved steak, vegetables, and juices as directed below.

STEP 5 Serve remaining steak, vegetables, and broth over hot cooked rice.

TO STORE RESERVES Place steak, vegetables, and juices in an airtight container. Seal and chill for up to 3 days. Use in Warm Soba Noodle Salad, page 19.

NUTRITION FACTS

PER SERVING
568 CAL., 16 G TOTAL FAT
(6 G SAT. FAT), 85 MG CHOL.,
647 MG SODIUM,
48 G CARBO., 3 G FIBER,
52 G PRO.

DAILY VALUES
81% VIT. A, 96% VIT. C,
9% CALCIUM, 29% IRON

EXCHANGES
½ VEGETABLE, 1½ STARCH,
1½ OTHER CARBO.,
6½ LEAN MEAT

warm soba noodle salad

SOBA NOODLES ARE NATIVE JAPANESE NOODLES MADE OF BUCKWHEAT FLOUR AND WHEAT FLOUR. LOOK FOR THEM IN THE ETHNIC OR PASTA SECTION OF YOUR SUPERMARKET OR NATURAL FOOD STORE. HINT: FOR ADDED FLAIR, TOP THE PREPARED SALAD WITH A SPLASH OF SOY SAUCE.

8	ounces dry soba noodles
1	cup frozen edamame (green soybeans)
	Reserved steak mixture from Asian Flank Steak* (see recipe, page 18)
1 ½	cups chopped yellow sweet pepper (1 ½ cups)
1	8-ounce can sliced water chestnuts, drained
¼	cup sliced green onion (2)
¼	cup chopped cashews
	Soy sauce (optional)

STEP 1 In a Dutch oven cook noodles in boiling salted water for 5 minutes. Add edamame; return to boiling. Cook for 3 to 5 minutes more or until noodles are tender. Drain.

STEP 2 Meanwhile, in a very large skillet heat reserved steak mixture over medium heat until heated through, stirring occasionally. Stir in noodle mixture, sweet pepper, and water chestnuts; heat through. Sprinkle with green onion and cashews. If desired, serve with soy sauce.

* There should be 12 ounces reserved steak, ¾ cup reserved vegetables, and 1¾ cups reserved cooking juices.

START TO FINISH
30 MINUTES

MAKES
4 (2-CUP) SERVINGS

NUTRITION FACTS
PER SERVING
716 CAL., 21 G TOTAL FAT (5 G SAT. FAT), 51 MG CHOL., 640 MG SODIUM, 90 G CARBO., 8 G FIBER, 50 G PRO.

DAILY VALUES
54% VIT. A, 382% VIT. C, 39% CALCIUM, 39% IRON

EXCHANGES
1 VEGETABLE, 4 STARCH, 1½ OTHER CARBO., 5 LEAN MEAT, ½ FAT

beef, bean & corn fajitas

JUST WHEN YOU THOUGHT YOU HAD EXPERIENCED EVERY KIND OF TAKE ON FAJITAS, HERE COMES A HEAD-TURNING VERSION. THE SOMETHING-EXTRA SECRET IS IN THE CRUNCHY, CREAMY, AND REFRESHING CUCUMBER SALAD TOPPING.

PREP
15 MINUTES

COOK
8 HOURS (LOW) OR
4 HOURS (HIGH)

MAKES
6 SERVINGS + RESERVES

2	large red onions, cut into thin wedges (4 cups)
2	pounds beef stew meat, cut into ¾-inch cubes
2	teaspoons chili powder
1	teaspoon garlic salt
2	cups frozen whole kernel corn
1	15- to 16-ounce can black beans, rinsed and drained
2	14.5-ounce cans Mexican-style stewed tomatoes, cut up
½	of a small cucumber, seeded and chopped
½	of a small jicama, peeled and chopped
¼	cup snipped fresh cilantro
12	7- to 8-inch flour tortillas, warmed*
½	cup dairy sour cream and/or purchased guacamole

STEP 1 Place red onion in a 5- or 6-quart slow cooker. In a medium bowl toss beef with chili powder and garlic salt; add to cooker. Top beef with corn, beans, and undrained tomatoes.

STEP 2 Cover and cook on low-heat setting for 8 to 9 hours or on high-heat setting for 4 to 4½ hours.

STEP 3 Using a slotted spoon, remove beef and vegetables from cooker. Reserve half of the beef and vegetable mixture (about 4 cups) and 1 cup of the cooking juices; store as directed below.

STEP 4 Stir together cucumber, jicama, and cilantro. Divide remaining beef and vegetables among tortillas. Top with cucumber mixture and sour cream.

* To warm tortillas, wrap in foil and place in a 350°F oven for 15 minutes.

TO STORE RESERVES Place beef and vegetable mixture and 1 cup cooking juices in an airtight container. Seal and chill for up to 3 days. (Or freeze for up to 3 months. Thaw in refrigerator overnight before using.) Use in Cheesy Double-Corn & Beef Squares, page 21.

NUTRITION FACTS
PER SERVING
406 CAL., 11 G TOTAL FAT
(4 G SAT. FAT), 52 MG CHOL.,
711 MG SODIUM,
53 G CARBO., 4 G FIBER,
25 G PRO.

DAILY VALUES
14% VIT. A, 38% VIT. C,
13% CALCIUM, 27% IRON

EXCHANGES
1 VEGETABLE, 3 STARCH,
2 LEAN MEAT, ½ FAT

cheesy double-corn & beef squares

IF YOU ENJOYED THE ZESTY FLAVORS OF THE BEEF, BEAN & CORN FAJITAS, YOU'LL ALSO LOVE THEM IN THIS SAUCY BEEF AND VEGGIE CASSEROLE. IT'S TOPPED WITH CILANTRO-SPECKED CORN BREAD AND PEPPER JACK CHEESE.

Nonstick cooking spray

Reserved beef and vegetable mixture from Beef, Bean & Corn Fajitas*
(see recipe, page 20)

¼	cup tomato paste
1	8-ounce package corn muffin mix
¼	cup snipped fresh cilantro
⅓	cup milk
1	egg
1	cup shredded Monterey Jack cheese with jalapeño peppers or Monterey Jack cheese (4 ounces)
½	cup bottled salsa

STEP 1 Lightly coat a 2-quart square baking dish with cooking spray. Set aside.

STEP 2 In a large saucepan stir together reserved beef and vegetable mixture and tomato paste. Heat over medium heat for 5 minutes or just until bubbly, stirring occasionally.

STEP 3 In a medium bowl stir together muffin mix and cilantro. In a small bowl whisk together milk and egg. Add to muffin mix mixture; stir just until combined.

STEP 4 Pour hot beef mixture into the prepared dish; sprinkle with ½ cup of the cheese. Spoon batter over top; spread gently to cover. Sprinkle with remaining cheese.

STEP 5 Bake, uncovered, in a 400°F oven for 20 minutes or until a wooden toothpick inserted into the center of the corn bread comes out clean. Cut into squares and serve with salsa.

* There should be 4 cups beef and vegetable mixture combined with 1 cup cooking juices.

PREP
15 MINUTES

COOK
5 MINUTES

BAKE
20 MINUTES

OVEN
400°F

MAKES
4 SERVINGS

NUTRITION FACTS
PER SERVING
661 CAL., 21 G TOTAL FAT (8 G SAT. FAT), 147 MG CHOL., 1,394 MG SODIUM, 76 G CARBO., 5 G FIBER, 45 G PRO.

DAILY VALUES
19% VIT. A, 44% VIT. C, 30% CALCIUM, 34% IRON

EXCHANGES
1 VEGETABLE, 5 STARCH, 4 LEAN MEAT, 1 FAT

wine-braised beef brisket

GOT THE WEEKNIGHT "WHAT'S FOR DINNER" BLUES? YOU'LL SING ANOTHER TUNE WHEN YOU COME HOME TO A TENDER BRISKET WITH A WINE-ENHANCED SAUCE. SERVE WITH MASHED POTATOES FOR COMFORT FOOD AT ITS FINEST.

PREP
30 MINUTES

COOK
10 HOURS (LOW) OR
5 HOURS (HIGH)

MAKES
6 SERVINGS + RESERVES

1	4-pound fresh beef brisket
2	cups thinly sliced carrot (4 medium)
1	cup finely chopped onion (1 large)
1	cup dry red wine
1/3	cup tomato paste
2	tablespoons quick-cooking tapioca
1	tablespoon Worcestershire sauce
2	teaspoons garlic salt
2	teaspoons liquid smoke
1 1/2	teaspoons chili powder
3	cups hot cooked mashed potatoes

STEP 1 Trim fat from beef. If necessary, cut beef to fit in a 4- or 5-quart slow cooker. Place carrot and onion in cooker. Top with beef. In a medium bowl stir together wine, tomato paste, tapioca, Worcestershire sauce, garlic salt, liquid smoke, and chili powder; pour over brisket in cooker.

STEP 2 Cover and cook on low-heat setting for 10 to 12 hours or on high-heat setting for 5 to 6 hours.

STEP 3 Remove beef from cooker. Using a slotted spoon, remove vegetables from cooker. Reserve half of the beef (about 1 pound), 1 cup of the vegetables, and 1 cup of the cooking juices; store as directed below. Slice remaining beef; serve with vegetables, cooking juices, and mashed potatoes.

TO STORE RESERVES Place beef in an airtight container. Place vegetables and cooking juices in a second airtight container. Seal and chill for up to 3 days. Use in Brisket Pie, page 23.

NUTRITION FACTS
PER SERVING
355 CAL., 11 G TOTAL FAT
(4 G SAT. FAT), 96 MG CHOL.,
641 MG SODIUM,
25 G CARBO., 3 G FIBER,
33 G PRO.

DAILY VALUES
46% VIT. A, 16% VIT. C,
4% CALCIUM, 21% IRON

EXCHANGES
1 1/2 STARCH, 4 LEAN MEAT

brisket pie

STAY ON THE COMFORT-FOOD BUS! TRANSFORM YOUR LEFTOVER HOME-COOKED BRISKET INTO A DELIGHTFULLY HEARTY AND MOIST CASSEROLE OF CHOPPED BEEF AND VEGGIES TOPPED WITH TALL GOLDEN BISCUITS.

Reserved Wine-Braised Beef Brisket* (see recipe, page 22)

1	cup frozen whole kernel corn
½	cup chopped sweet green pepper (1 small)
1	cup shredded cheddar cheese (4 ounces)
1	cup milk
2	eggs, slightly beaten
2	cups packaged biscuit mix
¼	teaspoon onion salt

STEP 1 Chop the reserved beef (about 4 cups). In a large saucepan combine chopped beef, reserved vegetables and juices, the corn, sweet pepper, and ³⁄₄ cup of the cheese. Bring to a boil, stirring occasionally; transfer to a 2-quart rectangular baking dish.

STEP 2 In a small bowl stir together milk and eggs. In a medium bowl stir together biscuit mix and onion salt. Add milk mixture to biscuit mixture and whisk until nearly smooth. Pour batter over hot beef mixture in baking dish.

STEP 3 Bake, uncovered, in a 350°F oven about 30 minutes or until top is lightly browned. Sprinkle with remaining cheese. Let stand for 10 minutes before serving.

* There should be about 1 pound reserved beef, 1 cup reserved vegetables, and 1 cup reserved cooking juices.

PREP
25 MINUTES

BAKE
30 MINUTES

STAND
10 MINUTES

OVEN
350°F

MAKES
6 SERVINGS

NUTRITION FACTS PER SERVING
577 CAL., 25 G TOTAL FAT (10 G SAT. FAT), 188 MG CHOL., 1,046 MG SODIUM, 42 G CARBO., 2 G FIBER, 43 G PRO.

DAILY VALUES
55% VIT. A, 22% VIT. C, 26% CALCIUM, 29% IRON

EXCHANGES
3 STARCH, 5 LEAN MEAT, 1½ FAT

braised corned beef dinner

THIS IS SLOW COOKING AT ITS BEST! EVERYTHING—MAIN DISH AND SIDES—COOKS UP TOGETHER FOR A MEAL YOU'LL LOOK FORWARD TO COMING HOME TO ALL DAY. BE SURE TO USE LIGHT BEER BECAUSE REGULAR BEER CAN MAKE THE DISH TASTE A LITTLE BITTER.

PREP
15 MINUTES

COOK
10 HOURS (LOW) OR
5 HOURS (HIGH)

MAKES
4 SERVINGS + RESERVES

4	medium red potatoes, quartered
4	carrots, peeled and cut into 1½-inch pieces
2	medium onions, peeled and cut into thin wedges
2	teaspoons dried thyme, crushed
1	bay leaf
1	3-pound corned beef brisket, juices and spices reserved
1	12-ounce bottle light beer

STEP 1   In a 5- or 6-quart slow cooker, place potato, carrot, onion, thyme, and bay leaf. Trim fat from beef and place beef on top of vegetables. Pour the reserved juices and spices from brisket and the beer over beef and vegetables in cooker.

STEP 2   Cover and cook on low-heat setting for 10 to 11 hours or on high-heat setting for 5 to 5½ hours.

STEP 3   Discard bay leaf. Thinly slice beef across the grain. Reserve half of the sliced beef (about 1 pound); store as directed below. Using a slotted spoon, remove vegetables from slow cooker; reserve broth. Serve remaining sliced beef with vegetables. Drizzle some broth over top; pass remaining broth.

TO STORE RESERVES Place beef in an airtight container. Seal and chill for up to 2 days. Use in Reuben Panini, page 25.

**NUTRITION FACTS
PER SERVING**
478 CAL., 21 G TOTAL FAT
(6 G SAT. FAT), 86 MG CHOL.,
1,195 MG SODIUM,
37 G CARBO., 5 G FIBER,
29 G PRO.

DAILY VALUES
135% VIT. A, 106% VIT. C,
7% CALCIUM, 31% IRON

EXCHANGES
½ VEGETABLE, 2½ STARCH,
3 MEDIUM-FAT MEAT, 1 FAT

reuben panini

REUBEN SANDWICHES ARE A CLASSIC—AND ONE OF THE MOST
BELOVED—WAY TO USE LEFTOVER CORNED BEEF. THE BEVERAGE
OF CHOICE IS ALSO A NO-BRAINER: A BEER WOULD BE PERFECT!
ROUND OUT THE MEAL WITH A GOOD DELI POTATO SALAD.

¼   cup bottled Thousand Island salad dressing
8   slices rye bread
     Reserved beef from Braised Corned Beef Dinner* (see recipe, page 24)
1   cup canned sauerkraut, rinsed and drained
4   slices Swiss cheese (3 to 4 ounces)

STEP 1   Spread 1 tablespoon dressing on each of 4 slices of bread. Top each
with sliced corned beef, ¼ cup sauerkraut, cheese, and remaining bread.

STEP 2   Lightly grease the rack of a covered indoor electric grill. Preheat
grill to medium heat. Place sandwiches on grill rack; close the lid. Grill for
5 to 10 minutes or until bread is toasted and cheese is melted. (Or lightly
grease a large heavy skillet. Heat skillet over medium heat. Place sandwiches,
half at a time if necessary, in skillet; top with a heavy cast-iron skillet. Cook
for 5 to 10 minutes or until bread is toasted and cheese is melted, turning
once halfway through cooking time.)

* There should be about 1 pound reserved beef.

PREP
10 MINUTES

GRILL
5 MINUTES

MAKES
4 SERVINGS

NUTRITION FACTS
PER SERVING
594 CAL., 34 G TOTAL FAT
(10 G SAT. FAT), 110 MG
CHOL., 3,176 MG SODIUM,
35 G CARBO., 8 G FIBER,
36 G PRO.

DAILY VALUES
4% VIT. A, 66% VIT. C,
23% CALCIUM, 27% IRON

EXCHANGES
2½ STARCH, 4 MEDIUM-FAT
MEAT, 2 FAT

five-spice beef short ribs

FORGET TAKEOUT! THE FLAVORS THAT DRAW YOU TO YOUR FAVORITE ASIAN RESTAURANT CAN BE READY AND WAITING AT HOME WITH THE RIGHT MIX OF INGREDIENTS AND YOUR SLOW COOKER.

PREP
25 MINUTES

COOK
11 HOURS (LOW) OR
5½ HOURS (HIGH)

MAKES
4 SERVINGS + RESERVES

6	pounds beef short ribs
1	large red onion, cut into thin wedges
2	tablespoons quick-cooking tapioca
⅔	cup beef broth
¼	cup soy sauce
¼	cup rice vinegar
2	tablespoons honey
1	tablespoon five-spice powder
1	teaspoon ground ginger
4	cloves garlic, minced
2	cups hot cooked rice

STEP 1 Trim fat from beef; set ribs aside. Place onion wedges in a 5- or 6-quart slow cooker. Sprinkle with tapioca. Place beef ribs on top. In a medium bowl stir together broth, soy sauce, vinegar, honey, five-spice powder, ginger, and garlic. Pour over beef in cooker.

STEP 2 Cover and cook on low-heat setting for 11 to 12 hours or on high-heat setting for 5½ to 6 hours.

STEP 3 Using a slotted spoon, remove ribs and onion from cooker; set aside. Pour cooking liquid into a 1-quart glass measure. Skim fat from liquid; discard fat. Reserve half of the beef, half of the onion, and half of the cooking liquid; store as directed below.

STEP 4 Serve remaining beef, onion, and liquid over hot cooked rice.

TO STORE RESERVES Place ribs with meat on in an airtight container. Place onion and cooking liquid in a second airtight container. Seal and chill for up to 3 days. (Or freeze for up to 3 months. Thaw in refrigerator overnight before using.) Use in Asian Beef Stew, page 27.

NUTRITION FACTS
PER SERVING
369 CAL., 12 G TOTAL FAT
(5 G SAT. FAT), 79 MG CHOL.,
628 MG SODIUM,
33 G CARBO., 1 G FIBER,
30 G PRO.

DAILY VALUES
1% VIT. A, 4% VIT. C,
4% CALCIUM, 25% IRON

EXCHANGES
1½ STARCH, ½ OTHER
CARBO., 4 LEAN MEAT

asian beef stew

PARLAY THE INTRIGUING FLAVORS AND TENDER, RICH BEEF OF THE FIVE-SPICE BEEF SHORT RIBS INTO A SERIOUSLY GOOD STEW THAT'S CHOCK-FULL OF COLORFUL VEGETABLES AND TAKES ONLY MINUTES START TO FINISH.

1	14-ounce can beef broth
½	of a 16-ounce package frozen pepper stir-fry vegetables (yellow, green, and red sweet peppers and onion)
8	ounces tiny new potatoes, sliced ¼ inch thick
1	cup thinly sliced carrot (2 medium)
	Reserved Five-Spice Beef Short Ribs* (see recipe, page 26)
4	green onions, bias-sliced into 1-inch pieces

STEP 1 In a large saucepan or Dutch oven bring broth to boiling. Add frozen stir-fry vegetables, potato, and carrot. Return to boiling; reduce heat. Cover and simmer for 10 minutes.

STEP 2 Meanwhile, remove beef from reserved ribs and trim off the fat; discard fat and bones. Chop the beef. Remove and discard any fat from the reserved cooking liquid. Add beef, cooking liquid and onion, and green onion to vegetables in saucepan. Return to boiling; reduce heat. Cover and simmer about 5 minutes more or until vegetables are tender.

* There should be about 4 reserved ribs and about 1 cup reserved cooking liquid mixed with ½ cup reserved onion.

START TO FINISH
20 MINUTES

MAKES
4 TO 6 SERVINGS

NUTRITION FACTS
PER SERVING
349 CAL., 12 G TOTAL FAT
(5 G SAT. FAT), 79 MG CHOL.,
1,026 MG SODIUM,
27 G CARBO., 3 G FIBER,
32 G PRO.

DAILY VALUES
76% VIT. A, 63% VIT. C,
6% CALCIUM, 28% IRON

EXCHANGES
1½ VEGETABLE, ½ STARCH,
½ OTHER CARBO., 4 LEAN MEAT

1

moroccan short ribs

IGNORED FOR TOO MANY YEARS, SHORT RIBS HAVE MADE A COMEBACK, THANKS TO BISTRO CHEFS WHO HAVE REDISCOVERED THEIR SUCCULENT APPEAL. THE RICH BEEF IS SLOWLY SIMMERED WITH MOROCCAN SPICES FOR COMPANY-WORTHY RESULTS.

PREP
35 MINUTES

COOK
10 HOURS (LOW) OR
5 HOURS (HIGH)
+ 30 MINUTES

MAKES
6 SERVINGS

3 ¼	to 3½ pounds boneless beef short ribs
1 ½	teaspoons garlic salt
1	teaspoon ground turmeric
1	teaspoon ground cumin
½	teaspoon ground coriander
¼	teaspoon black pepper
2	large onions, cut into thin wedges
1	cup thinly sliced carrot (2 medium)
2	tablespoons quick-cooking tapioca
1	14.5-ounce can diced tomatoes with basil and garlic
2	8- or 9-ounce packages frozen artichoke hearts, thawed
4	cups hot cooked couscous
⅓	cup pine nuts, toasted and chopped

STEP 1 Trim fat from ribs; set aside. In a small bowl stir together garlic salt, turmeric, cumin, coriander, and pepper; set aside.

STEP 2 In a 5- or 6- quart slow cooker place onion and carrot; sprinkle with tapioca. Place short ribs on top of vegetables; sprinkle with spices. Pour undrained tomatoes and ¼ cup water over ribs in cooker.

STEP 3 Cover and cook on low-heat setting for 10 hours or on high-heat setting for 5 hours.

STEP 4 If using low-heat setting, turn to high-heat setting. Add artichoke hearts. Cover and cook for 30 minutes. Using a slotted spoon, remove 12 ounces of the short ribs and 1¼ cups of the vegetables (be sure vegetables are well drained); store as directed below.

STEP 5 Serve remaining rib mixture over couscous. Sprinkle with pine nuts.

TO STORE RESERVES Place beef and vegetables in separate airtight containers. Seal and chill for up to 3 days. Use in Moroccan Pita Pizzas, page 29.

NUTRITION FACTS
PER SERVING
456 CAL., 17 G TOTAL FAT
(6 G SAT. FAT), 84 MG CHOL.,
497 MG SODIUM,
39 G CARBO., 5 G FIBER,
36 G PRO.

DAILY VALUES
32% VIT. A, 14% VIT. C,
8% CALCIUM, 30% IRON

EXCHANGES
1 VEGETABLE, 2 STARCH,
4 LEAN MEAT, 1 FAT

moroccan pita pizzas

MAKE THE MOROCCAN SHORT RIBS FOR COMPANY ONE NIGHT, THEN SERVE LEFTOVERS IN THIS EXOTIC KNIFE-AND-FORK PIZZA FOR A SPECIAL WEEKEND LUNCH. YOU'LL LOVE THE WAY THE HUMMUS AND FETA CHEESE ADD EXTRA ZIP.

4	pita bread rounds
½	of a 7-ounce container roasted red pepper hummus
	Reserved beef and vegetables from Moroccan Short Ribs* (see recipe, page 28)
1½	cups crumbled feta cheese with garlic and herbs (6 ounces)
¼	cup pine nuts

STEP 1 Spread one side of pita rounds with hummus; arrange, hummus sides up, on a large baking sheet.

STEP 2 Coarsely chop reserved short ribs; arrange ribs and vegetables on pita rounds. Sprinkle with feta cheese and pine nuts.

STEP 3 Bake, uncovered, in a 425°F oven for 10 to 12 minutes or until heated through.

* There should be 12 ounces reserved beef and 1¼ cups reserved vegetables.

PREP
15 MINUTES

BAKE
10 MINUTES

OVEN
425°F

MAKES
4 SERVINGS

NUTRITION FACTS
PER SERVING
668 CAL., 30 G TOTAL FAT (12 G SAT. FAT), 122 MG CHOL., 1,434 MG SODIUM, 55 G CARBO., 6 G FIBER, 45 G PRO.

DAILY VALUES
36% VIT. A, 16% VIT. C, 34% CALCIUM, 41% IRON

EXCHANGES
1 VEGETABLE, 3 STARCH, 4½ LEAN MEAT, 3½ FAT

spicy beef
sloppy joes

SLOPPY JOES, A FAVORITE SATURDAY LUNCH OR QUICK WEEKNIGHT DINNER, GET A TEX-MEX MAKEOVER! HINT: CHOOSE HOTTER OR MILDER SALSA, DEPENDING ON HOW HIGH UP ON THE HEAT SCALE YOU WANT TO GO!

PREP
20 MINUTES

COOK
8 HOURS (LOW) OR
4 HOURS (HIGH)

MAKES
6 SERVINGS + RESERVES

2	pounds lean ground beef
2	16-ounce jars salsa
3	cups sliced fresh mushrooms (8 ounces)
1½	cups shredded carrot (3 medium)
1½	cups finely chopped red and/or green sweet pepper
⅓	cup tomato paste
2	teaspoons dried basil, crushed
1	teaspoon dried oregano, crushed
½	teaspoon salt
¼	teaspoon cayenne pepper
4	cloves garlic, minced
6	kaiser rolls, split and toasted

STEP 1   In a large skillet cook beef over medium heat until brown, stirring to break meat into small pieces. Drain off fat. In a 5- or 6-quart slow cooker stir together cooked beef, the salsa, mushrooms, carrot, sweet pepper, tomato paste, basil, oregano, salt, cayenne pepper, and garlic.

STEP 2   Cover and cook on low-heat setting for 8 to 10 hours or on high-heat setting for 4 to 5 hours.

STEP 3   Reserve 5 cups of the meat mixture; store as directed below. Serve remaining meat mixture on toasted kaiser rolls.

TO STORE RESERVES Place meat mixture in an airtight container. Seal and chill for up to 3 days. (Or freeze for up to 3 months. Thaw in refrigerator overnight before using.) Use in Spicy Beef Taco Salad, page 31.

NUTRITION FACTS
PER SERVING
294 CAL., 8 G TOTAL FAT
(3 G SAT. FAT), 36 MG CHOL.,
756 MG SODIUM,
37 G CARBO., 3 G FIBER,
18 G PRO.

DAILY VALUES
37% VIT. A, 42% VIT. C,
8% CALCIUM, 20% IRON

EXCHANGES
1 VEGETABLE, 2 STARCH,
1½ MEDIUM-FAT MEAT

spicy beef
taco salad

RIFE WITH AN ARRAY OF FLAVORS, TEXTURES, AND COLORS, TACO SALADS ARE TERRIFIC ONE-DISH MEALS. THIS ONE IS ALSO A GREAT WAY TO SNEAK A FEW FIBER-PACKED BLACK BEANS INTO YOUR DINNER.

MEAL

2

	Reserved meat mixture from Spicy Beef Sloppy Joes* (see recipe, page 30)
1	15-ounce can black beans, rinsed and drained
1	2.25-ounce can sliced, pitted ripe olives, drained
1	teaspoon Mexican or taco seasoning
6	baked crisp salad shells
9	cups torn iceberg lettuce
1	cup shredded cheddar cheese (4 ounces)
1	cup chopped tomato (2 medium)
⅓	cup dairy sour cream

STEP 1   In a large saucepan stir together reserved meat mixture, the beans, olives, and seasoning. Heat to boiling; reduce heat. Simmer, covered, for 10 minutes.

STEP 2   To serve, place salad shells on serving plates; fill with lettuce. Add meat mixture. Evenly top with cheese, tomato, and sour cream.

* There should be 5 cups reserved meat mixture.

PREP
20 MINUTES

COOK
10 MINUTES

MAKES
6 SERVINGS

NUTRITION FACTS
PER SERVING
495 CAL., 26 G TOTAL FAT
(10 G SAT. FAT), 84 MG
CHOL., 1,181 MG SODIUM,
41 G CARBO., 9 G FIBER,
32 G PRO.

DAILY VALUES
81% VIT. A, 81% VIT. C,
25% CALCIUM, 29% IRON

EXCHANGES
2 VEGETABLE, 2 STARCH,
3 MEDIUM-FAT MEAT,
1½ FAT

chipotle meatballs

HERE'S A CURE FOR THE COMMON PASTA-AND-MEATBALL COMBO. LIVEN THE DISH UP WITH A ZIPPY BEER AND CHIPOTLE-SPIKED SAUCE! ORZO, A RICE-SHAPE PASTA, MAKES A GOOD CHOICE FOR THE PASTA OPTION.

PREP
35 MINUTES

BAKE
25 MINUTES

COOK
4 HOURS (LOW) OR
2 HOURS (HIGH)

MAKES
4 SERVINGS + RESERVES

2	eggs, lightly beaten
1 ⅓	cups ketchup
¾	cup quick-cooking rolled oats
1 ¼	to 1 ½ teaspoons ground chipotle chile pepper
½	teaspoon garlic powder
½	teaspoon salt
1	pound lean ground beef
1	pound ground pork
1	12-ounce can beer
¼	cup packed brown sugar
1	tablespoon quick-cooking tapioca, crushed
8	ounces desired dried pasta

STEP 1 In a large bowl stir together eggs, ⅓ cup of the ketchup, the oatmeal, 1 teaspoon of the chile powder, the garlic powder, and salt. Add beef and pork; mix well. Shape meat mixture into 32 balls. Place meatballs in a 15×10×1-inch baking pan. Bake, uncovered, in a 350°F oven for 25 minutes; drain off fat.

STEP 2 In a 3½- or 4-quart slow cooker stir together beer, the remaining 1 cup ketchup, the brown sugar, tapioca, and ¼ to ½ teaspoon of the remaining chile powder. Place meatballs on top of sauce in cooker.

STEP 3 Cover and cook on low-heat setting for 4 to 5 hours or on high-heat setting for 2 to 2½ hours. Using a slotted spoon, remove meatballs from cooker. Reserve half the meatballs (16 meatballs) and ½ cup of the sauce; store as directed below.

STEP 4 Prepare pasta according to package directions. Serve remaining meatballs and sauce over pasta.

TO STORE RESERVES Place meatballs and sauce in two separate airtight containers. Seal and chill for up to 3 days. (Or freeze for up to 3 months. Thaw in refrigerator overnight before using.) Use in Meatball Hoagies, page 33.

NUTRITION FACTS
PER SERVING
544 CAL., 12 G TOTAL FAT
(5 G SAT. FAT), 115 MG
CHOL., 827 MG SODIUM,
76 G CARBO., 3 G FIBER,
28 G PRO.

DAILY VALUES
14% VIT. A, 15% VIT. C,
4% CALCIUM, 23% IRON

EXCHANGES
3 STARCH, 2 OTHER CARBO.,
2½ MEDIUM-FAT MEAT

meatball hoagies

THE MEATBALLS PACK A GREAT COMBINATION OF SWEET AND HEAT—IF YOU ENJOYED THEM IN THE CHIPOTLE MEATBALLS RECIPE, YOU'LL LOVE THEM IN A SANDWICH TOPPED WITH IRRESISTIBLY MELTY MONTEREY JACK CHEESE!

Reserved Chipotle Meatballs* (see recipe, page 32)

4   hoagie buns

1   cup shredded Monterey Jack cheese (4 ounces)

STEP 1   In a small saucepan bring reserved sauce to a simmer over medium heat. Reduce heat; keep warm.

STEP 2   Place reserved meatballs in a single layer on a microwave-safe plate and microwave on 100 percent power (high) for 2 to 3 minutes or until hot.

STEP 3   Place split hoagie buns on a baking sheet and broil 4 to 6 inches from the heat for 3 minutes or until toasted. Split meatballs in half; arrange on hoagie buns. Drizzle with warm sauce. Sprinkle with cheese. Return filled hoagies to oven and broil about 2 minutes or until cheese melts. Serve immediately.

* There should be 1/2 cup sauce and 16 meatballs.

PREP
10 MINUTES

COOK
2 MINUTES

BROIL
5 MINUTES

MAKES
4 SERVINGS

NUTRITION FACTS
PER SERVING
761 CAL., 28 G TOTAL FAT (12 G SAT. FAT), 140 MG CHOL., 1,321 MG SODIUM, 89 G CARBO., 5 G FIBER, 38 G PRO.

DAILY VALUES
12% VIT. A, 7% VIT. C, 33% CALCIUM, 35% IRON

EXCHANGES
4 1/2 STARCH, 1 1/2 OTHER CARBO., 3 1/2 MEDIUM-FAT MEAT, 1 1/2 FAT

1

classic meat loaf

HERE IT IS—THE KETCHUP- AND BROWN-SUGAR-TOPPED MEAT LOAF BELOVED BY GENERATIONS! GO AHEAD—SERVE IT WITH MASHED POTATOES AND GRAVY AND CANNED GREEN BEANS FOR A TASTY TRIP DOWN MEMORY LANE. NOTE THAT YOU'LL NEED A LARGE OVAL SLOW COOKER FOR THIS RECIPE.

PREP
30 MINUTES

COOK
7 HOURS (LOW) OR
3½ HOURS (HIGH)

MAKES
6 SERVINGS + RESERVES

3	beaten eggs
¾	cup milk
2	cups soft bread crumbs
1	cup finely chopped onion (1 large)
2	teaspoons salt
½	teaspoon black pepper
1½	pounds lean ground beef
1½	pounds ground pork
¼	cup ketchup
2	tablespoons packed brown sugar
1	teaspoon dry mustard

STEP 1 In a large bowl combine eggs and milk; stir in bread crumbs, onion, salt, and pepper. Add beef and pork; mix well. Shape into two 5-inch round loaves.

STEP 2 Tear off two 18-inch square pieces of heavy foil. Cut each into thirds. Fold each piece of foil in half lengthwise to make strips. Crisscross three of the strips and place one meat loaf on center of strips. Bring up ends of strips and transfer loaf to a 6- or 7-quart slow cooker. Repeat with remaining foil strips and meat loaf.

STEP 3 Cover and cook on low-heat setting for 7 to 8 hours or on high-heat setting for 3½ to 4 hours.

STEP 4 Use foil strips to remove one meat loaf; discard foil strips. Store meat loaf as directed below. Transfer second meat loaf to a serving platter; discard foil strips. In a small bowl stir together ketchup, brown sugar, and dry mustard; spread over meat loaf on platter.

TO STORE RESERVES Place meat loaf in an airtight container. Seal and chill for up to 3 days. (Or freeze for up to 3 months. Thaw in refrigerator overnight before using.) Use in Meat Loaf Parmesan, page 35.

NUTRITION FACTS
PER SERVING
239 CAL., 11 G TOTAL FAT
(4 G SAT. FAT), 116 MG
CHOL., 617 MG SODIUM,
13 G CARBO., 0 G FIBER,
20 G PRO.

DAILY VALUES
4% VIT. A, 4% VIT. C,
5% CALCIUM, 12% IRON

EXCHANGES
1 OTHER CARBO.,
2½ MEDIUM-FAT MEAT

meat loaf parmesan

IF YOU ENJOY CHICKEN PARMESAN AND EGGPLANT PARMESAN, WHY NOT GIVE THE PARMESAN TREATMENT TO MEAT LOAF, TOO? THE SIDE DISH ACCOMPANIMENT COULD GO EITHER WAY: GO ITALIAN WITH PASTA OR AMERICAN WITH MASHED POTATOES.

Reserved Classic Meat Loaf* (see recipe, page 34)

2	eggs, beaten
¼	cup milk
½	cup seasoned fine dry bread crumbs
¼	cup grated Parmesan cheese
1	26- to 28-ounce jar spaghetti or pasta sauce
1	cup shredded mozzarella cheese (4 ounces)

STEP 1 Slice reserved meat loaf into 6 slices; set aside. In a shallow bowl stir together eggs and milk. In another shallow bowl stir together bread crumbs and Parmesan cheese. Dip meat loaf slices, one at a time, into egg mixture, then dredge in bread crumb mixture to coat. Place slices in a single layer in a 3-quart rectangular baking dish.

STEP 2 Bake, uncovered, in a 350°F oven for 20 minutes. Remove from oven and pour spaghetti sauce evenly over meat loaf; sprinkle with cheese. Bake about 15 minutes more or until sauce is heated through and cheese is melted.

* There should be one meat loaf.

PREP
15 MINUTES

BAKE
35 MINUTES

OVEN
350°F

MAKES
6 SERVINGS

NUTRITION FACTS
PER SERVING
469 CAL., 22 G TOTAL FAT
(9 G SAT. FAT),
205 MG CHOL., 33 G CARBO.,
4 G FIBER, 31 G PRO.

DAILY VALUES
17% VIT. A, 6% VIT. C,

EXCHANGES
½ VEGETABLE, 2 OTHER
CARBO., 4 MEDIUM-FAT MEAT

1

adobo pork tostadas

THE SMOKY FLAVOR OF THE CANNED CHIPOTLE CHILES AND THE
SPICE OF THE ADOBO SAUCE ARE THE KEYS TO THE SMOKY-SPICY
FLAVOR IN THESE ATTRACTIVELY LAYERED TOSTADAS.

PREP
30 MINUTES

COOK
10 HOURS (LOW) OR
5 HOURS (HIGH)

MAKES
4 SERVINGS + RESERVES

1	3- to 3½-pound boneless pork shoulder roast
1	15-ounce can tomato sauce
½	cup chicken broth
2	tablespoons finely chopped canned chipotle peppers in adobo sauce
6	cloves garlic, minced (1 tablespoon)
½	teaspoon ground cumin
½	teaspoon ground coriander
¼	teaspoon black pepper
1	cup canned refried beans
8	corn tostada shells
1	cup shredded lettuce
1	cup chopped tomato (2 medium)
1	avocado, halved, seeded, peeled, and sliced
1	cup queso fresco cheese, crumbled (4 ounces)
½	cup dairy sour cream

NUTRITION FACTS
PER SERVING
680 CAL., 36 G TOTAL FAT
(12 G SAT. FAT),
144 MG CHOL.,
988 MG SODIUM,
40 G CARBO., 8 G FIBER,
48 G PRO.

DAILY VALUES
35% VIT. A, 25% VIT. C,
29% CALCIUM, 25% IRON

EXCHANGES
1 VEGETABLE, 2½ STARCH,
5½ LEAN MEAT, 2½ FAT

STEP 1 Trim fat from roast; cut pork into chunks. Place pork in a 4- or 5-quart slow cooker. Stir together tomato sauce, broth, chipotle peppers, garlic, ¼ teaspoon salt, cumin, coriander, and black pepper; pour over pork in cooker.

STEP 2 Cover and cook on low-heat setting for 10 to 12 hours or high-heat setting for 5 to 6 hours.

STEP 3 Remove pork from cooker. Using 2 forks, shred pork. Reserve half of the pork (about 3 cups) and 2 cups of the sauce; store as directed below. Mix remaining pork with ¼ cup of the sauce. Discard any remaining sauce.

STEP 4 Spread refried beans over tostada shells. Top with pork mixture. Divide lettuce, tomato, avocado, and cheese among tostadas. Top with sour cream.

TO STORE RESERVES Place shredded pork and sauce in separate airtight containers. Seal and chill for up to 3 days. (Or freeze for up to 3 months. Thaw in refrigerator overnight before using.) Use in Chipotle Pork Tamale Casserole, page 37.

chipotle pork
tamale casserole

POLENTA USED TO BE A LITTLE TRICKY TO MAKE. THEN ALONG CAME CONVENIENT TUBES OF REFRIGERATED POLENTA, WHICH IS A TERRIFIC INGREDIENT IN CASSEROLES THAT ARE INSPIRED BY MEXICAN TAMALES.

1	16-ounce tube refrigerated cooked polenta, sliced ½ inch thick
	Reserved pork and sauce from Adobo Pork Tostadas* (see recipe, page 36)
1	cup shredded cheddar cheese (4 ounces)
½	cup chopped tomato (1 medium)
¼	cup sliced green onion (2)

STEP 1 In a 2-quart square baking dish arrange polenta slices, overlapping as necessary. Top with reserved pork. Remove layer of fat from sauce. Spoon ⅓ cup of the sauce over pork.

STEP 2 Bake, covered, in a 375°F oven for 30 minutes. Top with cheese. Bake, uncovered, about 5 minutes more, or until cheese is melted. Meanwhile, heat remaining sauce. Sprinkle tomato and onion over casserole. Serve with warm sauce.

* There should be 3 cups shredded reserved pork and 2 cups reserved sauce.

PREP
15 MINUTES

BAKE
35 MINUTES

OVEN
375°F

MAKES
4 SERVINGS

NUTRITION FACTS
PER SERVING
488 CAL., 21 G TOTAL FAT (10 G SAT. FAT), 143 MG CHOL., 1,215 MG SODIUM, 27 G CARBO., 4 G FIBER, 44 G PRO.

DAILY VALUES
12% VIT. A, 10% VIT. C, 24% CALCIUM, 16% IRON

EXCHANGES
2 STARCH, 5½ LEAN MEAT, ½ FAT

barbecue
pulled pork

PORK SHOULDER ROAST IS A PRIME CANDIDATE FOR THE SLOW
COOKER BECAUSE THE ALL-DAY SIMMERING HELPS IT BECOME
RICHER AND MORE TENDER OVER TIME.

PREP
15 MINUTES

COOK
12 HOURS (LOW) OR
6 HOURS (HIGH)

MAKES
8 SERVINGS + RESERVES

1	4-pound boneless pork shoulder roast
1	sweet onion, cut into thin wedges
1	12-ounce bottle chili sauce
1	cup cola
½	cup ketchup
2	tablespoons yellow mustard
1	tablespoon chili powder
1	tablespoon cider vinegar
2	teaspoons ground cumin
3	cloves garlic, minced
1	teaspoon paprika
¼	teaspoon crushed red pepper
8	hamburger buns, split and toasted

STEP 1 In a 5- or 6-quart slow cooker place pork roast and onion. In a medium bowl stir together chili sauce, cola, ketchup, mustard, chili powder, vinegar, cumin, garlic, paprika, ½ teaspoon salt, ½ teaspoon black pepper, and crushed red pepper. Pour over pork in cooker.

STEP 2 Cover and cook on low-heat setting for 12 to 13 hours or on high heat setting for 6 to 6½ hours.

STEP 3 Remove roast from cooker; remove onion with a slotted spoon. Set cooking liquid aside. When pork is cool enough to handle, thinly slice or shred it; combine pork with onion. Reserve half of the pork mixture (about 3½ cups); store as directed below.

STEP 4 Add enough of the reserved cooking liquid to moisten remaining pork. (If necessary, return pork mixture to cooker. Cover and cook on high-heat setting for 15 minutes more to heat through.) Serve on toasted buns.

TO STORE RESERVES Place pork mixture in an airtight container. Seal and refrigerate for up to 3 days. Use in Pulled Pork Turnovers, page 39.

NUTRITION FACTS
PER SERVING
332 CAL., 10 G TOTAL FAT
(3 G SAT. FAT), 76 MG CHOL.,
760 MG SODIUM,
31 G CARBO., 3 G FIBER,
27 G PRO.

DAILY VALUES
9% VIT. A, 11% VIT. C,
9% CALCIUM, 18% IRON

EXCHANGES
1½ STARCH, ½ OTHER
CARBO., 3½ LEAN MEAT

pulled pork turnovers

TRANSFORM THE BARBECUE PULLED PORK INTO LOVELY LITTLE TURNOVERS WITH A SOFT, TENDER PASTRY. THEY'LL TASTE GREAT WITH A STEAMING BOWL OF CHEESE SOUP FOR A CASUAL SATURDAY LUNCH OR A WARMING SUNDAY NIGHT SUPPER.

Reserved Barbecue Pulled Pork* (see recipe, page 38)

1   16.3-ounce package (8) refrigerated Southern-style biscuits

1   egg

1   tablespoon water

Bottled barbecue sauce, warmed (optional)

STEP 1   In a medium saucepan bring reserved pork mixture to a simmer.

STEP 2   On a lightly floured surface, roll each of the biscuits into a 6-inch round. In a small bowl whisk together egg and water. On half of each biscuit round place a scant ½ cup of pork mixture. Brush edges of biscuit with egg mixture. Fold dough over pork mixture and seal edges with the tines of a fork. Place turnovers on a lightly greased baking sheet.

STEP 3   Bake, uncovered, in a 350°F oven for 15 to 17 minutes or until golden brown. If desired, serve with warmed barbecue sauce.

* There should be about 3½ cups reserved pork mixture.

PREP
20 MINUTES

BAKE
15 MINUTES

OVEN
350°F

MAKES
8 SERVINGS

NUTRITION FACTS
PER SERVING
411 CAL., 18 G TOTAL FAT (5 G SAT. FAT), 102 MG CHOL., 1,153 MG SODIUM, 34 G CARBO., 2 G FIBER, 28 G PRO.

DAILY VALUES
9% VIT. A, 11% VIT. C, 7% CALCIUM, 19% IRON

EXCHANGES
1½ STARCH, ½ OTHER CARBO., 3½ LEAN MEAT, 1½ FAT

southwestern-style green chili

SOME LIKE IT HOT! IF YOU'RE IN THAT CROWD, LOOK FOR A HOTTER-STYLE GREEN CHILE ENCHILADA SAUCE FOR THIS THICK AND HEARTY CHILI.

PREP
25 MINUTES

COOK
10 HOURS (LOW) OR
5 HOURS (HIGH)

MAKES
6 (1⅓-CUP) SERVINGS
+ RESERVES

3	pounds boneless pork shoulder roast
2	16-ounce cans pinto beans or Great Northern beans, rinsed and drained
2	11-ounce cans tomatillos, drained and coarsely chopped
2	10-ounce cans green chile enchilada sauce
2	4.5-ounce cans diced green chile peppers, undrained
1	cup chopped onion (2 medium)
1	teaspoon dried oregano, crushed
1	teaspoon garlic powder
1	teaspoon ground cumin
	Dairy sour cream (optional)
	Snipped fresh cilantro (optional)

STEP 1 Trim fat from roast. Cut roast into 1-inch pieces. In a 5- or 6-quart slow cooker stir together pork, pinto beans, tomatillos, enchilada sauce, undrained chile peppers, onion, oregano, garlic powder, and cumin.

STEP 2 Cover and cook on low-heat setting for 10 to 11 hours or on high-heat setting for 5 to 5½ hours.

STEP 3 Reserve 3 cups of the chili; store as directed below. If desired, top remaining chili with sour cream and cilantro.

TO STORE RESERVES Place chili in an airtight container. Seal and chill for up to 3 days. Use in Huevos Rancheros Verdes, page 41.

NUTRITION FACTS
PER SERVING
384 CAL., 11 G TOTAL FAT
(3 G SAT. FAT), 107 MG
CHOL., 1,364 MG SODIUM,
30 G CARBO., 7 G FIBER,
40 G PRO.

DAILY VALUES
8% VIT. A, 23% VIT. C,
9% CALCIUM, 28% IRON

EXCHANGES
1 VEGETABLE, 1½ STARCH,
4½ LEAN MEAT

huevos rancheros verdes

WITH SOUTHWESTERN-STYLE GREEN CHILI READY AND WAITING IN THE FRIDGE, YOU'RE JUST MINUTES TO A FLAVOR-PACKED WEEKEND BRUNCH. OR SERVE THE DISH FOR A QUICK AND SATISFYING SUPPER AFTER A BUSY WEEKDAY.

	Reserved Southwestern-Style Green Chili* (see recipe, page 40)
3	tablespoons cooking oil
6	6-inch corn tortillas
6	eggs
1	tablespoon water
¾	cup shredded Monterey Jack cheese (3 ounces)
	Snipped fresh cilantro (optional)

STEP 1   In a medium saucepan heat reserved chili over medium-low heat about 10 minutes or until bubbly, stirring occasionally. Keep warm.

STEP 2   In a large skillet heat oil over medium-high heat. Cook tortillas, one at a time, in hot oil about 2 minutes each or until browned, turning once. Drain tortillas on paper towels. Reserve remaining oil in skillet. Reduce heat to medium.

STEP 3   Carefully break eggs into skillet. When whites are set, add water. Cover skillet and cook eggs to desired doneness (3 to 4 minutes for soft-set yolks or 4 to 5 minutes for firm-set yolks).

STEP 4   To serve, place a tortilla on each plate. Spoon ½ cup hot chili onto each tortilla; top each with a cooked egg. Sprinkle with cheese and, if desired, cilantro.

* There should be 3 cups reserved chili.

START TO FINISH
25 MINUTES

MAKES
6 SERVINGS

NUTRITION FACTS
PER SERVING
400 CAL., 21 G TOTAL FAT (7 G SAT. FAT), 264 MG CHOL., 659 MG SODIUM, 26 G CARBO., 4 G FIBER, 26 G PRO.

DAILY VALUES
10% VIT. A, 8% VIT. C, 20% CALCIUM, 24% IRON

EXCHANGES
½ VEGETABLE, 1½ STARCH, 3 LEAN MEAT, 2 FAT

balsamic-sauced pork roast

HERE, SUCCULENT PORK SHOULDER GETS SIMMERED FOR HOURS IN A TOMATO-BASED SAUCE SPIKED WITH DEEPLY FLAVORED BALSAMIC VINEGAR. THE RESULTS ARE SATISFYINGLY DOWN-HOME AND A LITTLE GOURMET.

PREP
25 MINUTES

COOK
12 HOURS (LOW) OR
6 HOURS (HIGH)

MAKES
6 SERVINGS + RESERVES

1	4-pound boneless pork shoulder roast
2	teaspoons dried Italian seasoning
1	teaspoon seasoned salt
¼	teaspoon black pepper
2	large onions, halved and thinly sliced
4	cloves garlic, minced
¼	cup quick-cooking tapioca
2	14.5-ounce cans Italian-style stewed tomatoes
¼	cup balsamic vinegar
3	cups hot cooked noodles (about 8 ounces dry)

STEP 1 Trim fat from meat. If necessary, cut meat to fit in a 5- or 6-quart slow cooker. Sprinkle meat with Italian seasoning, salt, and pepper. In slow cooker place onion and garlic; sprinkle with tapioca. Top onion with meat. In a small bowl stir together undrained tomatoes and the vinegar; pour over meat in cooker.

STEP 2 Cover and cook on low-heat setting for 12 to 14 hours or on high-heat setting for 6 to 7 hours.

STEP 3 Remove meat from cooker. Reserve one-third of the meat (about 14 ounces); store as directed below. Skim fat from cooking liquid; reserve 1½ cups cooking liquid; store as directed below.

STEP 4 Cut remaining meat into 6 slices. Serve remaining sliced meat and juices over hot cooked noodles.

TO STORE RESERVES Place meat and cooking liquid in separate airtight containers. Seal and chill for up to 3 days. (Or freeze for up to 3 months. Thaw in refrigerator overnight before using.) Use in Pork & Noodles, page 43.

NUTRITION FACTS
PER SERVING
455 CAL., 13 G TOTAL FAT
(4 G SAT. FAT), 157 MG
CHOL., 662 MG SODIUM,
37 G CARBO., 1 G FIBER,
45 G PRO.

DAILY VALUES
1% VIT. A, 24% VIT. C,
5% CALCIUM, 24% IRON

EXCHANGES
½ VEGETABLE, 2 STARCH,
3 LEAN MEAT

pork & noodles

BEEF AND NOODLES RANK RIGHT UP THERE AS A FAVORITE COMFORT FOOD. NOW SHAKE THINGS UP A BIT WITH PORK FOR A DINNER THAT'S NICELY FAMILY-FRIENDLY BUT ALSO PLEASANTLY UNEXPECTED.

Reserved meat and liquid from Balsamic-Sauced Pork Roast*
(see recipe, page 42)

3   cups hot cooked noodles
1   12-ounce jar mushroom gravy
1   16-ounce bag frozen cut green beans, thawed

STEP 1   Cube leftover meat. In a large saucepan combine meat, reserved juices, the noodles, gravy, and beans. Cook just until mixture comes to a boil, stirring occasionally. Cover and cook for 3 to 5 minutes or until beans are crisp-tender.

* There should be about 14 ounces reserved meat and 1½ cups reserved cooking liquid.

START TO FINISH
25 MINUTES

MAKES
6 (1⅓-CUP) SERVINGS

NUTRITION FACTS
PER SERVING
331 CAL., 8 G TOTAL FAT
(2 G SAT. FAT), 92 MG CHOL.,
674 MG SODIUM,
37 G CARBO., 3 G FIBER,
27 G PRO.

DAILY VALUES
7% VIT. A, 26% VIT. C,
6% CALCIUM, 19% IRON

EXCHANGES
1 VEGETABLE, 2 STARCH,
2½ LEAN MEAT

sage-scented pork chops

WHAT MAKES THIS DISH SPECIAL IS ITS SAUCE—JUST BEFORE SERVING, THE RICHLY FLAVORED COOKING LIQUID GETS AN ADDED FLAVOR BOOST WITH TWO SIMPLE STIR-INS: DIJON-STYLE MUSTARD AND CARAWAY SEEDS.

PREP
30 MINUTES

COOK
4 HOURS (LOW) OR
2 HOURS (HIGH)

MAKES
6 SERVINGS + RESERVES

10	boneless pork loin chops, cut ¾ inch thick (about 3½ pounds)
2	teaspoons dried sage, crushed
1	teaspoon black pepper
½	teaspoon salt
2	tablespoons cooking oil
1	medium onion, thinly sliced
½	cup chicken broth
⅓	cup dry white wine or apple juice
3	tablespoons quick-cooking tapioca, crushed
½	of a medium head green cabbage, cut into ½-inch-wide strips
1	tablespoon Dijon-style mustard
1	teaspoon caraway seeds
	Salt and black pepper

STEP 1 Trim fat from chops. Stir together sage, 1 teaspoon pepper, and ¼ teaspoon salt. Rub sage mixture onto one side of the chops. In a very large skillet brown chops, half at a time, on both sides in hot oil over medium heat.

STEP 2 In a 6- or 7-quart slow cooker place onion, broth, wine, and tapioca. Add the browned chops to cooker. Top with cabbage.

STEP 3 Cover and cook on low-heat setting for 4 to 5 hours or on high-heat setting for 2 to 2½ hours.

STEP 4 Reserve 4 chops; store as directed below. Transfer remaining 6 chops to a platter; cover and keep warm. Using a slotted spoon, transfer cabbage and onion to a serving bowl. Stir mustard and caraway seeds into remaining juices in cooker. Season sauce to taste with salt and pepper. Spoon sauce over pork and cabbage to serve.

TO STORE RESERVES Place meat in an airtight container. Seal and chill for up to 3 days. (Or freeze for up to 3 months. Thaw in refrigerator overnight before using.) Use in Pork & Potato Gratin with Gruyère Cheese, page 45.

NUTRITION FACTS
PER SERVING
300 CAL., 12 G TOTAL FAT
(4 G SAT. FAT), 87 MG CHOL.,
351 MG SODIUM,
9 G CARBO., 1 G FIBER,
37 G PRO.

DAILY VALUES
2% VIT. A, 20% VIT. C,
6% CALCIUM, 9% IRON

EXCHANGES
1 VEGETABLE, 5 LEAN MEAT

pork & potato gratin with gruyère cheese

IF YOU LIKE SCALLOPED HAM AND POTATOES, GIVE THIS A TRY. INSTEAD OF HAM, RICH BITS OF COOKED PORK LOIN CHOPS GIVE THE CLASSIC A NICE CHANGE OF TASTE.

½	cup chopped onion (1 medium)
3	tablespoons butter
3	tablespoons all-purpose flour
¾	teaspoon salt
½	teaspoon black pepper
¼	teaspoon ground nutmeg
1¾	cups milk
1¼	cups shredded Gruyère cheese (5 ounces)
2	pounds round red or white potatoes, peeled and thinly sliced (5 to 6 potatoes) (do not use russet potatoes)
	Reserved Sage-Scented Pork Chops* (see recipe, page 44), chopped

STEP 1 For sauce, in a medium saucepan cook onion in hot butter over medium heat until tender. Stir in flour, salt, pepper, and nutmeg. Cook and stir for 1 minute. Add milk all at once. Cook and stir until thickened and bubbly. Add cheese; cook and stir until melted.

STEP 2 In a greased 2½- to 3-quart rectangular baking dish or au gratin dish spread half of the potato. Top with all of the chopped reserved meat; cover with half of the sauce. Repeat potato and sauce layers.

STEP 3 Bake, covered, in a 375°F oven about 45 minutes or until potato is tender. Let stand for 10 minutes before serving.

* There should be 4 reserved pork chops (about 1 pound).

PREP
30 MINUTES

BAKE
45 MINUTES

STAND
10 MINUTES

OVEN
375°F

MAKES
6 SERVINGS

NUTRITION FACTS
PER SERVING
488 CAL., 24 G TOTAL FAT (12 G SAT. FAT), 109 MG CHOL., 618 MG SODIUM, 29 G CARBO., 2 G FIBER, 37 G PRO.

DAILY VALUES
12% VIT. A, 29% VIT. C, 40% CALCIUM, 11% IRON

EXCHANGES
2 STARCH, 4½ LEAN MEAT, 2 FAT

cider braised pork roast & apples

PORK AND APPLES ARE A CLASSIC, AND THEY COOK UP BEAUTIFULLY TOGETHER IN THE SLOW COOKER. THE APPLE-LIKE TONES SOMETIMES PRESENT IN CHARDONNAY WINE WOULD PAIR NICELY WITH THIS; IF YOU PREFER RED WINE, TRY A PINOT NOIR.

PREP
30 MINUTES

COOK
8 HOURS (LOW)
4 HOURS (HIGH)

MAKES
6 SERVINGS + RESERVES

1	3-pound boneless pork top loin roast
½	teaspoon salt
½	teaspoon dried thyme, crushed
½	teaspoon dried sage, crushed
¼	teaspoon black pepper
2	tablespoons cooking oil
4	red, yellow, and/or green apples, cored and each cut into 6 wedges
⅓	cup chopped shallot
1	tablespoon bottled minced garlic or 6 cloves garlic, minced
3	tablespoons quick-cooking tapioca
¾	cup chicken broth
¾	cup apple cider or juice
3	cups hot cooked rice

NUTRITION FACTS

PER SERVING
407 CAL., 12 G TOTAL FAT
(3 G SAT. FAT), 67 MG CHOL.,
303 MG SODIUM,
43 G CARBO., 2 G FIBER,
30 G PRO.

DAILY VALUES
3% VIT. A, 9% VIT. C,
5% CALCIUM, 13% IRON

EXCHANGES
1 FRUIT, 2 STARCH,
3½ LEAN MEAT, 1 FAT

STEP 1   Trim fat from meat. In a small bowl stir together salt, thyme, sage, and pepper. Sprinkle spice mixture over meat; rub in with your fingers. In a large skillet brown meat on all sides in hot oil over medium heat.

STEP 2   In a 6- or 7-quart slow cooker place apple, shallot, and garlic; sprinkle with tapioca. Place meat on top of apple mixture in cooker. Pour broth and apple cider over meat.

STEP 3   Cover and cook on low-heat setting for 8 to 10 hours or high-heat setting for 4 to 5 hours.

STEP 4   Reserve 1 pound of the meat; store as directed below. Slice remaining pork; serve with apples and hot cooked rice. Spoon some of the cooking liquid over all.

TO STORE RESERVES   Place meat in an airtight container. Cover and chill for up to 3 days. (Or freeze for up to 3 months. Thaw in refrigerator overnight before using.) Use in Pork & Berry Salad, page 47.

pork & berry salad

PAIRED WITH SWEET BERRIES, LEFTOVER PORK HITS A HOME RUN IN THIS MAIN-DISH SALAD. HINT: THE SALAD LOOKS PRETTIER WHEN THE PORK IS SLICED BUT IS EASIER TO EAT WHEN PORK IS CHOPPED. FOR KIDS, CHOP IT; WHEN SERVING ADULTS, GO FOR THE SLICED OPTION.

PREP
20 MINUTES

MAKES
6 SERVINGS

Reserved meat from Cider Braised Pork Roast & Apples* (see recipe, page 46)

6   cups torn mixed greens

3   cups mixed berries, such as sliced strawberries, blueberries, and/or raspberries

½   cup bottled balsamic vinaigrette or your favorite vinaigrette

STEP 1   Chop or slice meat. Arrange greens on individual plates. Top with meat and berries. Drizzle with vinaigrette.

* There should be 1 pound reserved pork.

NUTRITION FACTS
PER SERVING
236 CAL., 11 G TOTAL FAT
(2 G SAT. FAT), 66 MG CHOL.,
371 MG SODIUM, 9 G CARBO.,
2 G FIBER, 24 G PRO.

DAILY VALUES
6% VIT. A, 75% VIT. C,
4% CALCIUM, 8% IRON

EXCHANGES
½ VEGETABLE, ½ FRUIT,
3 LEAN MEAT, ½ FAT

mojo pork roast

A WINNING COMBINATION OF JUST THE RIGHT SEASONINGS—
INCLUDING ORANGE MARMALADE, HONEY, LIME, GARLIC, AND
CHIPOTLE PEPPER—WILL HELP YOUR SLOW COOKER GET ITS
MOJO WORKING, TRANSFORMING A PORK ROAST INTO SOMETHING
MAGICALLY YUMMY!

PREP
25 MINUTES

COOK
5 HOURS (LOW) OR
2½ HOURS (HIGH)

MAKES
6 SERVINGS + RESERVES

	Nonstick cooking spray
1	3½- to 4-pound boneless pork top loin roast (single loin)
1	12-ounce jar orange marmalade
½	cup finely chopped onion (1 medium)
1	tablespoon honey
½	teaspoon finely shredded lime peel
1	tablespoon lime juice
2	cloves garlic, minced
1	chipotle pepper in adobo sauce, finely chopped
1	teaspoon ground cumin
½	teaspoon salt
½	teaspoon dried oregano, crushed
¼	teaspoon black pepper
½	cup chicken broth

NUTRITION FACTS
PER SERVING
354 CAL., 9 G TOTAL FAT
(3 G SAT. FAT), 97 MG CHOL.,
292 MG SODIUM,
29 G CARBO., 1 G FIBER,
39 G PRO.

DAILY VALUES
1% VIT. A, 6% VIT. C,
6% CALCIUM, 9% IRON

EXCHANGES
1 STARCH, 1 OTHER CARBO.,
5 LEAN MEAT

STEP 1 Lightly coat a 4- or 5-quart slow cooker with cooking spray. Trim fat from meat. If necessary, cut meat to fit into cooker. Place meat in prepared cooker. In a small bowl stir together marmalade, onion, honey, lime peel, lime juice, garlic, chipotle pepper, cumin, salt, oregano, and black pepper. Spread mixture over meat in cooker; pour broth around meat.

STEP 2 Cover and cook on low-heat setting for 5 to 5½ hours or on high-heat setting for 2½ to 3 hours.

STEP 3 Remove meat from cooker. Reserve 12 ounces of the meat; store as directed below. Slice remaining meat. If desired, strain cooking liquid. Drizzle meat with a little cooking liquid.

TO STORE RESERVES Place meat in an airtight container. Seal and chill for up to 3 days. (Or freeze for up to 3 months. Thaw in refrigerator overnight before using.) Use in Cuban Pork Sandwiches, page 49.

cuban pork sandwiches

WARM, OOZY, AND CHOCK-FULL OF LIVELY INGREDIENTS, CUBAN PORK SANDWICHES HAVE BECOME A HIT THROUGHOUT THE COUNTRY. THIS RECIPE SHOWS HOW EASY IT IS TO MAKE THIS POPULAR DELIGHT.

⅓   cup mayonnaise or salad dressing

½   of a canned chipotle pepper in adobo sauce, finely chopped
      Reserved Mojo Pork Roast* (see recipe, page 48)

12   ½-inch slices crusty country bread or 12 slices white or
      whole wheat bread

12   slices Monterey Jack cheese (12 ounces)

6   thin lengthwise slices dill pickle

6   thin slices red onion (optional)

3   tablespoons butter, softened

PREP
20 MINUTES

BROIL
4 MINUTES

MAKES
6 SANDWICHES

STEP 1 In a small bowl stir together mayonnaise and chipotle pepper; set aside. Cut reserved pork into 6 slices; place slices in a 1½-quart covered casserole. Microwave on 100 percent power (high) for 2 to 3 minutes or until heated through, rearranging slices once halfway through cooking.

STEP 2 Spread mayonnaise mixture evenly on 6 slices of bread. Top each with a slice of cheese, a slice of meat, a pickle slice, a red onion slice (if using), and another slice of cheese. Top with remaining 6 slices of bread. Spread tops of sandwiches with half of the butter.

STEP 3 Place 3 of the sandwiches, buttered sides down, on the unheated rack of a broiler pan. Spread remaining butter on sandwiches. Broil sandwiches 4 to 5 inches from the heat for 4 to 5 minutes or until bread is toasted and cheese is melted, turning sandwiches once halfway through broiling. Remove sandwiches from pan. Repeat with remaining sandwiches.

STEP 4 Cut sandwiches in half to serve.

* There should be 12 ounces reserved meat.

NUTRITION FACTS
PER SERVING
691 CAL., 39 G TOTAL FAT (18 G SAT. FAT), 118 MG CHOL., 974 MG SODIUM, 45 G CARBO., 2 G FIBER, 39 G PRO.

DAILY VALUES
13% VIT. A, 3% VIT. C, 50% CALCIUM, 17% IRON

EXCHANGES
2 STARCH, 1 OTHER CARBO., 5 LEAN MEAT, 4 FAT

1

pork chops & saucy beans mexicana

SOME DISHES HAVE A WAY OF TRANSFORMING A WEEKNIGHT DINNER INTO A COZY FAMILY PARTY. POWERHOUSE INGREDIENTS, SUCH AS CHILE PEPPERS, GARLIC, AND SPICES ARE THE KEY TO THE FESTIVE ANGLE IN THIS DISH.

PREP
15 MINUTES

COOK
8 HOURS (LOW) OR
4 HOURS (HIGH)

MAKES
4 SERVINGS + RESERVES

1	15-ounce can black beans, rinsed and drained
1	14.5-ounce can diced tomatoes
1	10-ounce package frozen whole kernel corn
1	cup chopped onion (1 large)
1	7-ounce can diced green chile peppers, drained
4	cloves garlic, minced
1	to 2 fresh jalapeño or serrano chile peppers, seeded and finely chopped*
1	tablespoon chili powder
2	teaspoons dried oregano, crushed
1	teaspoon ground cumin
¼	teaspoon salt
8	boneless loin blade pork chops, cut ½ inch thick (about 2½ to 3 pounds)
	Shredded cheddar cheese, thinly sliced green onion, snipped fresh cilantro, lime wedges, and/or dairy sour cream (optional)

STEP 1 In a 4- or 5-quart slow cooker stir together beans, undrained tomatoes, corn, onion, green chile peppers, garlic, jalapeño peppers, chili powder, oregano, cumin, and salt. Place pork chops on bean mixture.

STEP 2 Cover and cook on low-heat setting for 8 to 10 hours or on high-heat setting for 4 to 5 hours. Reserve 4 pork chops and 3 cups bean mixture; store as directed below. Place the remaining chops in four shallow bowls. Spoon 1 cup bean mixture over each chop. If desired, sprinkle with cheese, green onion, cilantro, lime wedges, and/or sour cream.

TO STORE RESERVES Place pork chops and reserved bean mixture in separate airtight containers. Seal and chill for up to 3 days. Use in Tamale Pie Casserole, page 51.

* Because hot peppers, such as jalapeños, contain volatile oils that can burn your skin and eyes, avoid direct contact with chiles as much as possible. Wear plastic or rubber gloves. If your bare hands do touch the peppers, wash them well with soap and water.

NUTRITION FACTS
PER SERVING
239 CAL., 4 G TOTAL FAT
(1 G SAT. FAT), 65 MG CHOL.,
599 MG SODIUM,
21 G CARBO., 4 G FIBER,
32 G PRO.

DAILY VALUES
8% VIT. A, 34% VIT. C,
10% CALCIUM, 13% IRON

EXCHANGES
1½ STARCH,
4 VERY LEAN MEAT

tamale pie casserole

IN THIS SATISFYING CASSEROLE, A GOLDEN CORN BREAD TOPPING NICELY COMPLEMENTS THE BOLD FLAVORS OF THE SAUCY MEAT-AND-BEAN STEW UNDERNEATH.

Reserved Pork Chops & Saucy Beans Mexicana* (see recipe, page 50)

1	2.25-ounce can sliced, pitted ripe olives, drained
2	tablespoons tomato paste
1	cup cornmeal
½	cup all-purpose flour
1	teaspoon baking powder
¼	teaspoon salt
¾	cup milk
1	egg, beaten
3	tablespoons cooking oil
¾	cup shredded Mexican cheese blend (3 ounces)
	Dairy sour cream (optional)

PREP
15 MINUTES

BAKE
25 MINUTES

STAND
5 MINUTES

OVEN
400°F

MAKES
4 SERVINGS

STEP 1 Chop reserved pork chops. In a medium saucepan combine reserved bean mixture and the chopped pork. Stir in olives and tomato paste; cook over medium heat until heated through. Pour pork mixture into a greased 2-quart rectangular baking dish; set aside.

STEP 2 In a medium bowl stir together cornmeal, flour, baking powder, and salt. In a small bowl whisk together milk, egg, and oil. Add to cornmeal mixture, stirring until combined. Stir in cheese. Spread cornmeal mixture evenly over pork and bean mixture.

STEP 3 Bake, uncovered, in a 400°F oven for 25 to 30 minutes or until top is completely set and begins to brown. Let stand for 5 minutes before serving. If desired, serve with sour cream.

* There should be 4 reserved pork chops and 3 cups reserved bean mixture.

NUTRITION FACTS PER SERVING
657 CAL., 25 G TOTAL FAT (7 G SAT. FAT), 141 MG CHOL., 1,166 MG SODIUM, 65 G CARBO., 8 G FIBER, 45 G PRO.

DAILY VALUES
14% VIT. A, 37% VIT. C, 32% CALCIUM, 24% IRON

EXCHANGES
4 STARCH, 5 LEAN MEAT, 1 FAT

asian pork ribs

THIS LUSCIOUS, FORK-TENDER DISH HAS A NICE LITTLE GINGER AND GARLIC KICK, MAKING IT JUST THE TICKET WHEN YOU WANT YOUR RIBS SERVED WITH SOME ATTITUDE.

PREP
15 MINUTES

COOK
9 HOURS (LOW) OR
4½ HOURS (HIGH)

MAKES
4 SERVINGS + RESERVES

1	cup bias-sliced carrot (2 medium)
1	8-ounce can bamboo shoots, drained
1	8-ounce can sliced water chestnuts, drained
1	medium onion, cut into thin wedges
2	pounds boneless country-style pork ribs
4	cups coarsely chopped cabbage (½ medium head)
1	11.5-ounce jar stir-fry sauce
2	tablespoons quick-cooking tapioca
1	teaspoon ground ginger
3	cloves garlic, minced
2	cups hot cooked rice
	Chow mein noodles (optional)

STEP 1   In a 5- or 6-quart slow cooker stir together carrot, bamboo shoots, water chestnuts, and onion. Place pork ribs on top. Place cabbage on ribs. In a small bowl stir together stir-fry sauce, tapioca, ginger, and garlic. Pour over ribs and cabbage in cooker.

STEP 2   Cover and cook on low-heat setting for 9 to 10 hours or on high-heat setting for 4½ to 5 hours.

STEP 3   Reserve half of the pork and vegetable mixture (about 3½ cups); store as directed below. Serve remaining pork and vegetable mixture over hot cooked rice. If desired, sprinkle with chow mein noodles.

TO STORE RESERVES   Place pork and vegetable mixture in an airtight container. Seal and chill for up to 3 days. (Do not freeze.) Use in Giant Wontons, page 53.

NUTRITION FACTS
PER SERVING
388 CAL., 11 G TOTAL FAT
(3 G SAT. FAT), 73 MG CHOL.,
987 MG SODIUM,
45 G CARBO., 2 G FIBER,
18 G PRO.

DAILY VALUES
34% VIT. A, 24% VIT. C,
15% CALCIUM, 14% IRON

EXCHANGES
1 VEGETABLE, 1½ STARCH,
1 OTHER CARBO.,
3 MEDIUM-FAT MEAT

giant wontons

IF YOU LOVE WONTONS AS AN APPETIZER, WHY NOT MAKE THEM INTO A MAIN-DISH EVENT? THESE ARE SEDUCTIVE—PORK AND VEGGIES STUFFED IN A DELICATE WRAP, FRIED UNTIL CRISP, AND TOPPED WITH AN EXQUISITE PLUM SAUCE.

Reserved pork and vegetables from Asian Pork Ribs* (see recipe, page 52)

1	egg
1	tablespoon water
1	16-ounce package egg roll wrappers (15)
	Cooking oil for deep-fat frying
1	cup plum jam
⅓	cup sliced green onion (3)
1	tablespoon soy sauce
1	tablespoon rice vinegar
1	teaspoon ground ginger
½	teaspoon toasted sesame oil
⅛	teaspoon crushed red pepper

STEP 1 Coarsely chop reserved pork and vegetable mixture; set aside. In a small bowl beat together egg and water. Place an egg roll wrapper on a work surface with a point toward you. In the center of the wrapper spoon about ¼ cup of the pork mixture. Fold bottom point over filling; tuck it under the filling. Roll the wrapper once to enclose filling; leave about 1 inch unrolled at the top of the wrapper. Moisten the right-hand corner of wrapper with a small amount of egg mixture. Pick up the right- and left-hand corners of the wrapper and bring toward you, below the filling. Overlap the right- and left-hand corners; press together to seal. Repeat with remaining wrappers and filling.

STEP 2 In a large heavy saucepan or deep-fat fryer heat 2 inches of cooking oil to 365°F. Fry wontons, three at a time, in hot oil for 2 to 3 minutes or until golden. Drain on paper towels. Keep warm in a 200°F oven while frying remaining wontons .

STEP 3 In a small saucepan combine plum jam, green onion, soy sauce, rice vinegar, ginger, sesame oil, and crushed red pepper. Cook and stir over low heat 5 minutes or until jam melts. Serve warm with plum sauce.

* There should be about 3¼ cups reserved pork and vegetable broth.

PREP
35 MINUTES

COOK
2 MINUTES PER BATCH
PLUS 5 MINUTES FOR SAUCE

MAKES
15 GIANT WONTONS

NUTRITION FACTS
PER SERVING
243 CAL., 8 G TOTAL FAT
(2 G SAT. FAT), 35 MG CHOL.,
396 MG SODIUM,
33 G CARBO., 1 G FIBER,
9 G PRO.

DAILY VALUES
10% VIT. A, 10% VIT. C,
5% CALCIUM, 5% IRON

EXCHANGES
1½ STARCH, 1 OTHER CARBO.,
1 MEDIUM-FAT MEAT, ½ FAT

barbecued country-style ribs

YOU KNEW YOU COULD MAKE BARBECUE RIBS IN YOUR SLOW COOKER, BUT YOU JUST HAVEN'T GOTTEN YOUR HANDS ON A GREAT RECIPE. WELL, HERE IT IS! SERVE THESE WITH PREPARED TWICE-BAKED POTATOES PICKED UP FROM THE DELI OR FREEZER CASE FOR A HEARTY—AND WORTHY—ACCOMPANIMENT.

PREP
30 MINUTES

COOK
10 HOURS (LOW) OR
5 HOURS (HIGH)

MAKES
4 SERVINGS + RESERVES

4½	to 5 pounds boneless pork country-style ribs
1½	cups bottled barbecue sauce
½	cup chopped onion (1 medium)
½	cup chopped celery (1 stalk)
2	tablespoons yellow mustard
1	tablespoon packed brown sugar
1	tablespoon Worcestershire sauce
2	cloves garlic, minced
1	teaspoon dried thyme, crushed
2	cups hot cooked noodles

STEP 1 Trim fat from ribs. Place ribs in a 4- or 5-quart slow cooker. In a medium bowl stir together barbecue sauce, onion, celery, mustard, brown sugar, Worcestershire sauce, garlic, and thyme. Pour sauce over ribs in cooker.

STEP 2 Cover and cook on low-heat setting for 10 to 11 hours or on high-heat setting for 5 to 5½ hours.

STEP 3 Using a slotted spoon, remove ribs from sauce. Strain sauce; if necessary, skim fat from sauce. Serve half of the ribs and half of the sauce with the hot cooked noodles.

STEP 4 Using two forks, shred the remaining half of the ribs, trimming fat as necessary; store as directed below.

TO STORE RESERVES Place shredded pork (about 3 cups) and 1 cup sauce in an airtight container; stir to coat. Place remaining sauce in a second airtight container. Seal and chill for up to 3 days. (Or freeze for up to 3 months. Thaw in refrigerator overnight before using.) Use in Shredded Pork Sandwiches with Vinegar Slaw, page 55.

NUTRITION FACTS
PER SERVING
554 CAL., 22 G TOTAL FAT (7 G SAT. FAT), 189 MG CHOL., 632 MG SODIUM, 30 G CARBO., 2 G FIBER, 54 G PRO.

DAILY VALUES
2% VIT. A, 10% VIT. C, 9% CALCIUM, 26% IRON

EXCHANGES
1 STARCH, 1 OTHER CARBO., 7½ LEAN MEAT

shredded pork sandwiches with vinegar slaw

YUP—THESE SANDWICHES ARE EVERY BIT AS SATISFYINGLY DOWN-HOME AS YOU'D EXPECT WITH A COMBO OF SHREDDED PORK AND PUCKERY SLAW! HINT: IF YOU DON'T WANT TO MESS WITH MAKING YOUR OWN HOMEMADE SLAW, JUST PICK SOME UP FROM THE DELI—YOU'LL NEED ABOUT $1\frac{1}{2}$ CUPS.

PREP
25 MINUTES

CHILL
2 TO 24 HOURS

MAKES
4 SERVINGS

2	cups finely shredded green cabbage
¼	cup cider vinegar
3	tablespoons honey
¼	teaspoon salt
⅛	teaspoon black pepper
	Reserved meat and sauce from Barbecued Country-Style Ribs* (see recipe, page 54)
4	kaiser rolls or hoagie buns, split and toasted
	Bottled hot pepper sauce (optional)

STEP 1 In a medium bowl combine cabbage, vinegar, honey, salt, and pepper. Toss to combine. Cover and chill for 2 to 24 hours, stirring occasionally.

STEP 2 In a medium saucepan heat reserved meat mixture, covered, over medium heat about 10 minutes or until heated through, stirring occasionally. If desired, add some of the reserved sauce to moisten meat as desired. In a small saucepan, heat any remaining sauce over medium-low heat until heated through.

STEP 3 To serve, strain cabbage mixture, discarding liquid. Divide meat mixture among roll bottoms. Top with cabbage and roll tops. Pass reserved sauce and, if desired, bottled hot pepper sauce.

* There should be 3 cups reserved shredded pork mixed with 1 cup sauce and about 2 cups additional reserved sauce.

NUTRITION FACTS
PER SERVING
673 CAL., 23 G TOTAL FAT (7 G SAT. FAT), 162 MG CHOL., 1,089 MG SODIUM, 56 G CARBO., 3 G FIBER, 57 G PRO.

DAILY VALUES
3% VIT. A, 29% VIT. C, 15% CALCIUM, 31% IRON

EXCHANGES
3 STARCH, 1 OTHER CARBO., 7 LEAN MEAT

southwestern pork ribs

FOR A BRIGHT, SLIGHTLY SWEET ACCOMPANIMENT TO THESE SPICY RIBS, TOSS SALAD GREENS WITH A VINAIGRETTE SPIKED WITH SOME HONEY AND LIME AND TOP THE SALAD WITH ORANGES, RED ONIONS, AND ALMONDS.

PREP
20 MINUTES

COOK
8 HOURS (LOW) OR
4 HOURS (HIGH)

MAKES
4 SERVINGS + RESERVES

2	teaspoons chili powder
½	teaspoon salt
½	teaspoon onion powder
½	teaspoon garlic powder
½	teaspoon ground cumin
¼	teaspoon black pepper
⅛	teaspoon cayenne pepper
3	pounds boneless pork country-style ribs
2	medium yellow sweet peppers, cut into 1-inch strips
1	large sweet onion, cut into wedges
1	16-ounce bottle lime and garlic chunky salsa or other type salsa
1	8.8-ounce pouch cooked Spanish-style rice

STEP 1 In a small bowl stir together chili powder, salt, onion powder, garlic powder, cumin, black pepper, and cayenne pepper. Sprinkle over pork ribs; rub in with your fingers.

STEP 2 Place ribs in a 5- or 6-quart slow cooker. Add sweet pepper and onion. Pour salsa over ribs and vegetables in cooker.

STEP 3 Cover and cook on low-heat setting for 8 to 10 hours or on high-heat setting for 4 to 5 hours.

STEP 4 Meanwhile, prepare rice according to package directions. Chop enough of the ribs to equal 3 cups; store as directed below. Serve remaining ribs with prepared rice.

TO STORE RESERVES Place reserved pork in an airtight container. Seal and chill for up to 3 days. (Or freeze for up to 3 months. Thaw in refrigerator overnight before using.) Use in Enchiladas al Pastor, page 57.

NUTRITION FACTS
PER SERVING
485 CAL., 15 G TOTAL FAT (5 G SAT. FAT), 108 MG CHOL., 1,389 MG SODIUM, 44 G CARBO., 4 G FIBER, 37 G PRO.

DAILY VALUES
16% VIT. A, 257% VIT. C, 8% CALCIUM, 16% IRON

EXCHANGES
2 VEGETABLE, 2 STARCH, 4 LEAN MEAT, 1 FAT

enchiladas al pastor

AL PASTOR MEANS "IN THE STYLE OF THE SHEPHERD," AND THERE'S DEFINITELY A NICELY RUSTIC APPEAL TO THIS DISH. YOU'LL ALSO LIKE THE WAY IT QUICKLY COMES TOGETHER, THANKS TO TWO CONVENIENT MEXICAN-STYLE PRODUCTS: ENCHILADA SAUCE AND A MEXICAN CHEESE BLEND.

PREP
20 MINUTES

BAKE
15 MINUTES

OVEN
400°F

MAKES
4 SERVINGS

Reserved Southwestern Pork Ribs* (see recipe, page 56)

1   10-ounce can enchilada sauce

2   cups shredded Mexican cheese blend (8 ounces)

8   6-inch corn tortillas

Dairy sour cream (optional)

Shredded lettuce (optional)

STEP 1   In a medium bowl stir together reserved pork, half of the enchilada sauce, and half of the cheese. Warm tortillas according to package directions. Place ⅓ to ¼ cup of pork mixture on one end of each of the tortillas; roll up. Place filled tortillas, seam sides down, in a 2-quart rectangular baking dish. Top filled tortillas with remaining enchilada sauce and shredded cheese.

STEP 2   Bake, uncovered, in a 400°F oven about 15 minutes or until cheese melts and enchiladas are heated through. If desired, serve with sour cream and shredded lettuce.

* There should be 3 cups chopped reserved pork.

NUTRITION FACTS
PER SERVING
648 CAL., 34 G TOTAL FAT (15 G SAT. FAT), 158 MG CHOL., 1,010 MG SODIUM, 35 G CARBO., 3 G FIBER, 49 G PRO.

DAILY VALUES
9% VIT. A, 5% VIT. C, 42% CALCIUM, 26% IRON

EXCHANGES
2 STARCH, 4 LEAN MEAT, 2 HIGH-FAT MEAT, 1½ FAT

chunky italian sausage stew

AFTER A LONG DAY, SIT DOWN WITH A STEAMING BOWL OF STEW THAT'S CHOCK-FULL OF FAVORITE PIZZA FLAVORS. FOCACCIA BREAD FROM THE BAKERY WOULD BE AN EASY AND WELL-MATCHED ACCOMPANIMENT.

PREP
25 MINUTES

COOK
5 HOURS (LOW) OR
2½ HOURS (HIGH)

MAKES
6 SERVINGS + RESERVES

2	pounds hot or sweet bulk Italian sausage
12	ounces unsliced pepperoni, cut into ¾-inch chunks
4	large yellow sweet peppers, cut into thin strips
½	cup finely chopped onion (1 medium)
2	4-ounce cans (drained weight) sliced mushrooms, drained
1	2.5-ounce can sliced, pitted ripe olives, drained
¼	to ½ teaspoon crushed red pepper (optional)
1	26-ounce jar pasta sauce with mushrooms

STEP 1 In a very large skillet cook bulk sausage over medium heat until brown, stirring to break into bite-size pieces. Drain off fat.

STEP 2 In a 5- or 6-quart slow cooker stir together cooked sausage, pepperoni, sweet pepper, onion, mushrooms, olives, and, if desired, crushed red pepper. Pour pasta sauce over sausage mixture in cooker.

STEP 3 Cover and cook on low-heat setting for 5 to 6 hours or on high-heat setting for 2½ to 3 hours.

STEP 4 Using a slotted spoon, remove 3 cups stew mixture; store as directed below. Spoon remaining stew into bowls.

TO STORE RESERVES Place stew mixture in an airtight container. Seal and chill for up to 3 days. (Or freeze for up to 3 months. Thaw in refrigerator overnight before using.) Use in French Bread Pizza, page 59.

NUTRITION FACTS
PER SERVING
751 CAL., 47 G TOTAL FAT
(17 G SAT. FAT),
127 MG CHOL., 3,730 MG
SODIUM, 44 G CARBO.,
15 G FIBER, 37 G PRO.

DAILY VALUES
13% VIT. A, 402% VIT. C,
16% CALCIUM, 37% IRON

EXCHANGES
½ VEGETABLE, 3 OTHER
CARBO., 5 MEDIUM-FAT MEAT,
4 FAT

french bread pizza

ONCE YOU'VE GOT A LITTLE CHUNKY ITALIAN STEW STASHED AWAY, THERE'S NO NEED TO SETTLE FOR FROZEN PIZZA. FRESHLY MADE, ABUNDANTLY CHEESY, AND RIFE WITH ROBUST SAUSAGE FLAVOR, THIS HOMEMADE VERSION IS SO MUCH BETTER.

1   loaf French bread, cut in half lengthwise
     Reserved meat and vegetable mixture from Chunky Italian Sausage Stew*
       (see recipe, page 58)
1   8-ounce package shredded Italian blend cheeses

STEP 1 Preheat oven to 425°F. Place bread loaf halves, cut sides up, on an extra large baking sheet. Top with reserved meat and vegetable mixture. Sprinkle with cheese. Bake 15 to 20 minutes or until cheese is melted and bubbly.

* There should be 3 cups reserved meat and vegetable mixture.

PREP
10 MINUTES

BAKE
15 MINUTES

OVEN
425°F

MAKES
6 SERVINGS

NUTRITION FACTS
PER SERVING
577 CAL., 27 G TOTAL FAT
(12 G SAT. FAT),
69 MG CHOL.,
1,944 MG SODIUM,
54 G CARBO., 7 G FIBER,
28 G PRO.

DAILY VALUES
4% VIT. A, 134% VIT. C,
32% CALCIUM, 23% IRON

EXCHANGES
½ VEGETABLE, 2½ STARCH,
1 OTHER CARBO., 3 MEDIUM-
FAT MEAT, 2 FAT

fire-roasted tomato & italian sausage grinders

WHEN CANS OF FIRE-ROASTED DICED TOMATOES HIT GROCERY STORE SHELVES IN RECENT YEARS, CLEVER COOKS IMMEDIATELY STARTED USING THEM TO REV UP THEIR RECIPES. USE THEM TO ADD SOMETHING EXTRA TO THIS CLASSIC ITALIAN SANDWICH.

PREP
15 MINUTES

COOK
6 HOURS (LOW) OR
3 HOURS (HIGH)

BROIL
2 MINUTES

MAKES
6 SERVINGS + RESERVES

10	uncooked hot or sweet Italian sausage links (about 2½ pounds)
2	14.5-ounce cans fire-roasted diced tomatoes
1	28-ounce can crushed tomatoes
6	cloves garlic, minced
1	tablespoon balsamic vinegar
2	teaspoons dried basil, crushed
1	teaspoon dried oregano, crushed
½	teaspoon salt
½	teaspoon crushed red pepper
¼	teaspoon black pepper
6	each French-style rolls or hoagie buns, split
6	slices provolone cheese
¾	cup bottled roasted red sweet peppers, cut into thin strips

STEP 1 In a 5- or 6-quart slow cooker stir together sausage links, undrained diced tomatoes, undrained crushed tomatoes, garlic, vinegar, basil, oregano, salt, crushed red pepper, and black pepper.

STEP 2 Cover and cook on low-heat setting for 6 to 8 hours or on high-heat setting for 3 to 4 hours.

STEP 3 Reserve 4 sausage links and 3 cups sauce; store as directed below.

STEP 4 Place remaining sausage links on roll bottoms. Place ½ slice cheese over each sausage and ½ slice cheese on cut side of each roll top. Broil 4 to 5 inches from heat for 2 to 3 minutes or until cheese is melted and bubbly. Top with pepper strips and roll tops. Serve with remaining sauce for dipping.

TO STORE RESERVES Place sausages and sauce in separate airtight containers. Seal and chill for up to 3 days. Use in Sausage-Stuffed Manicotti, page 61.

NUTRITION FACTS
PER SERVING
859 CAL., 39 G TOTAL FAT
(17 G SAT. FAT), 96 MG
CHOL., 2,305 MG SODIUM,
81 G CARBO., 6 G FIBER,
37 G PRO.

DAILY VALUES
23% VIT. A, 117% VIT. C,
41% CALCIUM, 39% IRON

EXCHANGES
1 VEGETABLE, 5 STARCH,
3 MEDIUM-FAT MEAT, 4 FAT

sausage-stuffed manicotti

LOOKING FOR A WINE TO SERVE WITH THIS TANGY-YET-CREAMY DELIGHT? TRY A CHIANTI FROM ITALY—MANY GOOD ONES ARE AVAILABLE AT EVERYDAY PRICES. OR TRY A SANGIOVESE FROM CALIFORNIA; IT'S MADE FROM THE SAME GRAPE AS CHIANTI, BUT THE CALIFORNIA VERSIONS ARE SOMETIMES FRUITIER.

PREP
20 MINUTES

BAKE
30 MINUTES

OVEN
350°F

MAKES
6 SERVINGS

12   large manicotti shells
      Reserved sausages and sauce from Fire-Roasted Tomato & Italian Sausage
        Grinders* (see recipe, page 60)
1   15-ounce carton ricotta cheese
1   cup finely shredded Parmesan cheese (4 ounces)
2   teaspoons dried basil, crushed
1½   cups shredded smoked mozzarella cheese (6 ounces)

STEP 1   Cook manicotti shells according to package directions; drain. Cool manicotti in a single layer on a piece of greased foil.

STEP 2   Chop reserved sausages. In a medium bowl combine chopped sausage, ricotta, Parmesan cheese, and basil. Use a small spoon to fill manicotti shells with sausage mixture. Arrange filled shells in a 3-quart rectangular baking dish. Pour reserved sauce over filled shells. Sprinkle with smoked mozzarella.

STEP 3   Bake, covered, in a 350°F oven for 20 minutes. Uncover and bake about 10 minutes or until cheese is melted and bubbly.

* There should be 4 reserved sausages and 3 cups reserved sauce.

NUTRITION FACTS
PER SERVING
764 CAL., 46 G TOTAL FAT (22 G SAT. FAT), 145 MG CHOL., 1,696 MG SODIUM, 39 G CARBO., 3 G FIBER, 42 G PRO.

DAILY VALUES
31% VIT. A, 32% VIT C, 53% CALCIUM, 26% IRON

EXCHANGES
½ VEGETABLE, 2½ STARCH, 5 MEDIUM-FAT MEAT, 4 FAT

italian sausage sandwiches

THESE ZESTY SANDWICHES ARE REMINISCENT OF SOMETHING
YOU MIGHT ENJOY AT A LIVELY FESTIVAL HOSTED BY AN
ITALIAN-AMERICAN COMMUNITY.

PREP
25 MINUTES

COOK
7 HOURS (LOW) OR
3½ (HIGH)

BAKE
5 MINUTES

OVEN
350°F

MAKES
6 SERVINGS + RESERVES

3	large green and/or red sweet peppers, cut into bite-size strips
4	4.5-ounce jars (drained weight) sliced mushrooms, drained
1	26-ounce jar purchased marinara sauce
1	15-ounce can tomato sauce with garlic and onion
1	to 2 teaspoons crushed red pepper
8	uncooked Italian sausage links (about 1½ pounds)
6	hoagie buns or French-style rolls, split and toasted
1½	cups shredded mozzarella cheese (6 ounces)

STEP 1   In a 5 - or 6-quart slow cooker place sweet pepper and mushrooms. Stir in pasta sauce, tomato sauce, and crushed red pepper. Add sausage.

STEP 2   Cover and cook on low-heat setting for 7 to 8 hours or on high-heat setting for 3½ to 4 hours.

STEP 3   Reserve 2 sausages and 1¼ cups of the vegetable mixture; store as directed below.

STEP 4   To serve, place a sausage on each hoagie bun. Using a slotted spoon, spoon vegetable mixture over the sausages. Sprinkle with mozzarella cheese. Arrange sandwiches on a baking sheet. Bake, uncovered, in a 350°F oven for 5 to 10 minutes or until cheese melts. Serve any remaining sauce for dipping.

TO STORE RESERVES Place sausages and vegetable mixture in an airtight container. Seal and chill for up to 3 days. Use in Speedy Sausage Pizza, page 63.

NUTRITION FACTS
PER SERVING
830 CAL., 34 G TOTAL FAT
(13 G SAT. FAT), 80 MG
CHOL., 2,329 MG SODIUM,
94 G CARBO., 9 G FIBER,
33 G PRO.

DAILY VALUES
9% VIT. A, 101% VIT. C,
31% CALCIUM, 35% IRON

EXCHANGES
1½ VEGETABLE, 4½ STARCH,
1 OTHER CARBO., 2 HIGH-FAT
MEAT, 3 FAT

speedy sausage pizza

IT WILL TAKE LESS TIME TO MAKE THIS TERRIFIC HOMEMADE
PIZZA THAN IT WOULD TO HAVE A PIZZA DELIVERED. AND THIS
IS SO MUCH BETTER!

	Reserved sausages and vegetable mixture from Italian Sausage Sandwiches*
	(see recipe, page 62)
1	6-ounce can Italian-style tomato paste
½	cup pitted, sliced ripe and/or green olives
1	teaspoon fennel seeds, crushed
1	10-inch Italian bread shell
1½	cups shredded mozzarella cheese (6 ounces)

STEP 1 Cut reserved sausages into ¼-inch slices; set aside. In a large
saucepan heat reserved vegetable mixture over medium heat. Stir in
tomato paste, olives, fennel seeds, and the sausage slices. Cook over
medium heat, stirring occasionally, until thickened and heated through.

STEP 2 Spread hot sausage mixture evenly over the bread shell. Top with
cheese. Bake, uncovered, in a 375°F oven for 15 to 17 minutes or until cheese
melts and begins to brown.

* There should be 2 reserved sausages and 1¼ cups reserved vegetable mixture.

PREP
20 MINUTES

BAKE
15 MINUTES

OVEN
375°F

MAKES
6 SERVINGS

NUTRITION FACTS
PER SERVING
424 CAL., 21 G TOTAL FAT
(7 G SAT. FAT), 47 MG CHOL.,
1,305 MG SODIUM,
40 G CARBO., 3 G FIBER,
20 G PRO.

DAILY VALUES
6% VIT. A, 39% VIT. C,
26% CALCIUM, 19% IRON

EXCHANGES
1 VEGETABLE, 2½ STARCH,
1½ HIGH-FAT MEAT, 1 FAT

peppered sweet ham steaks

A NICE PEPPERY BITE CONTRASTS THE DISTINCTIVE SWEETNESS OF PINEAPPLE, MAPLE, AND EARTHY SPICES FOR A KICKY TAKE ON HAM STEAKS!

PREP
10 MINUTES

COOK
8 HOURS (LOW) OR
4 HOURS (HIGH)

MAKES
6 SERVINGS + RESERVES

1	16-ounce package peeled baby carrots
2	1½-pound cooked center-cut ham steaks
1	15.25-ounce can pineapple chunks (juice pack)
⅓	cup apple juice
⅓	cup pure maple syrup or maple-flavor syrup
⅓	cup raisins
¼	cup packed brown sugar
1	teaspoon coarsely ground black pepper
¼	teaspoon cayenne pepper
¼	teaspoon ground cloves
¼	teaspoon ground ginger

STEP 1 Place carrots in a 5- or 6-quart slow cooker; place ham on top. In a small bowl stir together undrained pineapple, apple juice, maple syrup, raisins, brown sugar, black pepper, cayenne pepper, cloves, and ginger. Pour over ham in cooker.

STEP 2 Cover and cook on low-heat setting for 8 to 9 hours or on high-heat setting for 4 to 4½ hours.

STEP 3 Reserve 12 ounces of the ham; store as directed below. Serve remaining ham with all of the carrots and pineapple mixture. Drizzle some of the cooking liquid over all; discard remaining cooking liquid.

TO STORE RESERVES Finely chop ham (2 cups); place in an airtight container. Seal and chill for up to 3 days. (Or freeze for up to 3 months. Thaw in refrigerator overnight before using.) Use in Ham Salad Sandwiches, page 65.

NUTRITION FACTS

PER SERVING
136 CAL., 13 G TOTAL FAT
(4 G SAT. FAT), 86 MG CHOL.,
2,032 MG SODIUM,
54 G CARBO., 5 G FIBER,
26 G PRO.

DAILY VALUES
165% VIT. A, 28% VIT. C,
10% CALCIUM, 15% IRON

EXCHANGES
1 VEGETABLE, 1 FRUIT,
2 OTHER CARBO., 3½ LEAN
MEAT, 1 FAT

ham salad sandwiches

FOR LUNCH, SERVE THE TANGY HAM SALAD AND CREAMY BRIE ON CROISSANTS OR BREAD—THE SANDWICHES GO WELL WITH A STEAMING BOWL OF POTATO SOUP. FOR EASY ENTERTAINING, FILL TEA ROLLS OR MINI BREADS OF YOUR CHOICE WITH THE HAM-AND-CHEESE DUO.

PREP
20 MINUTES

MAKES
6 SANDWICHES

Reserved ham from Peppered Sweet Ham Steaks* (see recipe, page 64)

½   cup finely chopped celery (1 stalk)

½   cup mayonnaise or salad dressing

¼   cup thinly sliced green onion (2)

1   tablespoon Dijon-style mustard

1   teaspoon snipped fresh chives, basil, or tarragon or ¼ teaspoon dried basil or tarragon, crushed

6   croissants, split, or 12 slices bread

1   4-ounce round Brie or Camembert cheese, sliced

STEP 1   In a medium bowl stir together chopped ham, celery, mayonnaise, green onion, mustard, and chives.

STEP 2   Place a scant $\frac{1}{2}$ cup ham salad on each croissant bottom or on each of 6 slices of bread. Top with sliced cheese and the roll tops or remaining bread slices.

* There should be 2 cups finely chopped reserved ham.

NUTRITION FACTS
PER SERVING
526 CAL., 37 G TOTAL FAT (14 G SAT. FAT), 96 MG CHOL., 1,451 MG SODIUM, 29 G CARBO., 2 G FIBER, 19 G PRO.

DAILY VALUES
13% VIT. A, 6% VIT. C, 8% CALCIUM, 11% IRON

EXCHANGES
2 STARCH, 2½ MEDIUM-FAT MEAT, 4 FAT

ham & potato stew

CONDENSED CREAM OF POTATO SOUP IS YOUR SHORTCUT SECRET
TO A RICH, HEARTY STEW YOU'LL LOVE ON A FROSTY NIGHT.

1	pound cooked ham, cut into cubes
1	pound red-skin potatoes, cut in 1-inch pieces
1	16-ounce package frozen small whole onions
1	16-ounce package peeled baby carrots
1	cup sliced celery (2 stalks)
2	10.75-ounce cans condensed cream of potato soup
1	14-ounce can chicken broth
1	teaspoon dried thyme, crushed
¼	teaspoon black pepper
1	cup frozen peas

STEP 1 In a 4- or 5-quart slow cooker stir together ham, potato, onions, carrots, and celery. Stir in soup, broth, thyme, and pepper.

STEP 2 Cover and cook on low-heat setting for 8 to 10 hours on high-heat setting for 4 to 5 hours. Stir in peas. Let stand for 5 minutes.

STEP 3 Reserve half (about 6 cups) of the stew; store as directed below.

TO STORE RESERVES Place stew in an airtight container. Seal and chill for up to 3 days. (Do not freeze.) Use in Ham Stew Pot Pies, page 67.

PREP
15 MINUTES

COOK
8 HOURS (LOW) OR
4 HOURS (HIGH)

STAND
5 MINUTES

MAKES
4 SERVINGS + RESERVES

NUTRITION FACTS
PER SERVING
257 CAL., 7 G TOTAL FAT
(3 G SAT. FAT), 29 MG CHOL.,
1,570 MG SODIUM,
33 G CARBO., 6 G FIBER,
14 G PRO.

DAILY VALUES
132% VIT. A, 28% VIT. C,
6% CALCIUM, 12% IRON

EXCHANGES
1 VEGETABLE, 1 STARCH,
½ OTHER CARBO., 1½ LEAN
MEAT, ½ FAT

ham stew pot pies

TENDER, FLAKY PIECRUST TOPS A HEARTY HAM STEW—NOBODY WILL BELIEVE THESE WHOLESOME LITTLE PIES ARE SO SIMPLE TO PREPARE!

½   of a 15-ounce package rolled refrigerated unbaked piecrust (1 crust)
    Reserved Ham & Potato Stew* (see recipe, page 68)
1   egg
1   tablespoon water

STEP 1 Let piecrust stand at room temperature according to package directions. Unroll piecrust and cut into quarters. Cut slits in the center of each piece; set aside.

STEP 2 In a large saucepan heat reserved stew over medium heat just until bubbly. Divide mixture among four 14- to 18-ounce individual casserole dishes. Place each piecrust piece over mixture in each casserole, tucking in any edges that hang over. Place casseroles in a 15×10×1-inch baking pan. In a small bowl whisk together egg and water. Brush each crust with egg mixture.

STEP 3 Bake, uncovered, in a 375°F oven about 30 minutes or until pastry is golden brown. Let stand for 10 minutes before serving.

* There should be about 6 cups reserved stew.

PREP
15 MINUTES

BAKE
30 MINUTES

STAND
10 MINUTES

OVEN
375°F

MAKES
4 SERVINGS

NUTRITION FACTS
PER SERVING
511 CAL., 22 G TOTAL FAT (9 G SAT. FAT), 102 MG CHOL., 1,804 MG SODIUM, 59 G CARBO., 6 G FIBER, 17 G PRO.

DAILY VALUES
133% VIT. A, 28% VIT. C, 7% CALCIUM, 13% IRON

EXCHANGES
1 VEGETABLE, 1½ STARCH, 2 OTHER CARBO., 1½ LEAN MEAT, 3½ FAT

1

ham & four cheese linguine

READY FOR SOMETHING IRRESISTIBLY RICH AND EASY? LET FOUR CHEESES, HAM, AND CREAM BUBBLE TO THE PERFECT CONSISTENCY IN YOUR SLOW COOKER FOR A TERRIFICALLY LUSCIOUS LINGUINE DISH. NOTE: AT FIRST, THE SAUCE MAY SEEM A LITTLE THIN, BUT IT THICKENS UP NICELY WHEN STIRRED WITH THE PASTA.

PREP
25 MINUTES

COOK
2 HOURS (LOW)

MAKES
4 SERVINGS + RESERVES

1	cup shredded Emmentaler cheese (4 ounces)
1	cup shredded Gruyère cheese (4 ounces)
1	cup crumbled blue cheese (4 ounces)
¾	cup finely shredded Parmesan cheese (3 ounces)
2	tablespoons all-purpose flour
1	pound cooked ham, coarsely chopped
2	cups whipping cream
12	ounces dried linguine
	Milk
	Finely shredded Parmesan cheese (optional)
	Toasted pine nuts (optional)

STEP 1 In a 3½- or 4-quart slow cooker combine Emmentaler, Gruyère, blue, and the ¾ cup Parmesan cheeses. Add flour; toss well to coat the cheeses. Stir in ham and whipping cream.

STEP 2 Cover and cook on low-heat setting for 2 to 2½ hours. Reserve 2 cups of the ham and cheese sauce; store as directed below.

STEP 3 Meanwhile, cook linguine according to package directions; drain. Add cooked pasta to remaining sauce in cooker; toss to combine. If necessary, stir in a little milk to thin. To serve, if desired, sprinkle with shredded Parmesan and pine nuts.

TO STORE RESERVES Place ham and cheese sauce in an airtight container. Seal and chill for up to 3 days. Use in Ham, Cheese & Broccoli Baked Potatoes, page 69.

NUTRITION FACTS
PER SERVING
914 CAL., 51 G TOTAL FAT (30 G SAT. FAT), 191 MG CHOL., 1,397 MG SODIUM, 71 G CARBO., 3 G FIBER, 41 G PRO.

DAILY VALUES
31% VIT. A, 5% VIT. C, 59% CALCIUM, 19% IRON

EXCHANGES
5 STARCH, 4 MEDIUM-FAT MEAT, 5 FAT

ham, cheese & broccoli baked potatoes

THE STUFFED BAKED POTATO GOES GOURMET—SO GOURMET, IN
FACT, THAT NO ONE WOULD EVER THINK THAT THE SAUCE WAS
MADE FROM LEFTOVERS YOU HAD STASHED IN THE FRIDGE!

4   large baking potatoes (8 to 10 ounces each)
     Reserved sauce from Ham & Four Cheese Linguine* (see recipe, page 68)
2   cups frozen broccoli florets, thawed

STEP 1 Scrub potatoes thoroughly with a brush; pat dry. Prick potatoes with
a fork. Bake potatoes in a 425°F oven for 40 to 45 minutes or until tender.
Meanwhile, in a small saucepan heat reserved ham and cheese sauce until
melted and smooth. Stir in broccoli; heat through.

STEP 2 Roll baked potatoes under your hand. Using a knife, cut an X in
the top of each potato. Press in and up on ends of potatoes. Spoon ham and
cheese sauce evenly over potatoes.

* There should be 2 cups reserved ham and cheese sauce.

PREP
10 MINUTES

BAKE
40 MINUTES

OVEN
425°F

MAKES
4 SERVINGS

NUTRITION FACTS
PER SERVING
540 CAL., 34 G TOTAL FAT
(20 G SAT. FAT), 127 MG
CHOL., 956 MG SODIUM,
36 G CARBO., 5 G FIBER,
25 G PRO.

DAILY VALUES
26% VIT. A, 114% VIT. C,
42% CALCIUM, 19% IRON

EXCHANGES
2½ STARCH, 2 MEDIUM-FAT
MEAT, 4 FAT

tagine-style lamb stew

A TAGINE IS A CLAY POT OFTEN USED IN MOROCCAN COOKING. DISHES MADE IN A TAGINE ARE USUALLY COOKED AT LOW TEMPERATURES FOR A LONG TIME, MAKING THEM ADAPT WELL TO THE SLOW COOKER.

PREP
30 MINUTES

COOK
10 HOURS (LOW) OR
5 HOURS (HIGH)

MAKES
4 SERVINGS + RESERVES

2	medium onions, cut into thin wedges
1 ½	cups sliced carrot (3 medium)
1	cup sliced celery (2 stalks)
6	cloves garlic, thinly sliced
⅓	cup quick-cooking tapioca, crushed
3	pounds lean boneless lamb, cut into ¾-inch cubes
2	tablespoons cooking oil
2	14-ounce cans beef broth
2	14.5-ounce cans stewed tomatoes, cut up
1	15-ounce can garbanzo beans, rinsed and drained
½	cup dry red wine (optional)
1	teaspoon dried thyme, crushed
½	teaspoon black pepper
¼	to ½ teaspoon cayenne pepper

STEP 1 In a 5- to 7-quart slow cooker place onion, carrot, celery, and garlic. Sprinkle tapioca over vegetables.

STEP 2 In a very large skillet brown meat, half at a time, in hot oil over medium heat. Drain off fat. Place meat on vegetables in cooker. Stir in broth, undrained tomatoes, garbanzo beans, wine (if desired), thyme, black pepper, and cayenne pepper.

STEP 3 Cover and cook on low-heat setting for 11 to 12 hours or on high-heat setting for 5½ to 6 hours. Reserve 6 cups of the stew; store as directed below.

TO STORE RESERVES Place stew in an airtight container. Seal and chill for up to 3 days. Use in Cheesy Shepherd's Pie, page 71.

NUTRITION FACTS
PER SERVING
413 CAL., 13 G TOTAL FAT (3 G SAT. FAT), 119 MG CHOL., 947 MG SODIUM, 29 G CARBO., 4 G FIBER, 43 G PRO.

DAILY VALUES
56% VIT. A, 9% VIT. C, 8% CALCIUM, 26% IRON

EXCHANGES
1½ VEGETABLE, 1½ STARCH, 5 LEAN MEAT

cheesy shepherd's pie

WITH THIS CLEVER PLAN-OVER, YOU GET TO DO A LITTLE CONTINENT HOPPING. HERE THE SPECIALTY OF MOROCCO GETS TRANSFORMED INTO A BRITISH FAVORITE FOR BEST-OF-BOTH-WORLDS RESULTS.

	Reserved Tagine-Style Lamb Stew* (see recipe, page 70)
2	tablespoons all-purpose flour
1	24-ounce package refrigerated mashed potatoes
½	cup shredded cheddar cheese (2 ounces)

STEP 1 In a large saucepan stir together reserved stew and the flour. Cook and stir over medium-high heat until bubbly.

STEP 2 Place stew in a 2½- to 3-quart round casserole dish. Place large spoonfuls of the potatoes on top of the hot stew. Bake, uncovered, in a 375°F oven for 20 minutes or until the potatoes are heated through. Sprinkle with cheese. Bake about 5 minutes more or until cheese melts.

* There should be 6 cups reserved stew.

PREP
15 MINUTES

BAKE
20 MINUTES

OVEN
375°F

MAKES
4 SERVINGS

NUTRITION FACTS
PER SERVING
558 CAL., 18 G TOTAL FAT (5 G SAT. FAT), 117 MG CHOL., 1,155 MG SODIUM, 51 G CARBO., 5 G FIBER, 44 G PRO.

DAILY VALUES
51% VIT. A, 57% VIT. C, 18% CALCIUM, 28% IRON

EXCHANGES
1½ VEGETABLE, 3 STARCH, 4½ LEAN MEAT, ½ FAT

slow-cooked lamb

STOP—DON'T TURN THE PAGE BECAUSE YOU SEE A LOT OF INGREDIENTS! MANY OF THESE ARE EASY-TO-MEASURE SEASONINGS THAT TAKE JUST SECONDS TO STIR TOGETHER AND TASTE WONDERFUL AFTER PLENTY OF MELDING TIME IN THE SLOW COOKER.

PREP
25 MINUTES

COOK
8 HOURS (LOW) OR
4 HOURS (HIGH)

MAKES
4 SERVINGS + RESERVES

6	cloves garlic, minced (1 tablespoon)
1	tablespoon garam masala
2	teaspoons ground cumin
1	teaspoon salt
½	teaspoon ground cinnamon
½	teaspoon black pepper
¼	teaspoon ground cardamom
2½	pounds lean boneless lamb, cut into ¾-inch pieces
4	cups sliced carrot (8 medium)
2	cups sliced celery (4 stalks)
3	large onions, halved and sliced
1	14-ounce can beef broth
½	cup water
½	cup raisins
3	tablespoons quick-cooking tapioca
2	cups hot cooked couscous

NUTRITION FACTS
PER SERVING
310 CAL., 4 G TOTAL FAT
(1 G SAT. FAT), 62 MG CHOL.,
602 MG SODIUM,
43 G CARBO., 5 G FIBER,
26 G PRO.

DAILY VALUES
134% VIT. A, 12% VIT. C,
8% CALCIUM, 18% IRON

EXCHANGES
1 VEGETABLE, ½ FRUIT,
2 STARCH, 2½ VERY
LEAN MEAT

STEP 1   In a large bowl stir together garlic, garam masala, cumin, salt, cinnamon, pepper, and cardamom. Add meat; toss to coat. Set aside.

STEP 2   In a 5- or 6-quart slow cooker stir together carrot, celery, onion, broth, water, and raisins. Sprinkle with tapioca. Place meat on top of vegetable mixture in cooker.

STEP 3   Cover and cook on low-heat setting for 8 to 10 hours or high-heat setting for 4 to 5 hours.

STEP 4   Reserve half of the meat and vegetable mixture (about 4 cups); store as directed below. Serve remaining mixture over hot cooked couscous.

TO STORE RESERVES Place meat and vegetable mixture in an airtight container. Seal and chill for up to 3 days. Use in Lamb & Polenta Casserole, page 73.

lamb & polenta casserole

IF YOU LOVE SHEPHERD'S PIE—A MEAT STEW TOPPED WITH A HEARTY MASHED POTATO LAYER—GIVE THIS RECIPE A TRY. INSTEAD OF POTATOES, IT'S TOPPED WITH CREAMY POLENTA AND A SPRINKLING OF CHEESE.

1   cup cornmeal

1   cup cold water

½   teaspoon salt

     Reserved Slow-Cooked Lamb* (see recipe, page 72)

1   14.5-ounce can diced tomatoes

½   cup shredded Colby and Monterey Jack cheese (2 ounces)

STEP 1   In a medium saucepan bring 2¾ cups water to boiling. Meanwhile, in a small bowl stir together cornmeal, 1 cup cold water, and the salt. Slowly add cornmeal mixture to boiling water, stirring constantly. Cook and stir until mixture returns to boiling; reduce heat. Simmer about 10 minutes or until mixture is very thick, stirring occasionally. Remove from heat and set aside.

STEP 2   In a large bowl stir together reserved lamb and vegetable mixture and the undrained tomatoes. Transfer mixture to a 2-quart square baking dish. Spoon cornmeal mixture over lamb mixture, spreading evenly. Cover with foil.

STEP 3   Bake in a 350°F oven for 45 minutes. Remove foil. Sprinkle with cheese. Bake, uncovered, for 10 minutes more or until heated through.

* There should be 4 cups reserved lamb and vegetable mixture.

PREP
25 MINUTES

BAKE
55 MINUTES

OVEN
350°F

MAKES
4 SERVINGS

NUTRITION FACTS PER SERVING
429 CAL., 9 G TOTAL FAT (4 G SAT. FAT), 74 MG CHOL., 1,158 MG SODIUM, 57 G CARBO., 7 G FIBER, 29 G PRO.

DAILY VALUES
138% VIT. A, 34% VIT. C, 22% CALCIUM, 21% IRON

EXCHANGES
2 VEGETABLE, ½ FRUIT, 3 STARCH, 2½ VERY LEAN MEAT, ½ FAT

greek lamb dinner

THIS RECIPE IS PERFECT FOR A SUNDAY NOON MEAL. PUT IT ON
AFTER BREAKFAST AND DO YOUR FAVORITE SUNDAY MORNING
THINGS WHILE IT COOKS.

PREP
25 MINUTES

COOK
8 HOURS (LOW) OR
4 HOURS (HIGH)

MAKES
4 SERVINGS + RESERVES

1	tablespoon dried minced onion
1	teaspoon garlic powder
1	teaspoon dried oregano, crushed
1	teaspoon finely shredded lemon peel
½	teaspoon salt
½	teaspoon dried mint, crushed
½	teaspoon dried rosemary, crushed
¼	teaspoon black pepper
2	2- to 2½-pound boneless lamb shoulder roasts
2	medium potatoes, quartered
4	medium carrots, halved
1	large onion, cut into wedges
½	cup chicken broth

STEP 1 In a small bowl stir together minced onion, garlic powder, oregano, lemon peel, salt, mint, rosemary, and pepper; set aside. Trim fat from roasts. Sprinkle onion mixture over roasts and rub in with your fingers; set aside.

STEP 2 In a 5- or 6-quart slow cooker place potato, carrot, and onion. Pour broth over vegetables. Top with roasts.

STEP 3 Cover and cook on low-heat setting for 8 to 10 hours or on high-heat setting for 4 to 5 hours.

STEP 4 Remove roasts and vegetables from cooker. Strain cooking juices; skim fat from juices. Reserve one of the roasts (1 to 1¼ pounds); store as directed below. Slice remaining roast. Serve with vegetables. Spoon some of the cooking juices over lamb and vegetables.

TO STORE RESERVES Shred lamb, trimming and discarding fat as needed. Place shredded lamb (about 3 cups) in an airtight container. Seal and chill for up to 3 days. (Or freeze for up to 3 months. Thaw in refrigerator overnight before using.) Use in Lamb Gyro Salads, page 75.

NUTRITION FACTS
PER SERVING
243 CAL., 5 G TOTAL FAT
(2 G SAT. FAT), 72 MG CHOL.,
392 MG SODIUM,
24 G CARBO., 4 G FIBER,
26 G PRO.

DAILY VALUES
133% VIT. A, 28% VIT. C,
6% CALCIUM, 19% IRON

EXCHANGES
1½ STARCH, 3 LEAN MEAT

lamb gyro salads

THE YOGURT-BASED SAUCE, WITH ITS CUCUMBER, MINT, AND GARLIC, IS BASED ON A GREEK SAUCE CALLED TZATZIKI. THIS CLASSIC COMBINATION IS AN EASY WAY TO ADD A SMOOTH, REFRESHING, TANGY CONTRAST TO RICH MEATS LIKE LAMB.

1	6-ounce carton plain low-fat yogurt
½	cup chopped, seeded cucumber
½	teaspoon dried mint, crushed, or 1 tablespoon snipped fresh mint
2	cloves garlic, minced
⅛	teaspoon salt
	Reserved meat from Greek Lamb Dinner* (see recipe, page 75)
3	large pita bread rounds, split in half horizontally
2	cups shredded lettuce
2	medium tomatoes, sliced
½	cup crumbled feta cheese or goat cheese

STEP 1   In a small bowl stir together yogurt, cucumber, mint, garlic, and salt; set aside.

STEP 2   Place shredded lamb in a microwave-safe 1-quart casserole; cover. Microwave on 100 percent power (high) for 2½ to 3½ minutes or until lamb is heated through, stirring once halfway through cooking.

STEP 3   Divide pita halves among 4 serving plates. Top with lettuce and tomato. Spoon lamb over tomato. Top with yogurt mixture and sprinkle with cheese.

* There should be about 3 cups shredded reserved lamb (1 to 1¼ pounds).

MEAL

2

START TO FINISH
20 MINUTES

MAKES
4 SERVINGS

NUTRITION FACTS
PER SERVING
364 CAL., 10 G TOTAL FAT
(5 G SAT. FAT), 91 MG CHOL.,
783 MG SODIUM,
34 G CARBO., 3 G FIBER,
33 G PRO.

DAILY VALUES
16% VIT. A, 28% VIT. C,
25% CALCIUM, 24% IRON

EXCHANGES
1 VEGETABLE, 2 STARCH,
3 LEAN MEAT

gingered lamb & chickpeas

THIS DISH WAS INSPIRED BY THE ENTICING CUISINE OF THE MEDITERRANEAN, WHERE LAMB, CHICKPEAS, AND EARTHY SPICES LIKE CORIANDER AND CUMIN ARE MUCH-LOVED INGREDIENTS.

PREP
20 MINUTES

COOK
8 HOURS (LOW) OR
4 HOURS (HIGH)

MAKES
4 SERVINGS + RESERVES

3	15-ounce cans garbanzo beans (chickpeas), rinsed and drained
1	14.5-ounce can diced tomatoes
1	cup finely chopped onion (2 medium)
¾	cup chicken broth
1	tablespoon balsamic vinegar
4	cloves garlic, minced
1	teaspoon ground ginger
1	teaspoon ground coriander
1	teaspoon ground cumin
½	teaspoon salt
¼	teaspoon black pepper
1	2½- to 3-pound boneless lamb leg
	Salt and black pepper

STEP 1 In a 5- or 6-quart slow cooker stir together chickpeas, un-drained tomatoes, onion, broth, vinegar, garlic, ginger, coriander, cumin, salt, and pepper. Trim fat from meat. Place meat on chickpea mixture in cooker. Sprinkle lightly with additional salt and pepper.

STEP 2 Cover and cook on low-heat setting for 8 to 10 hours or high-heat setting for 4 to 5 hours.

STEP 3 Reserve half of the meat (about 1 pound) and half of the chickpea mixture (about 4 cups); store as directed below. Place remaining chickpea mixture in a large bowl; mash slightly with a potato masher. Slice lamb and serve with chickpea mixture.

TO STORE RESERVES Place meat and chickpea mixture in separate airtight containers. Seal and chill for up to 3 days. Use in Gingered Hummus & Lamb Pitas, page 77.

NUTRITION FACTS
PER SERVING
393 CAL., 7 G TOTAL FAT
(2 G SAT. FAT), 92 MG CHOL.,
960 MG SODIUM,
42 G CARBO., 8 G FIBER,
38 G PRO.

DAILY VALUES
1% VIT. A, 24% VIT. C,
9% CALCIUM, 29% IRON

EXCHANGES
½ VEGETABLE, 2 STARCH,
4 LEAN MEAT

gingered hummus & lamb pitas

WITH A WHIR IN THE BLENDER, THE LEFTOVER CHICKPEA MIXTURE BECOMES A HUMMUS-LIKE SPREAD FOR THESE SANDWICHES. CUCUMBER, RADISHES, AND YOGURT ADD A FRESH, BRIGHT BITE.

Reserved Gingered Lamb & Chickpeas* (see recipe, page 76)

2	tablespoons olive oil
4	pita bread rounds, halved
½	cup chopped cucumber
½	cup chopped radishes
	Plain yogurt (optional)

STEP 1 Chop lamb (1½ cups), discarding excess fat, and place in a small saucepan. Heat, covered, over medium-low heat, stirring occasionally.

STEP 2 Meanwhile, for hummus, skim fat from chickpea mixture; drain mixture, reserving liquid. Place drained chickpea mixture, the oil, and ¼ cup of the drained liquid in a food processor or blender. Cover and process until nearly smooth.

STEP 3 Spoon about 2 tablespoons hummus inside each pita bread half.** Divide lamb mixture among pita bread halves. Top with cucumber, radishes, and, if desired, yogurt.

* There should be about 1 pound reserved meat and about 4 cups reserved chickpea mixture.

** Store any remaining hummus in the refrigerator for up to 1 week. Serve with toasted pita or tortilla chips.

START TO FINISH
25 MINUTES

MAKES
4 SERVINGS

NUTRITION FACTS
PER SERVING
436 CAL., 13 G TOTAL FAT (3 G SAT. FAT), 92 MG CHOL., 601 MG SODIUM, 40 G CARBO., 3 G FIBER, 36 G PRO.

DAILY VALUES
7% VIT. C, 8% CALCIUM, 26% IRON

EXCHANGES
½ VEGETABLE, 2½ STARCH, 4 LEAN MEAT

1

lamb curry
spicy & slow

CURRY POWDERS TYPICALLY BRING TOGETHER MORE THAN A HALF DOZEN SPICES INTO ONE EASY-TO-MEASURE BLEND. BRIGHT GREEN PEAS ARE A CLASSIC WAY TO ADD A LITTLE SWEETNESS AND SPARK TO THE SPICE'S WARM, EXOTIC FLAVORS.

PREP
20 MINUTES

COOK
8 HOURS (LOW) OR
4 HOURS (HIGH)

STAND
5 MINUTES

MAKES
4 SERVINGS + RESERVES

1	pound lean boneless lamb, cut into 1-inch cubes
2	10.75-ounce cans condensed cream of onion soup
2	cups cauliflower florets
8	ounces red-skin potatoes, cut into 1-inch pieces
1	14.5-ounce can diced tomatoes
2	medium carrots, cut into 1-inch pieces
1	medium Granny Smith apple, cut into 1-inch pieces
1	medium onion, cut into wedges
½	cup golden raisins
2	to 3 teaspoons curry powder
1	teaspoon ground ginger
½	teaspoon ground cumin
1	cup frozen peas
2	cups hot cooked couscous

STEP 1   In a 4- or 5-quart slow cooker stir together lamb, soup, cauliflower, potato, undrained tomatoes, carrot, apple, onion, raisins, curry powder, ginger, and cumin.

STEP 2   Cover and cook on low-heat setting for 8 to 10 hours or on high-heat setting for 4 to 5 hours. Stir in peas. Let stand for 5 minutes.

STEP 3   Using a slotted spoon, remove 3 cups of the lamb mixture; store as directed below. Serve remaining lamb mixture over hot cooked couscous.

TO STORE RESERVES Place lamb mixture in an airtight container. Seal and chill for up to 3 days. Use in Giant Curried Lamb Samosas, page 79.

NUTRITION FACTS
PER SERVING
394 CAL., 9 G TOTAL FAT
(3 G SAT. FAT), 54 MG CHOL.,
888 MG SODIUM,
58 G CARBO., 7 G FIBER,
22 G PRO.

DAILY VALUES
54% VIT. A, 54% VIT. C,
10% CALCIUM, 20% IRON

EXCHANGES
1 VEGETABLE, 3½ STARCH,
1½ LEAN MEAT

giant curried lamb samosas

SAMOSAS ARE SMALL MEAT- AND/OR VEGETABLE-FILLED PASTRIES THAT ARE TYPICALLY SERVED AS SNACKS OR APPETIZERS. HERE THEY'RE FOLDED INTO LARGER PORTIONS FOR MEAL-SIZE TURNOVERS MEANT TO BE ENJOYED WITH A KNIFE AND FORK.

1	15-ounce package rolled refrigerated unbaked piecrust (2 crusts)
	Reserved Lamb Curry Spicy & Slow* (see recipe, page 78)
1	egg, beaten
1	tablespoon water
1	6-ounce carton plain low-fat yogurt
¼	cup mango chutney
1	tablespoon snipped fresh mint

STEP 1 Let piecrusts stand at room temperature according to package directions to soften. Unroll piecrusts and cut each crust in half.

STEP 2 On each piece of piecrust place ¾ cup reserved lamb mixture. Fold crust over lamb mixture; crimp edges closed. Using a fork, poke a few holes in the top of each samosa to vent. Place samosas on a lightly greased baking sheet. In a small bowl whisk together egg and water. Brush tops of samosas with egg mixture.

STEP 3 Bake, uncovered, in a 425°F oven 15 to 20 minutes or until golden brown.

STEP 4 Meanwhile, in a small bowl stir together yogurt, chutney, and mint. Serve samosas with yogurt dipping sauce.

* There should be 3 cups reserved lamb mixture.

PREP
15 MINUTES

BAKE
15 MINUTES

OVEN
425°F

MAKES
4 SERVINGS

NUTRITION FACTS
PER SERVING
727 CAL., 35 G TOTAL FAT (14 G SAT. FAT), 108 MG CHOL., 1,052 MG SODIUM, 84 G CARBO., 4 G FIBER, 17 G PRO.

DAILY VALUES
36% VIT. A, 39% VIT. C, 15% CALCIUM, 15% IRON

EXCHANGES
½ VEGETABLE, 5½ STARCH, ½ LEAN MEAT, 5½ FAT

cook once eat twice

poultry

poultry is one of the most versatile meats on the planet. see how it stars here in everything from homespun stews to intriguing indian, mexican, cajun, and asian takes. then morph the leftover batch into salads, pot pies, fried rice, tostadas, casseroles, wraps, and more.

honey curry
chicken

IF YOU'RE NOT GENERALLY A FAN OF CURRY, YOU MIGHT CONSIDER GIVING THIS RECIPE A TRY ANYWAY. THE HONEY AND MUSTARD ADD DIMENSIONS OF FLAVOR THAT MIGHT MAKE THE SPICES MORE PLEASING TO YOUR PALATE.

PREP
15 MINUTES

COOK
5 HOURS (LOW) OR
2½ HOURS (HIGH)

MAKES
6 SERVINGS + RESERVES

1	large onion, halved and sliced
8	chicken breast halves with bone, skinned (about 4½ pounds total)
½	teaspoon salt
¼	teaspoon black pepper
¼	cup honey
¼	cup Dijon-style mustard
2	tablespoons butter, melted
1	tablespoon curry powder
2	large red sweet peppers, cut into bite-size strips
3	cups hot cooked white or brown rice

STEP 1 Place onion in a 5- or 6-quart slow cooker. Top with chicken. Sprinkle chicken with salt and pepper. In a small bowl stir together honey, mustard, butter, and curry powder; pour mixture over chicken in cooker. Add sweet pepper to cooker.

STEP 2 Cover and cook on low-heat setting for 5 to 6 hours or on high-heat setting for 2½ to 3 hours.

STEP 3 Remove chicken and vegetables from cooker. Strain cooking liquid. Reserve 2 chicken breasts, 1 cup vegetables, and ¼ cup cooking liquid; store as directed below. Serve remaining chicken and vegetables with hot cooked rice. Spoon some of the remaining cooking liquid over top to moisten.

TO STORE RESERVES Place chicken, vegetables, and cooking liquid in separate airtight containers. Seal and chill for up to 3 days. Use in Asian Chicken Salad, page 83.

NUTRITION FACTS
PER SERVING
367 CAL., 5 G TOTAL FAT
(2 G SAT. FAT), 104 MG
CHOL., 435 MG SODIUM,
36 G CARBO., 1 G FIBER,
43 G PRO.

DAILY VALUES
17% VIT. A, 72% VIT. C,
5% CALCIUM, 15% IRON

EXCHANGES
1½ STARCH, 1 OTHER CARBO.,
5 VERY LEAN MEAT

asian chicken salad

CHINESE CABBAGE—SOMETIMES CALLED NAPA CABBAGE—IS WORTH SEEKING OUT. ITS CRINKLY TEXTURE AND DELICATE FLAVOR WILL BRING A UNIQUE TWIST TO CHICKEN SALAD.

START TO FINISH
20 MINUTES

MAKES
4 SERVINGS

Reserved Honey Curry Chicken* (see recipe, page 82)

½ cup mayonnaise

3 cups shredded Chinese cabbage or iceberg lettuce

½ cup chopped carrot (1 medium)

½ cup chopped, peeled jicama or carrot

½ cup snow pea pods, thinly sliced lengthwise

½ cup chow mein noodles

STEP 1 In a small bowl whisk together reserved cooking liquid and mayonnaise until smooth; set aside. Remove reserved chicken meat from bones; discard bones. Chop chicken and reserved vegetables.

STEP 2 In a large bowl combine reserved chicken and vegetables, the cabbage, carrot, jicama, and pea pods. Stir mayonnaise mixture, then add to chicken mixture; toss to coat. Sprinkle noodles over chicken salad.

* There should be 2 reserved chicken breasts, 1 cup reserved vegetables, and ¼ cup reserved cooking liquid.

NUTRITION FACTS
PER SERVING
406 CAL., 27 G TOTAL FAT
(6 G SAT. FAT), 62 MG CHOL.,
439 MG SODIUM,
19 G CARBO., 3 G FIBER,
22 G PRO.

DAILY VALUES
64% VIT. A, 137% VIT. C,
8% CALCIUM, 9% IRON

EXCHANGES
1½ VEGETABLE, ½ OTHER
CARBO., 2½ VERY LEAN MEAT,
5½ FAT

kickin' chicken chili

WITH CHICKEN INSTEAD OF BEEF, WHITE BEANS INSTEAD OF RED, AND A WINDFALL OF COLORFUL VEGETABLES—NOT TO MENTION SOME GREEN SALSA FOR EXTRA KICK—THIS IS A WHOLE NEW BOWL OF CHILI!

PREP
25 MINUTES

COOK
4 HOURS (LOW) OR
2 HOURS (HIGH)

MAKES
4 (1½-CUP) SERVINGS
+ RESERVES

2	pounds skinless, boneless chicken breast halves or thighs, cut into 1-inch pieces
2	teaspoons ground cumin
¼	teaspoon salt
1	tablespoon olive oil or cooking oil
1	16-ounce jar green salsa
1	16-ounce package frozen pepper stir-fry vegetables (yellow, green, and red sweet peppers and onion)
1	15-ounce can cannellini beans (white kidney beans), rinsed and drained
1	14.5-ounce can diced tomatoes with onion and garlic
	Dairy sour cream (optional)
	Cheese (optional)

STEP 1 In a large bowl toss chicken with cumin and salt to coat. In a large skillet cook chicken, half at a time, in hot oil over medium heat until lightly browned. Drain off fat. Place chicken in a 4- or 5-quart slow cooker. Stir in salsa, stir-fry vegetables, beans, and undrained tomatoes.

STEP 2 Cover and cook on low-heat setting for 4 to 5 hours or on high-heat setting for 2 to 2½ hours. Reserve 3 cups of the mixture; store as directed below.

STEP 3 Serve remaining chili. If desired, top with sour cream and cheese.

TO STORE RESERVES Place chili in an airtight container. Seal and chill for up to 3 days. Use in Kickin' Chicken Taco Salad, page 85.

NUTRITION FACTS
PER SERVING
305 CAL., 5 G TOTAL FAT
(1 G SAT. FAT), 88 MG CHOL.,
914 MG SODIUM,
24 G CARBO., 6 G FIBER,
41 G PRO.

DAILY VALUES
10% VIT. A, 63% VIT. C,
10% CALCIUM, 18% IRON

EXCHANGES
1½ VEGETABLE, 1 STARCH,
4 VERY LEAN MEAT, 1 FAT

kickin' chicken taco salad

GIVE THE USUAL TACO SALAD EXTRA KICK BY STARTING WITH KICKIN' CHICKEN CHILI. IN A HURRY? USE A BAG OF LETTUCE AND DON'T BOTHER HALVING THE TOMATOES.

Reserved Kickin' Chicken Chili* (see recipe, page 84)

6   cups torn romaine lettuce
1   large avocado, halved, seeded, peeled, and chopped
1   cup grape tomatoes or cherry tomatoes, halved, if desired
1   cup chopped, peeled jicama
1 ½   cups coarsely crushed lime-flavor or plain tortilla chips
½   cup dairy sour cream
¼   cup snipped fresh cilantro

STEP 1 In a medium saucepan heat reserved chili over medium-low heat until hot. In a very large bowl combine lettuce, avocado, tomatoes, and jicama. Add heated chili; toss to combine. Divide among 4 large salad bowls. Sprinkle with chips.

STEP 2 In a small bowl stir together sour cream and cilantro; spoon evenly onto salads.

* There should be about 3 cups reserved chili.

MEAL 2

START TO FINISH
30 MINUTES

MAKES
4 SERVINGS

NUTRITION FACTS
PER SERVING
385 CAL., 19 G TOTAL FAT (5 G SAT. FAT), 54 MG CHOL., 565 MG SODIUM, 34 G CARBO., 9 G FIBER, 25 G PRO.

DAILY VALUES
120% VIT. A, 97% VIT. C, 14% CALCIUM, 18% IRON

EXCHANGES
3 VEGETABLE, 1 STARCH, 2½ VERY LEAN MEAT, 3 FAT

1

soy-ginger chicken & vegetables

RICE VINEGAR IS INTERCHANGEABLE WITH RICE WINE VINEGAR, SO USE WHICHEVER YOU HAVE ON HAND. EITHER WILL ADD A NICE, SLIGHTLY SWEET TANG TO THIS DISH. THE HONEY-ROASTED PEANUTS ARE OPTIONAL, BUT THE EXTRA TEXTURE THEY ADD IS A BONUS.

PREP
30 MINUTES

COOK
4 HOURS (LOW) OR
2 HOURS (HIGH)

MAKES
4 SERVINGS + RESERVES

$\frac{2}{3}$	cup water
$\frac{1}{4}$	cup thinly sliced green onion (2)
$\frac{1}{4}$	cup rice vinegar
$\frac{1}{4}$	cup soy sauce
$\frac{1}{4}$	cup hoisin sauce
2	tablespoons quick-cooking tapioca, crushed
4	cloves garlic, minced
1	teaspoon ground ginger
8	skinless, boneless chicken breast halves (2$\frac{1}{2}$ to 3 pounds)
1	16-ounce package frozen broccoli, carrots, and water chestnuts
2	cups hot cooked rice or vermicelli
	Thinly sliced green onion (optional)
	Chopped honey-roasted peanuts (optional)

NUTRITION FACTS
PER SERVING
367 CAL., 3 G TOTAL FAT
(1 G SAT. FAT), 82 MG CHOL.,
1,248 MG SODIUM,
41 G CARBO., 3 G FIBER,
39 G PRO.

DAILY VALUES
60% VIT. A, 39% VIT. C,
6% CALCIUM, 13% IRON

EXCHANGES
1 VEGETABLE, 2 STARCH,
$\frac{1}{2}$ OTHER CARBO.,
4$\frac{1}{2}$ VERY LEAN MEAT

STEP 1   In a small bowl stir together the water, the $\frac{1}{4}$ cup green onion, the rice vinegar, soy sauce, hoisin sauce, tapioca, garlic, and ginger. Transfer mixture to a 5- or 6-quart slow cooker. Place chicken on top of mixture in cooker. Place frozen vegetables on chicken.

STEP 2   Cover and cook on low-heat setting for 4 to 4$\frac{1}{2}$ hours or on high-heat setting for 2 to 2$\frac{1}{2}$ hours.

STEP 3   Reserve 4 of the chicken breast halves; store as directed below. Serve remaining chicken and all of the vegetables and sauce over hot cooked rice. If desired, top with additional sliced green onion and chopped peanuts.

TO STORE RESERVES   Place chicken in an airtight container. Seal and chill for up to 3 days. Use in Green Salad with Sliced Chicken, Pears & Blue Cheese, page 87.

green salad
with sliced chicken,
pears & blue cheese

THE PLUMP, TENDER, AND MOIST SLOW-COOKED CHICKEN OFFERS A TERRIFIC JUMP-START TO THIS SALAD. THEN, BLUE CHEESE, ALMONDS, AND A SPRIGHTLY VINAIGRETTE DRESSING COMBINE TO MAKE IT A SOPHISTICATED STANDOUT.

START TO FINISH
20 MINUTES

MAKES
4 SERVINGS

⅓ cup olive oil

¼ cup lemon juice

1 tablespoon honey

1 teaspoon Dijon-style mustard

⅛ teaspoon salt

1 pear, cored and thinly sliced

8 cups torn romaine lettuce, mesclun mix, or other torn mixed greens

Reserved chicken from Soy-Ginger Chicken & Vegetables*
  (see recipe, page 86), sliced*

½ cup crumbled blue cheese (2 ounces)

¼ cup sliced almonds, toasted

1 teaspoon cracked black pepper

STEP 1   For dressing, in a screw-top jar combine olive oil, lemon juice, honey, mustard, and salt. Cover and shake well. In a small bowl toss pear slices with 1 tablespoon of the dressing to prevent pears from browning.

STEP 2   Divide lettuce among 4 serving plates. Top with sliced chicken and pear slices. Drizzle with remaining dressing. Sprinkle with cheese, almonds, and cracked pepper.

* There should be 4 chicken breast halves.

NUTRITION FACTS PER SERVING
499 CAL., 30 G TOTAL FAT (6 G SAT. FAT), 95 MG CHOL., 614 MG SODIUM, 19 G CARBO., 5 G FIBER, 41 G PRO.

DAILY VALUES
134% VIT. A, 60% VIT. C, 18% CALCIUM, 16% IRON

EXCHANGES
1 VEGETABLE, 1 OTHER CARBO., 5½ LEAN MEAT, 2½ FAT

slow chicken
marsala

HAILING FROM SICILY, MARSALA IS A FORTIFIED WINE; ONE THAT HAS BEEN BOOSTED BY THE ADDITION OF SPIRITS. IT ADDS A NICE SMOKY FLAVOR AND TASTY RICHNESS TO THIS SLOW-COOKED VERSION OF THE ITALIAN CLASSIC.

PREP
25 MINUTES

COOK
7 HOURS (LOW) OR
3½ HOURS (HIGH)

MAKES
6 SERVINGS + RESERVES

3	medium onions, cut into thin wedges
6	medium carrots, cut into ½-inch pieces
4	stalks celery, cut into ½-inch pieces
2	6-ounce jars (drained weight) sliced mushrooms, drained
3	tablespoons quick-cooking tapioca, crushed
9	skinless, boneless chicken breast halves (about 3 pounds)
1	teaspoon salt
1	teaspoon dried thyme, crushed
½	teaspoon dried oregano, crushed
½	teaspoon black pepper
⅔	cup dry Marsala or dry white wine
½	cup chicken broth
3	cups hot mashed potatoes
	Grated Parmesan or Asiago cheese (optional)

NUTRITION FACTS

PER SERVING
352 CAL., 7 G TOTAL FAT
(2 G SAT. FAT), 99 MG CHOL.,
856 MG SODIUM,
29 G CARBO., 4 G FIBER,
39 G PRO.

DAILY VALUES
81% VIT. A, 17% VIT. C,
7% CALCIUM, 11% IRON

EXCHANGES
1 VEGETABLE, 1½ STARCH,
4½ VERY LEAN MEAT, 1 FAT

STEP 1   In a 6- or 7-quart slow cooker stir together onion, carrot, celery, and mushrooms; sprinkle with tapioca. Add chicken; sprinkle with salt, thyme, oregano, and pepper. Add Marsala and broth.

STEP 2   Cover and cook on low-heat setting for 7 to 8 hours or on high-heat setting for 3½ to 4 hours.

STEP 3   Reserve 3 chicken breast halves and 3 cups of the vegetable mixture; store as directed below. Serve remaining chicken and vegetable mixture with hot mashed potatoes. If desired, sprinkle generously with Parmesan cheese.

TO STORE RESERVES   Chop chicken (2 cups). Place chicken and vegetable mixture in an airtight container. Seal and chill for up to 3 days. Use in Creamy Chicken Pastry Shells, page 89.

creamy chicken pastry shells

START WITH YOUR RESERVED CHICKEN MARSALA MIXTURE AND SERVE IT OVER FLAKY PUFF PASTRY SHELLS—IF YOU LIKE THE CLASSIC IDEA OF CREAMED CHICKEN OVER BISCUITS, YOU'LL LOVE THIS VARIATION ON THE COMFORT-FOOD THEME!

START TO FINISH
20 MINUTES

MAKES
6 SERVINGS

1   10-ounce package frozen puff pastry shells (6 shells)

2   tablespoons butter, softened

2   tablespoons all-purpose flour

    Reserved Slow Chicken Marsala* (see recipe, page 88)

1   cup frozen peas

½   cup whipping cream, half-and-half, or light cream

    Snipped fresh Italian parsley (optional)

STEP 1   Bake pastry shells according to package directions; set aside.

STEP 2   In a large saucepan melt butter over medium heat; stir in flour until smooth. Add reserved chicken mixture and the peas. Cook and stir over medium heat until mixture is slightly thickened and bubbly. Add cream; stir until heated through.

STEP 3   Spoon chicken mixture into pastry shells and serve immediately. If desired, sprinkle with parsley.

* There should be about 5 cups reserved chopped chicken and vegetable mixture.

NUTRITION FACTS
PER SERVING
473 CAL., 28 G TOTAL FAT
(7 G SAT. FAT), 81 MG CHOL.,
615 MG SODIUM,
31 G CARBO., 3 G FIBER,
23 G PRO.

DAILY VALUES
77% VIT. A, 12% VIT. C,
5% CALCIUM, 8% IRON

EXCHANGES
1 VEGETABLE, 1½ STARCH,
2½ VERY LEAN MEAT, 5½ FAT

1

chicken with figs & blue cheese

THE SLOW COOKER IS OFTEN THE DOMAIN OF CLASSIC COMFORT FOOD, BUT YOUR COOKER CAN PRODUCE A MORE CONTEMPORARY DISH. FIGS, BALSAMIC VINEGAR, AND POLENTA ARE TRENDSETTING INGREDIENTS TODAY'S CHEFS LOVE.

PREP
25 MINUTES

COOK
5 HOURS (LOW) OR
2½ HOURS (HIGH)

MAKES
4 SERVINGS + RESERVES

1	cup chicken broth
¼	cup balsamic vinegar
1	tablespoon finely shredded orange peel
1	teaspoon salt
½	teaspoon black pepper
¼	teaspoon ground ginger
1	9-ounce package dried mission figs, stems removed
1	large onion, thinly sliced
2½	pounds skinless, boneless chicken thighs
1	16-ounce tube refrigerated cooked polenta
½	cup crumbled blue cheese (2 ounces)

STEP 1   In a small bowl stir together broth, vinegar, orange peel, salt, pepper, and ginger; set aside. Coarsely chop the figs. Place figs and onion in a 4- or 5-quart slow cooker. Top with chicken. Pour broth mixture over chicken in cooker.

STEP 2   Cover and cook on low-heat setting for 5 to 6 hours or on high-heat setting for 2½ to 3 hours.

STEP 3   Meanwhile, prepare polenta according to package directions for polenta mush. Using tongs, remove chicken from cooker. Chop enough of the chicken to equal 1½ cups; store as directed below. Transfer fig mixture to a serving bowl. Skim fat from fig mixture, if necessary. Serve remaining chicken thighs and the fig mixture with polenta mush. Sprinkle with cheese.

TO STORE RESERVES Place chopped chicken in an airtight container. Seal and chill for up to 3 days. (Or freeze for up to 3 months. Thaw in refrigerator overnight before using.) Use in Chicken Frittata, page 91.

NUTRITION FACTS
PER SERVING
592 CAL., 13 G TOTAL FAT
(5 G SAT. FAT), 164 MG
CHOL., 1,346 MG SODIUM,
71 G CARBO., 10 G FIBER,
47 G PRO.

DAILY VALUES
5% VIT. A, 15% VIT. C,
23% CALCIUM, 18% IRON

EXCHANGES
2 FRUIT, 2½ STARCH,
5 LEAN MEAT

chicken frittata

A FRITTATA IS AN OPEN-FACE ITALIAN OMELET. THIS ONE IS BAKED WITH THE CHICKEN AND FIG MIXTURE FOR A CLEVER DISH YOU WOULD EXPECT AT A STYLISH BRUNCH SPOT.

½   cup finely chopped onion (1 medium)

2   cloves garlic, minced

2   tablespoons butter

     Reserved chicken from Chicken with Figs & Blue Cheese* (see recipe, page 90)

8   eggs, beaten

¼   teaspoon salt

¼   teaspoon black pepper

¼   cup finely shredded or grated Parmesan cheese (1 ounce)

STEP 1   In a large nonstick ovenproof skillet cook onion and garlic in hot butter over medium heat about 5 minutes or until onion is tender. Stir in reserved chicken. Remove from heat.

STEP 2   Meanwhile, in a large bowl stir together eggs, salt, and pepper. Slowly pour eggs into skillet over chicken and vegetables.

STEP 3   Bake, uncovered, in a 350°F oven for 12 to 15 minutes or until set and a knife inserted near the center comes out clean. Sprinkle with cheese. Cut into wedges to serve.

* There should be 1½ cups chopped reserved chicken.

PREP
15 MINUTES

BAKE
12 MINUTES

OVEN
350°F

MAKES
4 SERVINGS

NUTRITION FACTS PER SERVING
349 CAL., 21 G TOTAL FAT (9 G SAT. FAT), 517 MG CHOL., 783 MG SODIUM, 4 G CARBO., 0 G FIBER, 34 G PRO.

DAILY VALUES
15% VIT. A, 9% VIT. C, 14% CALCIUM, 17% IRON

EXCHANGES
4½ LEAN MEAT, 2 FAT

herbed sherry chicken

THOUGH IT'S EASY ENOUGH TO MAKE ON A WEEKNIGHT, THE COMBINATION OF MUSHROOMS AND ASPARAGUS ADDS JUST ENOUGH ELEGANCE TO MAKE YOU FEEL LIKE YOU'RE TREATING YOURSELF TO SOMETHING SPECIAL. A GLASS OF CHARDONNAY WOULD GO PERFECTLY WITH THIS CREAMY DISH.

PREP
15 MINUTES

COOK
7 HOURS (LOW) OR
3½ HOURS (HIGH)
+ 15 MINUTES

MAKES
4 SERVINGS + RESERVES

1	cup thinly sliced onion (2 medium)
1	cup sliced fresh mushrooms
2	tablespoons quick-cooking tapioca
8	skinless, boneless chicken breast halves (about 2½ pounds)
¾	cup chicken broth
½	cup dry sherry
1	teaspoon salt
1	teaspoon dried thyme, crushed
¼	to ½ teaspoon black pepper
1	10-ounce package frozen cut asparagus
½	cup dairy sour cream
	Hot cooked rice
	Finely shredded Parmesan cheese

NUTRITION FACTS
PER SERVING
365 CAL., 7 G TOTAL FAT
(3 G SAT. FAT), 91 MG CHOL.,
554 MG SODIUM,
31 G CARBO., 1 G FIBER,
39 G PRO.

DAILY VALUES
10% VIT. A, 21% VIT. C,
12% CALCIUM, 14% IRON

EXCHANGES
½ VEGETABLE, 2 STARCH,
4½ VERY LEAN MEAT, 1 FAT

STEP 1   In a 4- or 5-quart slow cooker place onion and mushroom slices. Sprinkle with tapioca. Top with chicken. In a medium bowl stir together broth, sherry, salt, thyme, and pepper. Pour over chicken in cooker.

STEP 2   Cover and cook on low-heat setting for 7 to 8 hours or on high-heat setting for 3½ to 4 hours. If using low-heat setting, turn to high-heat setting. Stir in the asparagus. Cover and cook 15 minutes more.

STEP 3   Remove chicken from cooker. In a small bowl stir together sour cream and about ½ cup of hot cooking liquid. Stir mixture into remaining cooking liquid in cooker. Reserve 4 chicken breast halves and half of the sauce (2 cups); store as directed below. Serve remaining chicken and sauce with hot cooked rice. Top with Parmesan cheese.

TO STORE RESERVES Cut chicken into thin slices (1½ cups). Place chicken and sauce in separate airtight containers. Seal and chill for up to 3 days. Use in Chicken Biscuits & Gravy, page 93.

chicken
biscuits & gravy

GET READY FOR A CLASSIC! WHEN IT COMES TO LEFTOVER STRATEGIES, SERVING LEFTOVER CHICKEN IN A CREAM SAUCE OVER HOT BISCUITS IS AN OLDIE BUT GOODIE! THE PARMESAN CHEESE ADDS A LITTLE SOMETHING EXTRA WITHOUT DOMINATING THE DISH.

1	16.3-ounce package (8) refrigerated large biscuits
¼	cup thinly sliced green onion (2)
1	tablespoon butter
	Reserved sauce and chicken from Herbed Sherry Chicken* (see recipe, page 92)
½	cup finely shredded Parmesan cheese (2 ounces)

STEP 1 Bake biscuits according to package directions. Meanwhile, in a medium saucepan cook green onion in hot butter over medium heat for 2 to 3 minutes or until tender. Stir in reserved sauce. Cook and stir over medium heat until bubbly.

STEP 2 Stir in reserved chicken and the Parmesan cheese. Continue cooking over medium heat, stirring occasionally, until cheese melts and mixture is heated through. Serve immediately over 4 split biscuits (reserve remaining 4 biscuits for another use).

* There should be 2 cups reserved sauce and about 1½ cups reserved chicken.

PREP
15 MINUTES

COOK
10 MINUTES

MAKES
4 SERVINGS

NUTRITION FACTS
PER SERVING
501 CAL., 20 G TOTAL FAT (8 G SAT. FAT), 103 MG CHOL., 1,260 MG SODIUM, 33 G CARBO., 2 G FIBER, 43 G PRO.

DAILY VALUES
14% VIT. A, 23% VIT. C, 23% CALCIUM, 16% IRON

EXCHANGES
½ VEGETABLE, 2 STARCH, 5 VERY LEAN MEAT, 3½ FAT

creamy basil chicken

PANCETTA IS AN ITALIAN-STYLE BACON. UNLIKE MOST AMERICAN BACON IT IS NOT SMOKED; RATHER, IT'S SEASONED WITH PEPPER AND OTHER SPICES AND CURED WITH SALT.

PREP
25 MINUTES

COOK
6 HOURS (LOW) OR
3 HOURS (HIGH)
+ 30 MINUTES

MAKES
4 SERVINGS + RESERVES

2	cups sliced mushrooms
2	medium red and/or yellow sweet peppers, cut into strips
1	large onion, sliced
4	ounces cooked pancetta or bacon, chopped
8	cloves garlic, minced
3	tablespoons quick-cooking tapioca, crushed
8	skinless, boneless chicken breast halves (2½ to 3 pounds)
1	cup chicken broth
¼	cup dry white wine or vermouth
1	pound fresh asparagus or one 10-ounce package frozen cut asparagus, thawed
⅓	cup whipping cream (no substitutes)
½	cup snipped fresh basil or 1 tablespoon dried basil, crushed
2	cups hot cooked orzo pasta
	Snipped fresh basil
	Grated Parmesan cheese

NUTRITION FACTS
PER SERVING
556 CAL., 21 G TOTAL FAT
(9 G SAT. FAT), 132 MG
CHOL., 892 MG SODIUM,
43 G CARBO., 5 G FIBER,
47 G PRO.

DAILY VALUES
62% VIT. A, 177% VIT. C,
12% CALCIUM, 26% IRON

EXCHANGES
2 VEGETABLE, 2 STARCH,
4 VERY LEAN MEAT,
1 HIGH-FAT MEAT, 2½ FAT

STEP 1   In 5- or 6-quart slow cooker stir together mushrooms, sweet pepper, onion, pancetta, and garlic. Sprinkle with tapioca. Place chicken on top of mixture in cooker. Pour broth and wine over all.

STEP 2   Cover and cook on low-heat setting for 6 to 7 hours or on high-heat setting for 3 to 3½ hours.

STEP 3   Meanwhile, trim fresh asparagus; cut into 2-inch lengths. If using low-heat setting, turn to high-heat setting. Stir in asparagus, cream, and the ½ cup fresh basil or 1 tablespoon dried basil. Cover; cook 30 minutes more.

STEP 4   Reserve 4 breast halves; store as directed below. Serve remaining chicken, all of the vegetables, and sauce with hot cooked orzo. Sprinkle with additional fresh basil and Parmesan cheese.

TO STORE RESERVES Place chicken in an airtight container. Seal and chill for up to 3 days. (Or freeze for up to 3 months. Thaw in refrigerator overnight before using.) Use in Chicken & Wild Rice Chowder, page 95.

chicken & wild rice chowder

WILD RICE SOUP IS A SPECIALTY OF MINNESOTA, AND THERE ARE MANY WARMING VERSIONS THROUGHOUT THIS COOL-CLIMATE STATE. SOME OF THE BEST RECIPES INCLUDE CARROTS TO ADD A JOLT OF COLOR TO AN EARTHY MUSHROOM AND RICE MIX. AND HALF-AND-HALF OR LIGHT CREAM IS KEY FOR CREAMY CHOWDER.

PREP
20 MINUTES

COOK
25 MINUTES

MAKES
4 SERVINGS

1	cup sliced carrot (2 medium)
1	cup sliced celery (2 stalks)
1	cup quartered mushrooms
3	tablespoons butter
3	tablespoons all-purpose flour
2	14-ounce cans chicken broth
	Reserved chicken from Creamy Basil Chicken* (see recipe, page 94), chopped
¾	cup cooked wild rice
¼	teaspoon black pepper
1½	cups half-and-half or light cream
2	tablespoons dry sherry (optional)

STEP 1   In a large saucepan cook carrot, celery, and mushrooms in hot butter over medium heat until tender. Stir in flour. Add broth, chopped reserved chicken, the wild rice, and pepper. Cook and stir until mixture is bubbly and slightly thickened. Stir in half-and-half and, if using, sherry; heat through.

* There should be 4 chicken breast halves.

NUTRITION FACTS PER 2 CUPS
445 CAL., 22 G TOTAL FAT (13 G SAT. FAT), 140 MG CHOL., 1,019 MG SODIUM, 21 G CARBO., 2 G FIBER, 40 G PRO.

DAILY VALUES
113% VIT. A, 6% VIT. C, 14% CALCIUM, 10% IRON

EXCHANGES
1 VEGETABLE, 1 STARCH, 5 VERY LEAN MEAT, 3½ FAT

garlic & lemon chicken with leeks

LEEKS ARE RELATED TO ONIONS AND GARLIC, BUT THEIR FLAVOR IS MELLOWER, MAKING THEM MELD WELL WITH THE OTHER FLAVORS IN THIS DISH.

PREP
30 MINUTES

COOK
4 HOURS (LOW) OR
2 HOURS (HIGH)

MAKES
4 SERVINGS + RESERVES

⅓	cup all-purpose flour
½	teaspoon salt
½	teaspoon black pepper
6	large skinless, boneless chicken breast halves (2 ¼ to 2 ½ pounds)
3	tablespoons butter
2	cups thinly sliced leek (about 6)
10	cloves garlic, thinly sliced
2	tablespoons quick-cooking tapioca, crushed
¼	teaspoon salt
1	lemon
1 ½	cups chicken broth
2	cups hot cooked mashed potatoes

STEP 1 In a shallow dish stir together flour, ½ teaspoon salt, and the pepper. Dredge chicken in flour mixture to coat. In a large skillet melt butter over medium heat. Brown chicken, half at a time, in hot butter.

STEP 2 Meanwhile, place leek and garlic in a 4- or 5-quart slow cooker. Sprinkle with tapioca and ¼ teaspoon salt. Top with browned chicken. Finely shred enough lemon peel to make ½ teaspoon; store as directed below. Peel the lemon, removing all of the white pith; discard peel. Thinly slice the lemon; remove seeds. Place lemon slices on chicken. Pour broth over top.

STEP 3 Cover and cook on low-heat setting for 4 to 4½ hours or on high-heat setting for 2 to 2½ hours.

STEP 4 Reserve two chicken breast halves; store as directed below. Transfer the remaining 4 chicken breast halves to serving plates. Remove vegetables from cooker and divide among serving plates. Serve with mashed potatoes. If desired, spoon some cooking liquid over each serving.

TO STORE RESERVES Place lemon peel in a small airtight container. Place chicken in a second airtight container. Seal and chill for up to 3 days. Use in Chicken & Mushroom Risotto, page 97.

NUTRITION FACTS PER SERVING
454 CAL., 13 G TOTAL FAT (6 G SAT. FAT), 126 MG CHOL., 1,172 MG SODIUM, 38 G CARBO., 3 G FIBER, 44 G PRO.

DAILY VALUES
20% VIT. A, 34% VIT. C, 9% CALCIUM, 16% IRON

EXCHANGES
½ VEGETABLE, 2 STARCH, 5½ VERY LEAN MEAT, 2 FAT

chicken & mushroom risotto

TREATING YOUR FAMILY TO A RICH, CREAMY, AND MOIST MAIN-DISH RISOTTO IS MUCH EASIER THAN YOU THINK—ESPECIALLY WHEN YOU GET A JUMP-START WITH LEFTOVERS.

2	cups sliced fresh mushrooms
½	cup chopped onion (1 medium)
3	tablespoons olive oil
1¼	cups Arborio rice
2	14-ounce cans chicken broth
½	cup dry white wine
	Reserved chicken and lemon peel from Garlic & Lemon Chicken with Leeks* (see recipe, page 96), chopped
½	cup finely shredded Parmesan cheese (2 ounces)
¼	teaspoon black pepper
	Finely shredded Parmesan cheese and freshly ground black pepper (optional)

PREP
20 MINUTES

COOK
45 MINUTES

MAKES
4 SERVINGS

STEP 1 In a large saucepan cook mushrooms and onion in hot oil over medium heat about 8 minutes or until tender, stirring occasionally. Add rice; cook and stir until rice begins to brown. (Rice may stick to pan but will release when wine is added.)

STEP 2 Meanwhile, in another saucepan bring broth to boiling. Cover; reduce heat to low. Add wine to rice mixture, stirring to loosen rice from bottom of pan. Cook, uncovered, about 2 minutes or until wine is absorbed, stirring frequently. Add 1 cup of the broth. Continue to cook over medium heat, stirring frequently, until liquid is absorbed. Add another ½ cup of broth. Cook, stirring frequently, until liquid is nearly absorbed. Continue adding broth, ½ cup at a time, cooking after each addition until broth is nearly absorbed, stirring frequently. When all of the broth has been added, cook until mixture is creamy. (Total cooking time should take 25 to 30 minutes after the wine is absorbed.)

STEP 3 Stir in chopped chicken, the ½ cup cheese, reserved lemon peel, and ¼ teaspoon pepper. Cook, stirring frequently, until heated through but still creamy. If desired, sprinkle each serving with additional Parmesan cheese and pepper.

* There should be 2 reserved chicken breast halves and ¼ teaspoon reserved lemon peel.

NUTRITION FACTS PER SERVING
460 CAL., 18 G TOTAL FAT (5 G SAT. FAT), 66 MG CHOL., 1,128 MG SODIUM, 40 G CARBO., 1 G FIBER, 29 G PRO.

DAILY VALUES
3% VIT. A, 3% VIT. C, 15% CALCIUM, 21% IRON

EXCHANGES
½ VEGETABLE, 2½ STARCH, 3 VERY LEAN MEAT, 3 FAT

thai chicken over rice noodles

SWEET, SALTY, SPICY, AND SOUR—LIKE SO MANY THAI-INSPIRED DISHES, THIS RECIPE PUSHES ALL KINDS OF FLAVOR BUTTONS!

8	medium skinless, boneless chicken breast halves (about 2½ pounds)
1	14-ounce can chicken broth
¼	cup fish sauce
8	green onions, cut into ½-inch pieces
1	15-ounce can whole straw mushrooms, drained
1	large red sweet pepper, cut into 1-inch pieces
1	to 2 serrano chiles, seeded and finely chopped (see note, page 50)
1	tablespoon ground ginger
1	tablespoon bottled minced garlic or 6 cloves garlic, minced
1	14-ounce can unsweetened coconut milk
1½	cups bean sprouts
1	8-ounce package flat rice noodles
2	tablespoons cornstarch
	Chopped peanuts and snipped fresh cilantro

PREP
25 MINUTES

COOK
6 HOURS (LOW) OR
3 HOURS (HIGH)
+ 30 MINUTES

MAKES
4 SERVINGS

STEP 1 In a 4- or 5-quart slow cooker combine chicken, broth, fish sauce, green onion, mushrooms, sweet pepper, chile, ginger, and garlic.

STEP 2 Cover and cook on low-heat setting for 6 to 7 hours or high-heat setting for 3 to 3½ hours. If using low-heat setting, turn to high-heat setting. Add coconut milk and sprouts. Cover and cook for 30 minutes more.

STEP 3 Cook noodles for 5 to 7 minutes or until firm but tender. Drain; keep warm. Remove chicken from cooker; cover and set aside. Strain vegetables from cooking liquid. Reserve 4 pieces of chicken, 1½ cups vegetables, 2¼ cups cooking liquid, and 1 cup rice noodles; store as directed below.

STEP 4 In a saucepan stir together cornstarch and 2 tablespoons water; stir in remaining cooking liquid. Cook and stir until thickened and bubbly; cook and stir 2 minutes more. Toss remaining noodles and vegetables with sauce. Top with chicken; spoon sauce over top. Sprinkle with peanuts and cilantro.

TO STORE RESERVES Chop chicken; place chicken, vegetables, and cooking liquid in an airtight container. Snip noodles; place in an airtight container. Seal; chill for up to 3 days. Use in Thai Chicken & Coconut-Red Curry Soup, page 99.

NUTRITION FACTS
PER SERVING
577 CAL., 34 G TOTAL FAT
(26 G SAT. FAT), 83 MG
CHOL., 1,471 MG SODIUM,
29 G CARBO., 3 G FIBER,
40 G PRO.

DAILY VALUES
108% VIT. A, 95% VIT. C,
9% CALCIUM, 24% IRON

EXCHANGES
1 VEGETABLE, 1½ STARCH,
1½ VERY LEAN MEAT, 6 FAT

thai chicken & coconut-red curry soup

IF YOU'VE EVER ENJOYED TOM KA KAI, A SPECIALTY SOUP FROM THAILAND, YOU'LL KNOW EXACTLY WHERE THE INSPIRATION FOR THIS FASCINATING BOWL CAME FROM!

1½	cups sliced baby bok choy or bok choy
1	cup bias-sliced carrot (2 medium)
2	tablespoons cooking oil
	Reserved Thai Chicken over Rice Noodles* (see recipe, page 98)
1	14-ounce can unsweetened coconut milk
¾	cup chicken broth
1	tablespoon lime juice
2	teaspoons Thai red curry paste
¼	cup snipped fresh basil

STEP 1 In a large saucepan cook bok choy and carrot in hot oil over medium heat until crisp-tender. Add reserved chicken and vegetable mixture, reserved snipped rice noodles, the coconut milk, broth, lime juice, and curry paste; heat through. Stir in basil just before serving.

* There should be 4½ cups reserved chicken and vegetable mixture and 1 cup reserved rice noodles.

START TO FINISH
25 MINUTES

MAKES
4 SERVINGS

NUTRITION FACTS
PER SERVING
510 CAL., 17 G TOTAL FAT (10 G SAT. FAT), 83 MG CHOL., 1,153 MG SODIUM, 50 G CARBO., 3 G FIBER, 40 G PRO.

DAILY VALUES
18% VIT. A, 71% VIT. C, 6% CALCIUM, 21% IRON

EXCHANGES
½ VEGETABLE, 3 STARCH, 4 VERY LEAN MEAT, 2½ FAT

stewed chicken & andouille

ANDOUILLE (AN-DOO-EE) IS A SMOKY, SPICY SAUSAGE THAT'S OFTEN USED IN CAJUN SPECIALTIES. COMBINE IT WITH A JAR OF PICANTE SAUCE, AND YOU CAN EXPECT ANYTHING-BUT-TIMID RESULTS!

PREP
25 MINUTES

COOK
6 HOURS (LOW) OR
3 HOURS (HIGH)

MAKES
4 SERVINGS + RESERVES

1	pound andouille sausage, cut in ¾-inch slices
1	medium onion, cut into thin wedges
8	skinless chicken thighs (2½ to 3 pounds)
1	16-ounce jar picante sauce
⅓	cup water
2	tablespoons quick-cooking tapioca
2	teaspoons Worcestershire sauce
1	teaspoon dried thyme, crushed
2	cups frozen cut okra
6	ounces uncooked dry egg noodles

STEP 1   In a large skillet brown sausage over medium heat. Drain off fat.

STEP 2   In a 4- or 5-quart slow cooker place onion and chicken. Add browned sausage, picante sauce, the water, tapioca, Worcestershire sauce, and thyme to cooker; top with okra.

STEP 3   Cover and cook on low-heat setting for 6 to 7 hours or on high-heat setting 3 to 3½ hours.

STEP 4   Meanwhile, cook egg noodles according to package directions. Using a slotted spoon, reserve 4 thighs and 1 cup of the sausage; store as directed below. Serve remaining chicken mixture over noodles.

TO STORE RESERVES   Place chicken thighs and sausage in an airtight container. Seal and chill for up to 3 days. (Or freeze for up to 3 months. Thaw in refrigerator overnight before using.) Use in Bayou Shrimp & Rice, page 101.

NUTRITION FACTS
PER SERVING
419 CAL., 8 G TOTAL FAT
(2 G SAT. FAT), 154 MG
CHOL., 1,481 MG SODIUM,
50 G CARBO., 3 G FIBER,
36 G PRO.

DAILY VALUES
20% VIT. A, 12% VIT. C,
13% CALCIUM, 22% IRON

EXCHANGES
½ VEGETABLE, 3 STARCH,
4 LEAN MEAT

bayou shrimp & rice

IT'S SO EASY—COOK SOME RICE REVVED UP WITH PICANTE SAUCE, THEN STIR IN SHRIMP PLUS LEFTOVER STEWED CHICKEN AND ANDOUILLE. PRESTO! A FORMER CAJUN DISH BECOMES A CREOLE DISH REMINISCENT OF JAMBALAYA.

12	ounces fresh or frozen medium shrimp
	Reserved chicken and sausage from Stewed Chicken & Andouille*
	(see recipe, page 100)
2 ¼	cups water
1 ¼	cups bottled picante sauce
2	teaspoons Worcestershire sauce
1	cup long grain rice
	Salt (optional)
	Black pepper (optional)
	Bottled hot pepper sauce (optional)

STEP 1 Thaw shrimp, if frozen. Peel and devein shrimp. Remove chicken from bones; discard bones and chop meat. Set aside.

STEP 2 In a large skillet stir together the water, picante sauce, and Worcestershire sauce. Bring to boiling; add rice. Return to boiling; reduce heat. Cover and simmer for 15 minutes.

STEP 3 Add shrimp, chicken, and sausage to rice mixture. Return to boiling; reduce heat. Cover and simmer about 5 minutes more or until shrimp is opaque and rice is tender.

STEP 4 Remove from heat; season to taste with salt and black pepper. If desired, pass hot pepper sauce.

* There should be 4 chicken thighs and 1 cup sausage.

START TO FINISH
40 MINUTES

MAKES
4 SERVINGS

NUTRITION FACTS PER SERVING
437 CAL., 7 G TOTAL FAT (2 G SAT. FAT), 211 MG CHOL., 1,261 MG SODIUM, 45 G CARBO., 1 G FIBER, 44 G PRO.

DAILY VALUES
18% VIT. A, 9% VIT. C, 10% CALCIUM, 34% IRON

EXCHANGES
3 STARCH, 5 LEAN MEAT

chicken & succotash stew

SUCCOTASH IS A MIX OF LIMA BEANS AND CORN. WHY SUCH AN EXOTIC WORD FOR SUCH A SIMPLE BLEND? THE WORD WAS DERIVED FROM A TERM USED BY THE NARRAGANSETT NATIVE AMERICANS. HERE THE DUO ADDS COLOR AND HEARTINESS TO A CREAMY CHICKEN SOUP.

PREP
20 MINUTES

COOK
8 HOURS (LOW) OR
4 HOURS (HIGH)

MAKES
4 TO 6 SERVINGS + RESERVES

2½	pounds skinless, boneless chicken thighs, cut into 1-inch pieces
1	16-ounce package frozen baby lima beans, thawed
1	16-ounce package frozen whole kernel corn, thawed
2	10.75-ounce cans condensed cream of chicken soup
1	14-ounce can chicken or vegetable broth
2	cups thinly sliced carrot (4 medium)
1	cup chopped onion (1 large)
1	teaspoon dried sage, crushed
¼	teaspoon black pepper

STEP 1   In a 5- or 6-quart slow cooker stir together chicken, lima beans, corn, soup, broth, carrot, onion, sage, and pepper. Stir until combined.

STEP 2   Cover and cook on low-heat setting for 8 to 9 hours or on high-heat setting for 4 to 4½ hours. Reserve 6½ cups of the stew (about half); store as directed below. Serve remaining stew in bowls.

TO STORE RESERVES Place stew in an airtight container. Seal and chill for up to 3 days. Use in Quick Chicken Pot Pie, page 103.

NUTRITION FACTS
PER SERVING
402 CAL., 11 G TOTAL FAT
(3 G SAT. FAT), 120 MG
CHOL., 900 MG SODIUM,
38 G CARBO., 7 G FIBER,
37 G PRO.

DAILY VALUES
77% VIT. A, 24% VIT. C,
5% CALCIUM, 16% IRON

EXCHANGES
½ VEGETABLE, 2 STARCH,
4 LEAN MEAT

quick chicken pot pie

YOUR GRANDMOTHER OR GREAT-GRANDMOTHER MAY HAVE MADE A DISH SIMILAR TO THIS ONE. DURING THE GREAT DEPRESSION, SUCCOTASH WAS POPULAR SERVED IN A CASSEROLE AND TOPPED WITH A PIECRUST. THE COMFORTING, HOMEY STEW IS DUE FOR A REVIVAL!

Reserved Chicken & Succotash Stew* (see recipe, page 102)

1	**cup shredded cheddar cheese (4 ounces)**
2	**tablespoons cornstarch**
1	**7.5-ounce package (10) refrigerated biscuits, each biscuit quartered**

STEP 1 In a large saucepan stir together reserved stew, ³/₄ cup of the cheese, and the cornstarch. Heat and stir over medium heat just until mixture comes to boil. Simmer, uncovered, for 2 minutes.

STEP 2 Transfer stew mixture to a 3-quart rectangular baking dish. Top with biscuit quarters and sprinkle with remaining ¼ cup cheese.

STEP 3 Bake, uncovered, in a 400°F oven about 12 minutes or until biscuits are golden.

* There should be about 6½ cups reserved stew.

PREP
15 MINUTES

COOK
5 MINUTES

BAKE
12 MINUTES

OVEN
400°F

MAKES
6 SERVINGS

NUTRITION FACTS
PER SERVING
467 CAL., 19 G TOTAL FAT (7 G SAT. FAT), 100 MG CHOL., 1,110 MG SODIUM, 44 G CARBO., 5 G FIBER, 32 G PRO.

DAILY VALUES
55% VIT. A, 16% VIT. C, 18% CALCIUM, 16% IRON

EXCHANGES
½ VEGETABLE, 2½ STARCH, 3½ LEAN MEAT, 1½ FAT

szechwan chicken

THE SECRET TO THIS RECIPE'S APPEAL IS THE COMBO OF HOT BEAN SAUCE AND STIR-FRY SAUCE; THE DUO PAIRS FOR VERY TASTY RESULTS.

PREP
30 MINUTES

COOK
5 HOURS (LOW) OR
2½ HOURS (HIGH)

MAKES
4 SERVINGS + RESERVES

2	pounds skinless, boneless chicken thighs, cut into ½-inch pieces
1½	cups thinly sliced carrot (3 medium)
1½	cups thinly sliced celery (3 stalks)
1	8-ounce can (drained weight) straw mushrooms, drained
1	8-ounce can (drained weight) whole baby corn, drained
⅔	cup bottled stir-fry sauce
¼	cup hot bean sauce
1	tablespoon quick-cooking tapioca
6	cups hot cooked rice
¼	cup dry honey-roasted peanuts, coarsely chopped (optional)

STEP 1 In a 5- or 6-quart slow cooker stir together chicken, carrot, celery, mushrooms, corn, stir-fry sauce, bean sauce, and tapioca.

STEP 2 Cover and cook on low-heat setting for 5 to 7 hours or on high-heat setting for 2½ to 3 hours.

STEP 3 Using a slotted spoon, remove 3 cups of the chicken mixture and reserve 3 cups rice; store as directed below. Serve remaining chicken mixture and sauce over remaining hot cooked rice. If desired, sprinkle with nuts.

TO STORE RESERVES Place chicken mixture and rice in separate airtight containers. Seal and chill for up to 3 days. Use in Chicken Fried Rice, page 105.

NUTRITION FACTS
PER SERVING
386 CAL., 6 G TOTAL FAT (2 G SAT. FAT), 104 MG CHOL., 929 MG SODIUM, 47 G CARBO., 3 G FIBER, 33 G PRO.

DAILY VALUES
66% VIT. A, 9% VIT. C, 5% CALCIUM, 18% IRON

EXCHANGES
½ VEGETABLE, 2 STARCH, 1 OTHER CARBO., 3 LEAN MEAT

chicken fried rice

NO ONE WILL GUESS THAT THIS STARTS WITH LEFTOVERS—THE
FRESHLY FRIED EGG AND GREEN ONIONS REALLY FRESHEN UP
THE SZECHWAN CHICKEN YOU SAVED, RESULTING IN A BRIGHT
AND COLORFUL DISH.

Reserved chicken mixture and rice from Szechwan Chicken*
   (see recipe, page 104)

2	tablespoons cooking oil
3	eggs, lightly beaten
2	cloves garlic, minced
8	green onions, diagonally sliced into 1-inch pieces (about 1½ cups)
	Soy sauce (optional)

STEP 1 Place reserved chicken mixture in a large food processor; pulse to coarsely chop (or coarsely chop by hand); set aside.

STEP 2 Pour 1 tablespoon of the oil into a wok or large skillet. Heat over medium heat. Add eggs. Lift and tilt the wok to form a thin sheet of egg. Cook, without stirring, about 2 minutes or just until set. Slide the egg sheet onto a cutting board. Cut the cooked egg into thin strips. Set aside.

STEP 3 Pour remaining 1 tablespoon oil into the wok. (If necessary, add more oil during cooking.) Heat over medium-high heat. Add garlic; cook and stir for 15 seconds. Add green onion; cook and stir about 1¼ minutes more or until crisp-tender. Remove vegetables from the wok.

STEP 4 Add the cooked rice to the wok. Cook and stir for 2 to 3 minutes or until lightly browned. Return the vegetables and chicken mixture to the wok. Add egg strips. Cook and stir until well mixed and heated through. Serve immediately. If desired, serve with soy sauce.

* There should be 3 cups reserved chicken mixture and 3 cups reserved rice.

START TO FINISH
30 MINUTES

MAKES
4 SERVINGS

NUTRITION FACTS
PER SERVING
455 CAL., 15 G TOTAL FAT
(3 G SAT. FAT), 237 MG
CHOL., 755 MG SODIUM,
47 G CARBO., 3 G FIBER,
31 G PRO.

DAILY VALUES
59% VIT. A, 17% VIT. C,
8% CALCIUM, 22% IRON

EXCHANGES
½ VEGETABLE, 2 STARCH,
1 OTHER CARBO., 3½ LEAN
MEAT, 1 FAT

indian-spiced chicken thighs

AT FIRST GLANCE, SOME INDIAN-INSPIRED RECIPES LOOK SO LONG! BUT TAKE ANOTHER LOOK—MANY OF THE INGREDIENTS ARE SPICES, WHICH TAKE VERY LITTLE TIME TO MEASURE BUT ADD SO MUCH PLEASURE!

PREP
20 MINUTES

COOK
7 HOURS (LOW) OR
3½ HOURS (HIGH)

MAKES
6 SERVINGS + RESERVES

2	cups thinly sliced onion (4 medium)
¼	cup quick-cooking tapioca
4	teaspoons bottled minced garlic or 8 cloves garlic, minced
4	to 4½ pounds skinless, boneless chicken thighs (24 to 30)
1	tablespoon ground cumin
2	teaspoons salt
2	teaspoons curry powder
1½	teaspoons ground coriander
½	teaspoon ground cinnamon
¼	teaspoon ground cloves
¼	teaspoon cayenne pepper
¼	teaspoon black pepper
1	14-ounce can chicken broth
1	6-ounce carton plain yogurt
3	cups hot cooked Basmati rice
	Snipped fresh mint and/or toasted slivered almonds (optional)

STEP 1 Place onion in a 5- to 7-quart slow cooker; sprinkle with tapioca and garlic. Top with chicken. Sprinkle with cumin, salt, curry powder, coriander, cinnamon, cloves, cayenne, and black pepper. Pour broth over all.

STEP 2 Cover and cook on low-heat setting for 7 to 8 hours or on high-heat setting for 3½ to 4 hours.

STEP 3 Reserve half of the thighs (12 or 15) and half of onion mixture (about 2 cups); store as directed below. Transfer remaining chicken to a platter; cover and keep warm. Whisk yogurt into remaining onion mixture in cooker. Serve chicken and sauce with rice. If desired, sprinkle with mint and almonds.

TO STORE RESERVES Cut chicken into ¾-inch pieces; place chicken and onion mixture in an airtight container. Seal and chill for up to 3 days. Use in Coconut Chicken & Couscous, page 107.

NUTRITION FACTS
PER SERVING
347 CAL., 7 G TOTAL FAT
(2 G SAT. FAT), 123 MG
CHOL., 645 MG SODIUM,
33 G CARBO., 1 G FIBER,
35 G PRO.

DAILY VALUES
2% VIT. A, 10% VIT. C,
9% CALCIUM, 12% IRON

EXCHANGES
2 STARCH, 4 LEAN MEAT

coconut chicken & couscous

IF YOU ENJOYED THE INDIAN-SPICED CHICKEN THIGHS, YOU'RE IN FOR A TREAT! SIMPLY ADD SOME NUTTY-GOOD COCONUT MILK AND A LITTLE EXTRA SPICE, AND YOU'LL HAVE TONIGHT'S EQUALLY INTRIGUING MEAL READY IN MINUTES.

START TO FINISH
20 MINUTES

MAKES
6 SERVINGS

Reserved chicken and onion mixture from Indian-Spiced Chicken Thighs*
   (see recipe, page 106)
1   13.5- or 14-ounce can unsweetened coconut milk
4   teaspoons cornstarch
½   teaspoon curry powder
¼   cup raisins
3   cups hot cooked couscous
   Toasted shredded coconut (optional)

STEP 1   In a large saucepan heat reserved chicken and onion mixture over medium heat until hot. In a medium bowl stir together coconut milk, cornstarch, and curry powder; stir into chicken mixture. Stir in raisins.

STEP 2   Cook and stir over medium heat until thickened and bubbly. Cook and stir for 2 minutes more. Serve with hot cooked couscous. If desired, sprinkle with toasted coconut.

* There should be about 5½ cups reserved chicken and onion mixture.

NUTRITION FACTS
PER SERVING
466 CAL., 19 G TOTAL FAT
(12 G SAT. FAT), 121 MG
CHOL., 647 MG SODIUM,
37 G CARBO., 2 G FIBER,
36 G PRO.

DAILY VALUES
2% VIT. A, 10% VIT. C,
5% CALCIUM, 16% IRON

EXCHANGES
2½ STARCH, 4 LEAN MEAT,
1 FAT

chicken & turkey sausage soup

THIS RECIPE STARTS WITH SWEET PEPPERS, ONION, AND CELERY, A TRIO KNOWN AS THE "HOLY TRINITY" OF CAJUN AND CREOLE COOKING. THAT MEANS YOU CAN EXPECT A LIVELY DISH!

PREP
30 MINUTES

COOK
8 HOURS (LOW)
4 HOURS (HIGH)

MAKES
4 SERVINGS + RESERVES

1½   cups chopped red and/or green sweet pepper (2 medium)
1   cup chopped onion (2 medium)
1   cup chopped celery (2 stalks)
8   skinless, boneless chicken thighs, cut into bite-size pieces
1   tablespoon cooking oil (optional)
16   ounces smoked turkey sausage, cut lengthwise and sliced into ½-inch pieces
4   cloves garlic, minced
1   teaspoon dried thyme, crushed
1   teaspoon dried oregano, crushed
½   teaspoon salt
¼   to ½ teaspoon cayenne pepper
4   cups chicken broth

STEP 1   In a 4- or 5-quart slow cooker place sweet pepper, onion, and celery. If desired, in a large skillet brown chicken, half at a time, in hot oil over medium heat. Place chicken and sausage on top of vegetables in cooker. Add garlic, thyme, oregano, salt, and cayenne pepper. Pour broth over all.

STEP 2   Cover and cook on low-heat setting for 8 to 9 hours or high-heat setting for 4 to 4½ hours.

STEP 3   Skim fat from soup. Reserve 4 cups of the soup; store as directed below.

TO STORE RESERVES Place soup in an airtight container. Seal and chill for up to 3 days. (Or freeze for up to 3 months. Thaw in refrigerator overnight before using.) Use in Chicken, Sausage & Shrimp Gumbo, page 109.

NUTRITION FACTS
PER SERVING
267 CAL., 11 G TOTAL FAT
(3 G SAT. FAT), 129 MG
CHOL., 1,434 MG SODIUM,
8 G CARBO., 2 G FIBER,
33 G PRO.

DAILY VALUES
26% VIT. A, 115% VIT. C,
4% CALCIUM, 13% IRON

EXCHANGES
½ VEGETABLE, 4½ LEAN MEAT

chicken, sausage & shrimp gumbo

THE TICKET TO A GREAT GUMBO IS AN EXPERT ROUX—A MIXTURE OF FAT (EITHER OIL OR BUTTER) AND FLOUR THAT'S COOKED AND STIRRED TO A DARK REDDISH-BROWN COLOR. IT HELPS GIVE THE DISH A RICH, THICK TEXTURE AND FLAVOR.

3	tablespoons butter
3	tablespoons all-purpose flour
	Reserved Chicken & Turkey Sausage Soup* (see recipe, page 108)
1½	cups cooked rice
1	14.5-ounce can diced tomatoes
2	cups frozen cut okra, thawed
12	ounces cooked medium shrimp, peeled and deveined
	Bottled hot pepper sauce (optional)

STEP 1 For roux, in a heavy large saucepan melt butter over medium heat. Stir in flour until smooth. Cook and stir about 8 minutes or until mixture turns a dark reddish-brown color.

STEP 2 Add reserved soup, the cooked rice, undrained tomatoes, and the okra to saucepan. Bring to boiling; reduce heat. Simmer, uncovered, for 15 minutes. Add shrimp; heat through. If desired, serve with bottled hot pepper sauce.

* There should be 4 cups reserved soup.

START TO FINISH
35 MINUTES

MAKES
4 SERVINGS

NUTRITION FACTS PER SERVING
477 CAL., 17 G TOTAL FAT (7 G SAT. FAT), 275 MG CHOL., 1,401 MG SODIUM, 35 G CARBO., 4 G FIBER, 43 G PRO.

DAILY VALUES
27% VIT. A, 103% VIT. C, 15% CALCIUM, 31% IRON

EXCHANGES
½ VEGETABLE, 2 STARCH, 5 VERY LEAN MEAT, 3 FAT

chicken with fennel braised in white wine

THIS DISH IS FOR THOSE TIMES WHEN YOU'RE NOT LOOKING FOR "WOW," BUT SIMPLE, YET REFINED MEAL THAT WILL EASE YOU INTO A RELAXED EVENING AT THE END OF THE HECTIC DAY.

PREP
20 MINUTES

COOK
9 HOURS (LOW)
4½ HOURS (HIGH)

MAKES
4 SERVINGS + RESERVES

2	large fennel bulbs, trimmed and sliced (3 cups)
2	cups coarsely shredded carrot (4 medium)
¾	cup sliced celery (1 ½ stalks)
3	tablespoons quick-cooking tapioca, crushed
3 ½	to 4 pounds skinless, boneless chicken thighs (18 to 24)
2	teaspoons dried thyme, crushed
1	teaspoon salt
¼	teaspoon black pepper
⅔	cup dry white wine
⅔	cup chicken broth
2	cups hot cooked pasta or rice
	Grated Parmesan cheese (optional)
	Snipped fresh fennel leaves (optional)

STEP 1   In a 5- to 7-quart slow cooker place fennel slices, carrot, and celery. Sprinkle with tapioca. Top with chicken. Sprinkle with thyme, salt, and pepper. Add wine and broth.

STEP 2   Cover and cook on low-heat setting for 9 to 10 hours or on high-heat setting for 4¼ to 5 hours.

STEP 3   Reserve half of the chicken thighs (9 to 12) and 1¼ cups of the vegetable mixture; store as directed below. Serve remaining chicken and vegetable mixture over hot cooked pasta. If desired, sprinkle with Parmesan cheese and snipped fennel leaves.

TO STORE RESERVES Coarsely chop chicken (2¼ cups). Place chicken and vegetable mixture in an airtight container. Seal and chill for up to 3 days. Use in Quick Chicken & Dumplings, page 111.

NUTRITION FACTS
PER SERVING
417 CAL., 9 G TOTAL FAT (2 G SAT. FAT), 158 MG CHOL., 606 MG SODIUM, 33 G CARBO., 4 G FIBER, 45 G PRO.

DAILY VALUES
109% VIT. A, 22% VIT. C, 8% CALCIUM, 21% IRON

EXCHANGES
1 VEGETABLE, 1½ STARCH, 5 LEAN MEAT

quick chicken & dumplings

WHO SAYS COMFORT FOOD HAS TO BE TAME? HERE A LITTLE GARLIC, FENNEL, AND ROSEMARY CHARGE A CLASSIC DISH WITH LOADS OF FLAVOR!

	Reserved Chicken with Fennel Braised in White Wine* (see recipe, page 110)
1	15.25-ounce can whole kernel corn, drained
1	10.75-ounce can condensed cream of chicken or cream of mushroom soup
½	cup shredded cheddar cheese (2 ounces)
4	cloves garlic, minced
½	teaspoon dried rosemary, crushed
1	7.5-ounce package (10) refrigerated buttermilk biscuits

STEP 1 In a large saucepan stir together reserved chicken mixture, the corn, soup, cheese, garlic, and rosemary. Cook over medium heat until cheese melts and mixture is hot and bubbly. Transfer to a greased 2-quart square baking dish.

STEP 2 For dumplings, cut each biscuit into quarters. Arrange biscuit pieces on top of hot chicken mixture in dish.

STEP 3 Bake, uncovered, in a 375°F oven for 20 to 25 minutes or until bubbly and biscuits are lightly browned. Let stand for 10 minutes before serving.

* There should be about 5 cups reserved chicken and vegetable mixture.

PREP
10 MINUTES

COOK
10 MINUTES

BAKE
20 MINUTES

STAND
10 MINUTES

OVEN
375°F

MAKES
4 SERVINGS

NUTRITION FACTS
PER SERVING
499 CAL., 19 G TOTAL FAT (7 G SAT. FAT), 180 MG CHOL., 1,380 MG SODIUM, 31 G CARBO., 4 G FIBER, 48 G PRO.

DAILY VALUES
58% VIT. A, 26% VIT. C, 16% CALCIUM, 18% IRON

EXCHANGES
1 VEGETABLE, 1½ STARCH, 5½ LEAN MEAT, 1 FAT

lemon-herb chicken thighs

WHITE WINE, LEMON PEEL, AND MUSHROOMS ARE ALWAYS A WINNING TRIO TO FLAVOR CHICKEN. AND YOU CAN'T GO WRONG ADDING A LITTLE CREAM CHEESE TO THE MIX—THE RESULT IS A LUSCIOUSLY SAUCED DISH.

PREP
5 MINUTES

COOK
7 HOURS (LOW) OR
3½ HOURS (HIGH)

MAKES
4 SERVINGS + RESERVES

16	skinless, boneless chicken thighs (about 2¼ pounds)
2	10.75-ounce cans condensed golden mushrooms soup
½	of an 8-ounce tub cream cheese with chive and onions
½	cup dry white wine
1	tablespoon finely shredded lemon peel
2	teaspoons dried thyme, crushed
2	cups hot cooked pasta

STEP 1   Place the chicken in a 5- or 6- quart slow cooker. For sauce, in a medium bowl whisk together the soup, cream cheese, wine, lemon peel, and thyme. Pour over chicken in cooker.

STEP 2   Cover and cook on low-heat setting for 7 to 8 hours or on high-heat setting for 3½ to 4 hours. Skim fat from the surface.

STEP 3   Reserve half of the chicken (8 thighs) and sauce (about 2 cups); store as directed below. Serve remaining chicken and sauce over hot cooked pasta.

TO STORE RESERVES Place chicken thighs and sauce in an airtight container. Seal and chill for up to 3 days. Don't freeze.

NUTRITION FACTS
PER SERVING
371 CAL., 13 G TOTAL FAT
(5 G SAT. FAT), 119 MG
CHOL., 697 MG SODIUM,
27 G CARBO., 2 G FIBER,
31 G PRO.

DAILY VALUES
16% VIT. A, 7% VIT. C,
4% CALCIUM, 13% IRON

EXCHANGES
2 STARCH, 3½ LEAN MEAT,
½ FAT

chicken with spinach sauce

THIS RECIPE IS A NOD TO A GOOD OLD-FASHIONED DISH, CHICKEN À LA KING—CHICKEN IN A CREAM SAUCE SERVED OVER RICE OR TOAST. HERE FRESH SPINACH AND THE SPARK OF LEMON AND WINE FROM OTHER RECIPE INGREDIENTS ADD A PLEASING UPDATE.

Reserved Lemon-Herb Chicken Thighs* (see recipe, page 112)

1 4-ounce can (drained weight) sliced mushrooms, drained

3 cups shredded fresh spinach

4 English muffins, split, toasted, and cut into quarters

¼ cup finely shredded Parmesan cheese (1 ounce)

STEP 1 In a large saucepan or Dutch oven combine reserved chicken and sauce and the mushrooms. Bring to boiling over medium heat, stirring occasionally. Stir in spinach; cover and cook over medium-low heat for 1 to 2 minutes or until spinach wilts.

STEP 2 Serve chicken mixture over English muffin quarters and top with cheese.

* There should be 8 reserved thighs and about 2 cups reserved sauce.

NUTRITION FACTS
PER SERVING
433 CAL., 15 G TOTAL FAT
(6 G SAT. FAT), 122 MG
CHOL., 1,171 MG SODIUM,
35 G CARBO., 3 G FIBER,
35 G PRO.

DAILY VALUES
59% VIT. A, 18% VIT. C,
22% CALCIUM, 20% IRON

EXCHANGES
1 VEGETABLE, 2 STARCH,
4 LEAN MEAT, ½ FAT

sesame chicken

TOASTED SESAME OIL IS MADE FROM TOASTED SESAME SEEDS; RICH BROWN IN COLOR, WITH A CONCENTRATED FLAVOR, A LITTLE GOES A LONG WAY TO ADD A NICE, NUTTY INTRIGUE TO DISHES. REFRIGERATE THE OIL TO DELAY RANCIDITY.

PREP
25 MINUTES

COOK
6 HOURS (LOW) OR
3 HOURS (HIGH)

STAND
5 MINUTES

MAKES
4 SERVINGS + RESERVES

3	to 3 ½ pounds skinless, boneless chicken thighs or chicken breast halves
1	8-ounce can sliced mushrooms, drained
1	8-ounce can sliced water chestnuts
3	tablespoons honey
3	tablespoons rice vinegar
3	tablespoons quick-cooking tapioca, crushed
2	tablespoons frozen orange juice concentrate, thawed
4	teaspoons toasted sesame oil
1	tablespoon bottled minced garlic or 6 cloves garlic, minced
¾	teaspoon salt
1	large red or green sweet pepper, cut into strips
1	6-ounce package frozen snow pea pods, thawed
5	cups hot cooked rice
2	tablespoons toasted sesame seeds

NUTRITION FACTS
PER SERVING
516 CAL., 10 G TOTAL FAT
(1 G SAT. FAT), 98 MG CHOL.,
576 MG SODIUM,
59 G CARBO., 4 G FIBER,
46 G PRO.

DAILY VALUES
25% VIT. A, 141% VIT. C,
28% CALCIUM, 19% IRON

EXCHANGES
1½ VEGETABLE, 3 STARCH,
½ OTHER CARBO.,
5 VERY LEAN MEAT, 1 FAT

STEP 1   Place chicken in a 4- or 5-quart slow cooker. In a bowl stir together mushrooms, water chestnuts, honey, rice vinegar, tapioca, orange juice concentrate, sesame oil, garlic, and salt. Pour over chicken in cooker; top with sweet pepper.

STEP 2   Cover and cook on low-heat setting for 6 to 7 hours or on high-heat setting for 3 to 3¹/₂ hours. Turn off slow cooker; stir in pea pods. Let stand for 5 minutes.

STEP 3   Reserve half of the chicken and half of the rice; store as directed below. Serve remaining chicken with all of the vegetables and sauce over remaining hot cooked rice. Sprinkle with sesame seeds.

TO STORE RESERVES Coarsely chop chicken (2³/₄ cups). Place chicken and rice in separate airtight containers. Seal and chill for up to 3 days. (Or freeze for up to 3 months. Thaw in refrigerator overnight before using.) Use in Spicy Chicken Fried Rice, page 115.

spicy chicken fried rice

YOU'LL WONDER WHY YOU NEVER THOUGHT OF THIS BEFORE: COMBINE EXTRA RICE AND LEFTOVER CHINESE FARE WITH A FEW INGREDIENTS FOR A WHOLE NEW RECIPE. ATTENTION, EXPERIMENTAL COOKS: WHY NOT USE THIS BASIC CONCEPT TO INSPIRE YOUR OWN FRIED RICE CREATIONS!

2	tablespoons cooking oil
2	eggs, lightly beaten
1	cup chopped onion (2 medium)
1	cup chopped fresh mushrooms
	Reserved chicken and rice from Sesame Chicken* (see recipe, page 114)
⅓	cup reduced-sodium soy sauce
2	tablespoons water
½	teaspoon ground ginger
¼	teaspoon cayenne pepper
	Thinly sliced green onion
	Soy sauce

STEP 1 In a large skillet heat 1 tablespoon of the oil over medium heat. Add eggs; lift and tilt the skillet to form a thin layer of egg. Cook for 1 to 2 minutes or until eggs are set. Invert skillet over a baking sheet to remove cooked eggs; cut into short, narrow strips and set aside.

STEP 2 In the same skillet cook and stir the onion and mushrooms in the remaining 1 tablespoon oil until just tender. Add the reserved chicken; continue cooking until chicken is heated through. Stir in ⅓ cup soy sauce, the water, ginger, and cayenne pepper. Add the reserved cooked rice. Cook and stir for 3 to 4 minutes or until heated through. Stir in the egg strips. Sprinkle with sliced green onion. Serve with additional soy sauce.

* There should be 2¾ cups reserved chopped chicken and 2½ cups reserved cooked rice.

PREP
15 MINUTES

COOK
10 MINUTES

MAKES
4 SERVINGS

NUTRITION FACTS
PER SERVING
528 CAL., 15 G TOTAL FAT (3 G SAT. FAT), 204 MG CHOL., 1,109 MG SODIUM, 47 G CARBO., 1 G FIBER, 48 G PRO.

DAILY VALUES
6% VIT. A, 18% VIT. C, 7% CALCIUM, 19% IRON

EXCHANGES
½ VEGETABLE, 3 STARCH, 5½ VERY LEAN MEAT, 2 FAT

mole chicken on polenta

MOLE IS A DARK, SPICY MEXICAN SAUCE THAT CAN VARY FROM COOK TO COOK. MOST VERSIONS START WITH ONION, GARLIC, AND CHILES AND INCLUDE GROUND SEEDS AND CHOCOLATE. LOOK FOR PREPARED MOLE AT HISPANIC MARKETS OR IN THE SPECIALTY FOOD AISLE OF WELL-STOCKED SUPERMARKETS.

PREP
15 MINUTES

COOK
8 HOURS (LOW) OR
4 HOURS (HIGH)

MAKES
4 TO 6 SERVINGS + RESERVES

1	large onion, cut into thin wedges
2	tablespoons quick-cooking tapioca, ground
2½	pounds skinless, boneless chicken thighs
½	teaspoon salt
¼	teaspoon black pepper
2	14-ounce cans chicken broth
⅓	cup prepared mole sauce
2	tablespoons packed brown sugar
1	16-ounce tube refrigerated cooked polenta
	Snipped fresh cilantro

STEP 1 Place onion in a 4- or 5-quart slow cooker. Sprinkle with tapioca. Place chicken thighs on top. Sprinkle chicken with salt and pepper. In a large bowl stir together broth, mole sauce, and sugar; pour over chicken in cooker.

STEP 2 Cover and cook on low-heat setting for 8 to 9 hours or on high-heat setting for 4 to 4½ hours.

STEP 3 Meanwhile, prepare polenta according to package directions for polenta mush. Reserve half of the chicken, onions, and sauce (about 2 cups); store as directed below. Using a slotted spoon, spoon remaining chicken and onions over polenta. Drizzle with sauce; pass remaining sauce. Sprinkle each serving with cilantro.

TO STORE RESERVES Shred chicken; place chicken, onions, and sauce in an airtight container. Seal and chill for up to 3 days. Use in Mole Chicken Tostadas, page 117.

NUTRITION FACTS
PER SERVING
331 CAL., 7 G TOTAL FAT
(2 G SAT. FAT), 114 MG
CHOL., 1,096 MG SODIUM,
31 G CARBO., 4 G FIBER,
33 G PRO.

DAILY VALUES
11% VIT. A, 9% VIT. C,
3% CALCIUM, 9% IRON

EXCHANGES
2 STARCH, 4 LEAN MEAT

mole chicken tostadas

TOPPINGS OF TOMATOES, LETTUCE, AND ONIONS ARE VERY TYPICAL FOR TOSTADAS. IT'S WHAT'S UNDERNEATH—THE ENCHANTINGLY SPICED MOLE CHICKEN YOU'VE SET ASIDE— THAT REALLY MAKES THE DISH SING!

6	6-inch corn tortillas
	Reserved Mole Chicken on Polenta* (see recipe, page 116)
1 ½	cups chopped tomato (3 medium)
1 ½	cups shredded lettuce
½	cup sliced, pitted ripe olives
½	cup dairy sour cream

STEP 1 Wrap tortillas tightly in foil. Heat in a 350°F oven about 10 minutes or until heated through.

STEP 2 In a medium saucepan cook reserved chicken, onions, and sauce over medium heat until heated through. Use a slotted spoon to spoon chicken over each tortilla, reserving sauce. Top each tortilla with tomato, lettuce, olives, and sour cream. Drizzle each tostada with reserved sauce.

* There should be about 1 pound reserved chicken and onions and 2 cups reserved sauce.

PREP
20 MINUTES

BAKE
10 MINUTES

OVEN
350°F

MAKES
4 TO 6 SERVINGS

NUTRITION FACTS
PER SERVING
421 CAL., 15 G TOTAL FAT (5 G SAT. FAT), 125 MG CHOL., 821 MG SODIUM, 37 G CARBO., 4 G FIBER, 34 G PRO.

DAILY VALUES
48% VIT. A, 31% VIT. C, 12% CALCIUM, 26% IRON

EXCHANGES
½ VEGETABLE, 2 STARCH, 4 LEAN MEAT

chipotle stewed chicken

RECIPES OFTEN CALL FOR A SMALL AMOUNT OF CANNED CHIPOTLE PEPPERS; FORTUNATELY, YOU CAN FREEZE LEFTOVERS FOR FUTURE USE. JUST PACK IN A FREEZER CONTAINER AND COVER WITH SAUCE FROM THE CAN. SEAL, LABEL, AND FREEZE FOR UP TO 2 MONTHS, THEN THAW AS NEEDED IN THE REFRIGERATOR.

PREP
15 MINUTES

COOK
8 HOURS (LOW) OR
4 HOURS (HIGH)

MAKES
4 SERVINGS + RESERVES

2	medium red sweet peppers, cut into 1-inch pieces
1	medium onion, cut into thin wedges
2	tablespoons quick-cooking tapioca
8	chicken drumsticks, skinned
8	chicken thighs, skinned
1	14.5-ounce can diced tomatoes
1	6-ounce can tomato paste
2	to 3 tablespoons finely chopped canned chipotle peppers in adobo sauce
2	teaspoons sugar
1	teaspoon salt
2	16-ounce packages refrigerated mashed potatoes

STEP 1 In a 5- or 6-quart slow cooker place sweet pepper and onion. Sprinkle with tapioca. Top with all chicken pieces. In a medium bowl stir together undrained tomatoes, tomato paste, chipotle peppers, sugar, and salt. Pour over chicken in cooker.

STEP 2 Cover and cook on low-heat setting for 8 to 9 hours or on high-heat setting for 4 to $4\frac{1}{2}$ hours.

STEP 3 Reserve 4 thighs, 4 drumsticks, and 1 cup of sauce; store as directed below. Heat potatoes according to package directions; serve with remaining chicken and sauce.

TO STORE RESERVES Place chicken and sauce in separate airtight containers. Seal and chill for up to 3 days. Use in Wraps with Limed Cream, page 119.

NUTRITION FACTS PER SERVING
477 CAL., 9 G TOTAL FAT (2 G SAT. FAT), 136 MG CHOL., 1,110 MG SODIUM, 52 G CARBO., 4 G FIBER, 43 G PRO.

DAILY VALUES
31% VIT. A, 222% VIT. C, 8% CALCIUM, 22% IRON

EXCHANGES
2 VEGETABLE, 2½ STARCH, 4 LEAN MEAT

wraps with limed cream

AS A PAIR, LIME JUICE AND CILANTRO RANK RIGHT UP THERE AS ONE OF THE ALL-TIME-BEST WAYS TO ADD SPARK TO LEFTOVERS. TASTE THE DELICIOUS COMBO IN THIS SPRIGHTLY DISH.

	Reserved Chipotle Stewed Chicken* (see recipe, page 118)
¼	cup mayonnaise
¼	cup dairy sour cream
1	tablespoon lime juice
¼	teaspoon salt
4	10-inch flour tortillas
4	lettuce leaves
2	tablespoons snipped fresh cilantro (optional)
	Lime wedges

STEP 1 Remove chicken meat from bones; discard bones and shred chicken. In a large skillet heat shredded chicken and reserved sauce over medium heat until heated through.

STEP 2 Meanwhile, in a small bowl stir together mayonnaise, sour cream, lime juice, and salt. Warm tortillas according to package directions.

STEP 3 Place a lettuce leaf on each tortilla. Using a slotted spoon, spoon chicken mixture on tortillas just below center. Top each with 2 table-spoons of sour cream mixture and, if desired, sprinkle with cilantro. Fold bottom edge of a tortilla up and over filling. Fold one side in slightly, then roll up from the bottom. Repeat with remaining tortillas. Serve wraps with lime wedges.

* There should be 4 reserved chicken thighs, 4 reserved chicken drumsticks, and 1 cup reserved sauce.

START TO FINISH
15 MINUTES

MAKES
4 SERVINGS

NUTRITION FACTS
PER SERVING
486 CAL., 23 G TOTAL FAT (6 G SAT. FAT), 146 MG CHOL., 688 MG SODIUM, 28 G CARBO., 2 G FIBER, 39 G PRO.

DAILY VALUES
11% VIT. A, 42% VIT. C, 9% CALCIUM, 19% IRON

EXCHANGES
1 VEGETABLE, 1½ STARCH, 4 LEAN MEAT, 2½ FAT

buffalo chicken drumsticks with blue cheese dip

IF YOU LOVE THE FLAVORS OF BUFFALO CHICKEN WINGS AS AN APPETIZER, WHY NOT ENJOY THEM AS AN ENTRÉE? STEAMED RICE AND PEAS WOULD MAKE A NICE FOIL TO CUT THE HEAT— AND PASS PLENTY OF BLUE CHEESE DRESSING TOO!

PREP
30 MINUTES

COOK
6 HOURS (LOW) OR
3 HOURS (HIGH)

MAKES
4 SERVINGS + RESERVES

16	chicken drumsticks (about 4 pounds), skinned
1	16-ounce bottle buffalo wing hot sauce (2 cups)
¼	cup tomato paste
2	tablespoons white or cider vinegar
2	tablespoons Worcestershire sauce
1	8-ounce carton dairy sour cream
½	cup mayonnaise
½	cup crumbled blue cheese
¼	to ½ teaspoon cayenne pepper

STEP 1 Place drumsticks in a 4- or 5-quart slow cooker. In a medium bowl stir together hot sauce, tomato paste, vinegar, and Worcestershire sauce. Pour over chicken in cooker.

STEP 2 Cover and cook on low-heat setting for 6 to 8 hours or on high-heat setting for 3 to 4 hours.

STEP 3 Meanwhile, in a small bowl stir together sour cream, mayonnaise, blue cheese, and cayenne pepper. Reserve half of the blue cheese dip (³⁄₄ cup); store as directed below. Cover and chill the remaining dip until ready to serve.

STEP 4 Using a slotted spoon, remove drumsticks from cooker. Skim fat from cooking juices. Reserve 8 of the drumsticks and 1 cup of the cooking juices; store as directed below. Serve remaining drumsticks with some of the remaining cooking juices and the remaining blue cheese dip.

TO STORE RESERVES Place blue cheese mixture in an airtight container. Remove meat from drumsticks, discarding bones. Using two forks, shred chicken (2¼ to 3 cups). Place shredded chicken and the 1 cup cooking juices in a second airtight container. Seal and chill for up to 3 days. Use in Buffalo Chicken & Blue Cheese Pizza, page 121.

NUTRITION FACTS
PER SERVING
462 CAL., 27 G TOTAL FAT
(9 G SAT. FAT), 181 MG
CHOL., 2,049 MG SODIUM,
6 G CARBO., 0 G FIBER,
45 G PRO.

DAILY VALUES
15% VIT. A, 3% VIT. C,
10% CALCIUM, 13% IRON

EXCHANGES
½ OTHER CARBO.,
6 LEAN MEAT, 2 FAT

buffalo chicken & blue cheese pizza

NEXT TIME THERE'S A BIG GAME ON TV, ENJOY TWO ZESTY SPORTS-BAR FLAVORS—PIZZA AND BUFFALO CHICKEN WINGS— COMBINED IN ONE EASY DISH.

1	**14-ounce Italian bread shell**
	Reserved Buffalo Chicken Drumsticks with Blue Cheese Dip*
	(see recipe, page 120)
1 ½	**cups shredded mozzarella cheese (6 ounces)**
¼	**cup sliced green onion (2)**
	Hot pepper sauce (optional)

STEP 1 Place bread shell on a 14-inch pizza pan or large baking sheet. Bake in a 400°F oven for 5 minutes. Spread reserved blue cheese dip over partially baked crust, leaving a ¼-inch border around the edge. Sprinkle with half of the mozzarella cheese. Top with reserved chicken mixture and the green onion. Sprinkle with remaining cheese.

STEP 2 Bake about 15 minutes more or until pizza is heated through and cheese is melted. Cut into wedges. If desired, serve with hot pepper sauce.

* There should be ¾ cup reserved blue cheese dip and about 3½ to 4 cups reserved chicken mixture.

PREP
15 MINUTES

BAKE
20 MINUTES

OVEN
400°F

MAKES
4 SERVINGS

NUTRITION FACTS
PER SERVING
854 CAL., 43 G TOTAL FAT (15 G SAT. FAT), 219 MG CHOL., 2,860 MG SODIUM, 50 G CARBO., 2 G FIBER, 66 G PRO.

DAILY VALUES
22% VIT. A, 5% VIT. C, 42% CALCIUM, 26% IRON

EXCHANGES
3½ STARCH, 8 LEAN MEAT, 3 FAT

honey-mustard sauced turkey breast

THE MAGICAL COMBO OF HONEY AND MUSTARD MAKES QUITE A MARK IN THIS DISH, IMBUING THE POTATOES AND TURKEY WITH THEIR SWEETNESS AND TANG.

PREP
15 MINUTES

COOK
5½ HOURS (LOW)

MAKES
6 SERVINGS + RESERVES

	Nonstick cooking spray
2	20-ounce packages refrigerated shredded hash brown potatoes
1	teaspoon salt
¼	teaspoon ground black pepper
3½	to 4 pounds turkey tenderloins
¼	cup Dijon-style mustard
2	tablespoons honey
2	cloves garlic, minced
2	tablespoons butter, cut up and softened

STEP 1   Lightly coat the inside of a 6-quart slow cooker with cooking spray. Place potatoes in prepared cooker; sprinkle with half of the salt and half of the pepper. Place turkey on potatoes. Sprinkle turkey with remaining salt and pepper. In a small bowl stir together mustard, honey, and garlic; spoon over turkey, spreading evenly.

STEP 2   Cover and cook on low-heat setting for 5½ to 6½ hours until an instant-read thermometer inserted into turkey registers 170°F. Reserve half of the turkey (about 1½ pounds); store as directed below.

STEP 3   Transfer remaining turkey to a serving platter; cover and keep warm. Add butter to potatoes in cooker; mash with a potato masher. Slice and serve turkey with mashed potatoes.

TO STORE RESERVES Place turkey in an airtight container. Seal and chill for up to 3 days. (Or freeze for up to 3 months. Thaw in refrigerator overnight before using.) Use in Chutney-Glazed Turkey & Fruit Salad, page 123.

NUTRITION FACTS
PER SERVING
363 CAL., 4 G TOTAL FAT
(3 G SAT. FAT), 97 MG CHOL.,
214 MG SODIUM,
43 G CARBO., 2 G FIBER,
38 G PRO.

DAILY VALUES
2% VIT. A, 20% VIT. C,
3% CALCIUM, 9% IRON

EXCHANGES
2½ STARCH, 4 VERY LEAN
MEAT, ½ FAT

chutney-glazed
turkey & fruit salad

MEAL

2

CHUTNEY IS A TERRIFIC CONVENIENCE PRODUCT—THE SPICY CONDIMENT BRINGS TOGETHER A VARIETY OF FLAVORS WITH ONE EASY MEASURING STEP. SPREAD EXTRA CHUTNEY OVER CREAM CHEESE AND SERVE ALONGSIDE CRACKERS FOR A DELIGHTFUL PARTY SNACK.

START TO FINISH
25 MINUTES

MAKES
6 SERVINGS

1	9-ounce bottle mango chutney (¾ cup)
¼	cup salad oil
3	tablespoons orange juice
½	teaspoon curry powder
	Reserved Honey-Mustard Sauced Turkey Breast* (see recipe, page 122)
1	tablespoon olive oil
8	cups shredded leaf lettuce
2	cups fresh strawberries, hulled and sliced
2	mangoes, pitted, peeled, and cubed

STEP 1   Snip any large fruit pieces in the mango chutney. In a small bowl whisk together chutney, salad oil, orange juice, and curry powder; set aside.

STEP 2   Slice the reserved turkey crosswise into bite-size pieces. In a very large skillet cook and stir turkey in hot oil over medium-high heat for 2 to 3 minutes or until browned and heated through.

STEP 3   Divide shredded lettuce among 6 serving plates; top evenly with turkey, strawberries, and mango. Drizzle with some of the chutney mixture. Pass remaining chutney mixture.

*   There should be about 1½ pounds reserved turkey.

NUTRITION FACTS
PER SERVING
397 CAL., 13 G TOTAL FAT
(2 G SAT. FAT), 87 MG CHOL.,
491 MG SODIUM,
39 G CARBO., 4 G FIBER,
35 G PRO.

DAILY VALUES
127% VIT. A, 120% VIT. C,
8% CALCIUM, 17% IRON

EXCHANGES
1½ VEGETABLE, ½ FRUIT,
1½ OTHER CARBO.,
4½ VERY LEAN MEAT, 2 FAT

mushroom sauced turkey

CONDENSED CREAM OF CHICKEN SOUP IS OFTEN A SECRET WEAPON IN SLOW COOKER RECIPES—IT'S A SUREFIRE WAY TO CREATE RICH, CREAMY RESULTS. OF COURSE, ADDING A LITTLE ALFREDO PASTA SAUCE MIX DOESN'T HURT EITHER!

PREP
35 MINUTES

COOK
4 HOURS (LOW)

MAKES
6 SERVINGS + RESERVES

1	10.75-ounce can condensed cream of chicken soup
1	1.25-ounce package Alfredo pasta sauce mix
½	of an 8-ounce tub cream cheese with chives and onion
1	5-ounce can evaporated milk
½	cup water
2	pounds turkey breast tenderloins, cut into ¾-inch pieces
2	8-ounce cans (drained weight) sliced mushrooms, drained
2	cups shredded carrot (4 medium)
1	cup finely chopped onion (1 large)
1	pound dried angel hair pasta

STEP 1 In a 4- or 5-quart slow cooker stir together soup, pasta sauce mix, and cream cheese until blended. Gradually stir in evaporated milk and water. Add turkey, mushrooms, carrot, and onion.

STEP 2 Cover and cook on low-heat setting for 4 to 5 hours.

STEP 3 Meanwhile, cook pasta according to package directions.

STEP 4 Reserve half of the turkey mixture (about 4 cups) and half of the pasta (about 2½ cups); store as directed below. Serve remaining turkey mixture over remaining hot cooked pasta.

TO STORE RESERVES Place turkey mixture and pasta in separate airtight containers. Seal and chill for up to 3 days. Use in Turkey Tetrazzini, page 125.

NUTRITION FACTS

PER SERVING
336 CAL., 8 G TOTAL FAT
(4 G SAT. FAT), 61 MG CHOL.,
596 MG SODIUM,
39 G CARBO., 3 G FIBER,
26 G PRO.

DAILY VALUES
53% VIT. A, 4% VIT. C,
8% CALCIUM, 13% IRON

EXCHANGES
½ VEGETABLE, 2 STARCH,
½ OTHER CARBO., 3 VERY
LEAN MEAT, 1 FAT

turkey tetrazzini

THIS VERSION OF THE CLASSIC TURKEY DISH GETS A LITTLE
SOMETHING MORE, THANKS TO THE FROZEN ARTICHOKE HEARTS
AND WALNUTS.

Nonstick cooking spray

Reserved Mushroom Sauced Turkey* (see recipe, page 124)

2	8- or 9-ounce packages frozen artichoke hearts, thawed
½	cup milk
1	cup finely shredded Parmesan cheese (4 ounces)
¾	cup soft bread crumbs (1 slice bread)
⅓	cup chopped walnuts

STEP 1   Lightly coat a 3-quart rectangular baking dish with cooking spray.
Combine reserved turkey mixture, reserved pasta, the thawed artichoke
hearts, milk, and ¼ cup of the Parmesan cheese.

STEP 2   Bake, covered, in a 400°F oven for 30 minutes. Meanwhile,
combine remaining Parmesan cheese, the bread crumbs, and walnuts;
sprinkle over casserole. Bake, uncovered, about 15 minutes more or until
heated through and top is golden.

* There should be about 4 cups reserved turkey mixture and 2¼ cups
reserved pasta.

PREP
10 MINUTES

BAKE
45 MINUTES

OVEN
400°F

MAKES
6 SERVINGS

NUTRITION FACTS
PER SERVING
500 CAL., 17 G TOTAL FAT
(7 G SAT. FAT), 72 MG CHOL.,
924 MG SODIUM,
51 G CARBO., 8 G FIBER,
35 G PRO.

DAILY VALUES
58% VIT. A, 14% VIT. C,
33% CALCIUM, 18% IRON

EXCHANGES
1½ VEGETABLE, 2 STARCH,
½ OTHER CARBO.,
4 VERY LEAN MEAT, 3 FAT

rosemary turkey roast with vegetables

IF YOUR FAMILY LOVES TURKEY, WHY MAKE IT A HOLIDAY-ONLY TREAT? BONELESS TURKEY ROASTS ARE READILY AVAILABLE AND PERFECTLY SIZED FOR ANYTIME ENJOYMENT.

PREP
30 MINUTES

COOK
9 HOURS (LOW) OR
4½ HOURS (HIGH)

MAKES
6 SERVINGS + RESERVES

	Nonstick cooking spray
1	pound new potatoes, quartered
1	pound carrots, peeled and cut into 3-inch pieces
1	large onion, cut into ½-inch wedges
1	teaspoon dried rosemary, crushed
¼	teaspoon garlic powder
¼	teaspoon dried thyme, crushed
1	3-pound boneless turkey roast, thawed (do not remove cloth netting)*
	Chicken broth
¼	cup all purpose flour

STEP 1   Coat the inside of a 5- or 6-quart slow cooker with cooking spray. In prepared cooker, place potato, carrot, onion, ¼ cup water, 1 teaspoon salt, rosemary, garlic powder, thyme, and ¼ teaspoon pepper. Top with turkey.

STEP 2   Cover and cook on low-heat setting for 9 to 10 hours or on high-heat setting 4½ to 5 hours.

STEP 3   Remove turkey; place on cutting board. Cover turkey loosely with foil; let stand 15 minutes before removing netting and carving. Meanwhile, transfer vegetables to a serving platter; keep warm.

STEP 4   For gravy, strain cooking liquid into a 2-cup measure. Add enough chicken broth to strained liquid to equal 2 cups. In a medium saucepan whisk together the broth mixture and flour. Cook and stir over medium heat until thickened and bubbly. Cook and stir 1 minute more.

STEP 5   Reserve one-third of the turkey and 2 cups of vegetables; store as directed below. Serve remaining turkey and vegetables with gravy.

TO STORE RESERVES   Place turkey and vegetables in separate airtight containers. Seal and chill for up to 3 days. Use in Perfect Fit Turkey Pot Pie, page 127.

* Reserve giblets and/or gravy packet from turkey for another use.

NUTRITION FACTS
PER SERVING
270 CAL., 4 G TOTAL FAT
(1 G SAT. FAT), 81 MG CHOL.,
1,611 MG SODIUM,
29 G CARBO., 3 G FIBER,
29 G PRO.

DAILY VALUES
109% VIT. A, 18% VIT. C,
3% CALCIUM, 24% IRON

EXCHANGES
1 VEGETABLE, 1½ STARCH,
3½ VERY LEAN MEAT

perfect fit
turkey pot pie

COULD A HOMEMADE POT PIE BE ANY EASIER? ONE PAN DOES IT ALL—YOU COMBINE THE INGREDIENTS IN AN OVEN-GOING SKILLET, TOP WITH A REFRIGERATED PIECRUST, AND BAKE FOR A WARMING SUPPER WITH A FAMILY-FRIENDLY APPEAL.

½   **of a 15-ounce package rolled refrigerated unbaked piecrust (1 crust)**
     Reserved Rosemary Turkey Roast with Vegetables* (see recipe, page 126)
2   **10.75-ounce cans condensed cream of chicken soup**
1   **cup frozen peas**
1   **4-ounce jar diced pimiento**
⅛   **teaspoon black pepper**

STEP 1 Let piecrust stand at room temperature according to package directions.

STEP 2 Meanwhile, chop reserved turkey. In a large oven-going skillet stir together reserved turkey and vegetables, the soup, peas, undrained pimiento, and black pepper. Cook and stir over medium heat until mixture is bubbly. Remove from heat. Unroll piecrust and cut vents in crust to allow steam to escape. Carefully place pastry over the skillet, pressing the edge of the pastry into the edge of the skillet.

STEP 3 Bake, uncovered, in a 375°F oven for 40 to 45 minutes or until pastry is golden. Let stand for 10 minutes before serving.

* There should be about 12 ounces reserved turkey and 2 cups reserved vegetables.

PREP
25 MINUTES

BAKE
40 MINUTES

OVEN
375°F

MAKES
6 SERVINGS

NUTRITION FACTS
PER SERVING
406 CAL., 17 G TOTAL FAT
(6 G SAT. FAT), 55 MG CHOL.,
1,572 MG SODIUM,
43 G CARBO., 4 G FIBER,
19 G PRO.

DAILY VALUES
81% VIT. A, 43% VIT. C,
2% CALCIUM, 15% IRON

EXCHANGES
½ VEGETABLE, 2½ STARCH,
1½ VERY LEAN MEAT, 3 FAT

mexican turkey breast

IF YOU'VE NEVER TRIED AN ANCHO CHILE, NOW'S THE TIME—ITS RICH, SLIGHTLY FRUITY FLAVOR IS PERFECT FOR THIS DISH. DEEP REDDISH-BROWN IN COLOR, ANCHOS ARE THE SWEETEST VARIETY OF DRIED CHILE.

PREP
20 MINUTES

COOK
7 HOURS (LOW) OR
3½ HOURS (HIGH)

MAKES
4 SERVINGS + RESERVES

½	cup chicken broth
2	tablespoons quick-cooking tapioca
2	tablespoons ground ancho chile pepper or chili powder
2	teaspoons dried oregano, crushed
1	teaspoon garlic salt
½	teaspoon coarsely ground black pepper
¼	to ½ teaspoon cayenne pepper
2	tablespoons cooking oil
1	3½- to 4-pound turkey breast portion with bone
3	cups hot cooked mashed potatoes

STEP 1 Pour chicken broth into a 4½- to 6-quart slow cooker; sprinkle with tapioca. Set aside. In a small bowl stir together ground chile pepper, oregano, garlic salt, black pepper, and cayenne pepper. Stir in cooking oil to make a paste. Remove skin from turkey breast. Rub spice mixture over all sides of turkey. Place turkey in cooker.

STEP 2 Cover and cook on low-heat setting for 7 to 8 hours or on high-heat setting for 3½ to 4 hours.

STEP 3 Remove turkey from cooker, reserving cooking juices. Remove meat from bones. Reserve half of the turkey; store as directed below. Slice remaining half of the turkey and serve with mashed potatoes. Spoon some of the cooking juices over turkey and potatoes. Discard any remaining cooking juices.

TO STORE RESERVES Chop reserved turkey (about 3½ cups); place in an airtight container. Seal and chill for up to 3 days. (Or freeze for up to 3 months. Thaw in the refrigerator overnight before using.) Use in Mexican Turkey Casserole, page 129.

NUTRITION FACTS
PER SERVING
372 CAL., 10 G TOTAL FAT
(2 G SAT. FAT), 92 MG CHOL.,
775 MG SODIUM,
30 G CARBO., 3 G FIBER,
40 G PRO.

DAILY VALUES
18% VIT. A, 30% VIT. C,
6% CALCIUM, 14% IRON

EXCHANGES
2 STARCH, 5 VERY LEAN MEAT,
1 FAT

mexican
turkey casserole

IT'S EASY TO ADD EXTRA SPICY HEAT TO THIS RECIPE—JUST USE A SPICIER VERSION OF SALSA. AND IF YOU LOVE THE CONTRAST OF HOT AND COOL, BE SURE TO TOP EACH SERVING WITH SOUR CREAM TOO.

1	10-ounce can mild enchilada sauce
1	cup bottled mild salsa
6	6-inch corn tortillas
	Reserved Mexican Turkey Breast* (see recipe, page 128)
1 ½	cups shredded Monterey Jack cheese (6 ounces)
¼	cup dairy sour cream

STEP 1 In a medium bowl stir together enchilada sauce and salsa. In a 2-quart rectangular baking dish spread ½ cup of the salsa mixture. Arrange 2 tortillas in dish. Top evenly with half of the turkey and ½ cup of the cheese. Spoon ½ cup salsa mixture over turkey and cheese. Top with 2 more tortillas, followed by remaining turkey and ½ cup of the cheese. Spoon ½ cup salsa mixture over layers in dish. Top with remaining 2 tortillas. Spoon remaining salsa mixture over tortillas.

STEP 2 Cover and bake in a 375°F oven for 35 to 40 minutes or until heated through. Uncover and sprinkle with remaining ½ cup cheese. Bake, uncovered, about 1 minute more or until cheese is melted. Top each serving with sour cream.

* There should be about 3¼ cups reserved chopped turkey.

PREP
15 MINUTES

BAKE
35 MINUTES

MAKES
4 TO 6 SERVINGS

NUTRITION FACTS
PER SERVING
527 CAL., 21 G TOTAL FAT (10 G SAT. FAT), 133 MG CHOL., 1,190 MG SODIUM, 34 G CARBO., 3 G FIBER, 50 G PRO.

DAILY VALUES
33% VIT. A, 17% VIT. C, 40% CALCIUM, 25% IRON

EXCHANGES
2 STARCH, 6 LEAN MEAT, 1 FAT

bbq turkey kielbasa
& baked beans

IF YOUR CHILDREN LOVE BEENIE-WEENIES, BUT YOU'RE READY
TO GRADUATE YOUR FAMILY TO ANOTHER LEVEL, TRY THIS DISH.
IT HAS THE MAKINGS OF THE KID CLASSIC, BUT IT'S A LITTLE
MORE GROWN-UP.

PREP
10 MINUTES

COOK
6 HOURS (LOW) OR
3 HOURS (HIGH)

MAKES
4 SERVINGS + RESERVES

1	cup finely chopped onion (1 large)
1	cup ketchup
¾	cup packed brown sugar
3	tablespoons cider vinegar
3	tablespoons Worcestershire sauce
5	cloves garlic, minced
1	teaspoon chili powder
2	14.5-ounce cans navy beans, rinsed and drained
2	pounds turkey kielbasa, cut into four 4-inch lengths

STEP 1 In a medium bowl stir together onion, ketchup, brown sugar, vinegar, Worcestershire sauce, garlic, and chili powder.

STEP 2 In a 4- or 5-quart slow cooker place beans; top with half of the ketchup mixture. Place turkey kielbasa on bean mixture in cooker. Pour remaining ketchup mixture over top.

STEP 3 Cover and cook on low-heat setting for 6 to 8 hours or on high-heat setting for 3 to 4 hours.

STEP 4 Remove kielbasa from slow cooker. Reserve four of the kielbasa pieces; store as directed below.

TO STORE RESERVES Place kielbasa pieces in an airtight container. Seal and chill for up to 3 days. (Or freeze for up to 3 months. Thaw in refrigerator overnight before using.) Use in Turkey Kielbasa Sandwiches with Cabbage-Apple Slaw, page 131.

NUTRITION FACTS

PER SERVING
692 CAL., 11 G TOTAL FAT
(3 G SAT. FAT), 70 MG CHOL.,
2,864 MG SODIUM,
115 G CARBO., 13 G FIBER,
35 G PRO.

DAILY VALUES
15% VIT. A, 25% VIT. C,
17% CALCIUM, 44% IRON

EXCHANGES
2 STARCH, 5½ OTHER CARBO.,
4 LEAN MEAT

turkey kielbasa
sandwiches with cabbage-apple slaw

THE COLESLAW GETS EXTRA CRUNCH AND A LITTLE BIT OF FRUITY-SWEET TANG FROM A GRANNY SMITH APPLE. IT'S AN ABSOLUTELY PERFECT MATCH FOR THE HEARTY KIELBASA.

⅓   cup mayonnaise

¼   cup dairy sour cream

1   teaspoon cider vinegar

½   teaspoon dry mustard

½   teaspoon celery seed

2   cups thinly sliced red cabbage

1   cup chopped Granny Smith apple (1 large)

     Salt

     Black pepper

     Reserved kielbasa from BBQ Turkey Kielbasa & Baked Beans*
     (see recipe, page 130)

4   bratwurst or frankfurter buns

     Any variety mustard (optional)

STEP 1 In a medium bowl stir together mayonnaise, sour cream, vinegar, dry mustard, and celery seed; mix well. Add cabbage and apple; toss to coat. Season with salt and pepper. Cover and chill for at least 1 hour.

STEP 2 Place reserved kielbasa pieces on a microwave-safe plate; cook on 100 percent power (high) about 2 minutes or until heated through.

STEP 3 If desired, toast buns. Place a kielbasa piece in each bun. Top with some of the slaw mixture. Pass remaining slaw mixture. If desired, serve with mustard.

* There should be 4 pieces of reserved turkey kielbasa (4-inch lengths).

PREP
15 MINUTES

CHILL
1 HOUR

COOK
2 MINUTES

MAKES
4 SERVINGS

NUTRITION FACTS
PER SERVING
606 CAL., 41 G TOTAL FAT (10 G SAT. FAT), 37 MG CHOL., 1,921 MG SODIUM, 28 G CARBO., 3 G FIBER, 30 G PRO.

DAILY VALUES
10% VIT. A, 36% VIT. C, 9% CALCIUM, 12% IRON

EXCHANGES
½ VEGETABLE, 2 STARCH, 6½ LEAN MEAT, 5 FAT

sweet & sour turkey thighs

IF YOU'VE BEEN GETTING YOUR SWEET-AND-SOUR SAUCE FROM A JAR, TAKE JUST A FEW MINUTES MORE AND MAKE IT FROM SCRATCH. IT'S NOT DIFFICULT AT ALL, AND THE LITTLE EXTRA EFFORT ADDS A LOT OF GREAT TASTE TO THIS DISH.

PREP
20 MINUTES

COOK
6 HOURS (LOW) OR
3 HOURS (HIGH)

MAKES
4 TO 6 SERVINGS + RESERVES

6	pounds turkey thighs (6) or chicken thighs with bone
1	large onion, cut into thin wedges
2	tablespoons quick-cooking tapioca
1	teaspoon garlic powder
1	teaspoon lemon-pepper seasoning
½	teaspoon ground ginger
½	cup frozen pineapple juice concentrate, thawed
¼	cup red wine vinegar
¼	cup soy sauce
2	cups hot cooked rice

STEP 1 Remove and discard skin from turkey thighs; set turkey aside. Place onion in a 5- or 6-quart slow cooker. Sprinkle with tapioca. Top with turkey. Sprinkle turkey with garlic powder, lemon-pepper seasoning, and ginger. In a small bowl stir together pineapple juice concentrate, vinegar, and soy sauce; pour over turkey in cooker.

STEP 2 Cover and cook on low-heat setting for 6 to 7 hours or on high-heat setting for 3 to 3½ hours.

STEP 3 Remove turkey from cooker; strain ⅔ cup juices. Reserve two of the turkey thighs and the strained juices; store as directed below. Serve remaining turkey and unstrained juices with hot cooked rice.

TO STORE RESERVES Place turkey thighs and strained juices in separate air-tight containers. Seal and chill for up to 3 days. (Or freeze for up to 3 months. Thaw in refrigerator overnight before using.) Use in Turkey Cabbage Slaw, page 133.

NUTRITION FACTS
PER SERVING
510 CAL., 8 G TOTAL FAT (3 G SAT. FAT), 231 MG CHOL., 994 MG SODIUM, 43 G CARBO., 1 G FIBER, 63 G PRO.

DAILY VALUES
1% VIT. A, 20% VIT. C, 7% CALCIUM, 34% IRON

EXCHANGES
1½ STARCH, 1½ OTHER CARBO., 8 VERY LEAN MEAT, ½ FAT

turkey cabbage slaw

TRANSFORM LAST NIGHT'S DINNER INTO A BRIGHT, CRUNCHY SALAD FOR A LUNCH YOU'LL LOOK FORWARD TO ALL MORNING. IF YOU WANT TO TOTE IT TO THE OFFICE, PACK THE SALAD AND THE DRESSING SEPARATELY AND COMBINE THEM WHEN YOU'RE READY TO EAT.

PREP
25 MINUTES

CHILL
UP TO 1 HOUR

MAKES
4 SERVINGS

Reserved meat and juices from Sweet & Sour Turkey Thighs*
(see recipe, page 132)

⅓	cup salad oil
2	tablespoons rice vinegar
¼	teaspoon salt
⅛	teaspoon black pepper
1	3-ounce package ramen noodles (discard or reserve seasoning packet for another use)
6	cups shredded cabbage with carrot (coleslaw mix)
½	cup sliced green onion (4)
½	cup chopped walnuts or almonds, toasted

STEP 1   Remove turkey meat from bones; discard bones. Chop meat; set aside. Remove any fat from reserved juices. For dressing, in a small bowl whisk together reserved juices, oil, rice vinegar, salt, and pepper.

STEP 2   In a very large bowl break up ramen noodles. Add shredded cabbage with carrot, the green onion, and chopped turkey. Drizzle dressing over mixture; toss to coat. Cover and chill for up to 1 hour.

STEP 3   Sprinkle with nuts to serve.

* There should be 2 reserved turkey thighs and ⅔ cup reserved juices.

NUTRITION FACTS
PER SERVING
594 CAL., 36 G TOTAL FAT (5 G SAT. FAT), 116 MG CHOL., 670 MG SODIUM, 31 G CARBO., 4 G FIBER, 36 G PRO.

DAILY VALUES
33% VIT. A, 76% VIT. C, 10% CALCIUM, 19% IRON

EXCHANGES
1½ VEGETABLE, ½ STARCH, ½ OTHER CARBO., 4½ VERY LEAN MEAT, 7 FAT

turkey thighs in creamy mustard sauce

THE TURKEY COMES OUT JUICY AND TENDER AFTER A LONG, SLOW SIMMER WITH JUST THE RIGHT SEASONINGS. THE MUSTARD FLAVOR IS NICELY SUBTLE AND MELDS BEAUTIFULLY WITH THE CARAWAY SEEDS AND DRIED HERBS.

PREP
15 MINUTES

COOK
10 HOURS (LOW) OR
5 HOURS (HIGH)

MAKES
6 SERVINGS + RESERVES

½	cup Dijon-style mustard
¼	cup water
2	tablespoons quick-cooking tapioca
2	tablespoons honey
1	teaspoon dried dillweed
½	teaspoon salt
½	teaspoon dried thyme, crushed
½	teaspoon caraway seeds
¼	teaspoon black pepper
8	turkey thighs (about 6 pounds), skinned
	Salt and black pepper
½	cup dairy sour cream
3	cups hot cooked egg noodles

STEP 1 In a 5- to 7-quart slow cooker stir together mustard, water, tapioca, honey, dillweed, ½ teaspoon salt, the thyme, caraway seeds, and ¼ teaspoon pepper. Top with turkey. Lightly sprinkle turkey with additional salt and pepper.

STEP 2 Cover and cook on low-heat setting for 10 to 12 hours or on high-heat setting for 5 to 6 hours.

STEP 3 Reserve two of the turkey thighs; store as directed below. Transfer remaining turkey to a serving dish; cover and keep warm.

STEP 4 For sauce, strain cooking liquid into a medium bowl. Place sour cream in a small bowl. Slowly whisk about 1 cup of the strained cooking liquid into the sour cream. Whisk sour cream mixture into remaining cooking liquid. Serve turkey with sauce and hot cooked noodles.

TO STORE RESERVES Place turkey in an airtight container. Seal and chill for up to 3 days. (Or freeze for up to 3 months. Thaw in refrigerator overnight before using.) Use in Turkey Pasta Salad, page 135.

NUTRITION FACTS
PER SERVING
421 CAL., 10 G TOTAL FAT
(4 G SAT. FAT), 207 MG
CHOL., 704 MG SODIUM,
30 G CARBO., 1 G FIBER,
51 G PRO.

DAILY VALUES
3% VIT. A, 8% CALCIUM,
30% IRON

EXCHANGES
2 STARCH, 6 LEAN MEAT

turkey
pasta salad

MANY FLAVORS, COLORS, AND TEXTURES COMBINE FOR AN
IMMENSELY SATISFYING SALAD. IT WILL MAKE A PERFECT
QUICK LUNCH TO ENJOY ON A BUSY SATURDAY.

8	ounces dried tricolored rotini or bow tie pasta
	Reserved turkey from Turkey Thighs in Creamy Mustard Sauce*
	(see recipe, page 134)
1	cup frozen peas, thawed
1	6-ounce jar marinated artichoke hearts, drained and chopped
½	of a 12-ounce jar roasted red sweet peppers, drained and chopped (⅔ cup)
⅓	cup chopped walnuts, toasted
¼	cup sliced green onion (2)
⅛	to ¼ teaspoon crushed red pepper
¾	cup bottled Italian salad dressing

START TO FINISH
25 MINUTES

MAKES
6 SERVINGS

STEP 1 Cook pasta according to package directions; drain. Rinse pasta with cold water; drain again. Meanwhile, remove and discard bones from reserved turkey thighs; chop turkey.

STEP 2 In a large bowl combine cooked pasta, turkey, peas, artichoke hearts, sweet pepper, walnuts, green onion, crushed red pepper, and salad dressing. Toss gently to coat.

* There should be 2 reserved turkey thighs.

NUTRITION FACTS
PER SERVING
454 CAL., 19 G TOTAL FAT
(3 G SAT. FAT), 95 MG CHOL.,
671 MG SODIUM,
40 G CARBO., 3 G FIBER,
32 G PRO.

DAILY VALUES
11% VIT. A, 95% VIT. C,
5% CALCIUM, 24% IRON

EXCHANGES
2½ STARCH, 4 LEAN MEAT,
1 FAT

1

southwest-style bbq turkey thighs

SMALL AMOUNTS OF HERBS AND SPICES ADD UP TO BIG FLAVORS IN THIS BOLD AND SATISFYING DISH. YOU'LL APPRECIATE THE WAY THE TURKEY THIGHS COOK UP NICELY TENDER AFTER THE LONG, SLOW SIMMER.

PREP
25 MINUTES

COOK
10 HOURS (LOW) OR
5 HOURS (HIGH)

MAKES
6 SERVINGS + RESERVES

1	14.5-ounce can diced tomatoes
1	10-ounce can enchilada sauce
¼	cup red wine vinegar
1	cup chopped red or green sweet pepper (1 large)
1	tablespoon bottled minced garlic or 6 cloves garlic, minced
1	to 2 tablespoons finely chopped canned chipotle peppers in adobo sauce
3	tablespoons quick-cooking tapioca, crushed
2	teaspoons dried oregano, crushed
1	teaspoon ground cumin
¾	teaspoon salt
¼	teaspoon ground cinnamon
¼	to ½ teaspoon cayenne pepper (optional)
5	1-pound turkey thighs, skinned
3	cups hot cooked rice
	Dairy sour cream (optional)

STEP 1   In a 5- to 7-quart slow cooker stir together undrained tomatoes, the enchilada sauce, vinegar, sweet pepper, garlic, chipotle peppers, tapioca, oregano, cumin, salt, cinnamon, and, if desired, cayenne pepper. Add turkey, turning to coat.

STEP 2   Cover and cook on low-heat setting for 10 to 12 hours or on high-heat setting for 5 to 6 hours.

STEP 3   Skim fat from sauce. Reserve 2 turkey thighs and 1 cup of the sauce; store as directed below. Cut remaining thighs in half; remove and discard bones. Serve turkey and sauce with hot cooked rice and, if desired, sour cream.

TO STORE RESERVES Place turkey and sauce in separate airtight containers. Seal and chill for up to 3 days. (Or freeze for up to 3 months. Thaw in refrigerator overnight before using.) Use in Turkey & Shrimp Tortilla Soup, page 137.

NUTRITION FACTS
PER SERVING
406 CAL., 7 G TOTAL FAT
(2 G SAT. FAT), 184 MG
CHOL., 600 MG SODIUM,
33 G CARBO., 1 G FIBER,
49 G PRO.

DAILY VALUES
14% VIT. A, 63% VIT. C,
7% CALCIUM, 30% IRON

EXCHANGES
½ VEGETABLE, 2 STARCH,
6 VERY LEAN MEAT, ½ FAT

turkey & shrimp tortilla soup

THE TORTILLA CHIPS, GREEN ONIONS, CILANTRO, CHEESE, AND LIME ARE ALL OPTIONAL—BUT THEY'RE ALSO WHAT MAKE THIS DISH SO FESTIVE AND FUN. AND BECAUSE KIDS LOVE CHOICES, THE MORE GARNISH OPTIONS YOU BRING TO THE TABLE, THE MORE LIKELY YOU'LL ENTICE PICKY EATERS TO DIG IN.

START TO FINISH
30 MINUTES

MAKES
6 SERVINGS

8	ounces fresh or frozen medium shrimp, peeled, deveined, and halved lengthwise
	Reserved Southwest-Style BBQ Turkey Thighs* (see recipe, page 136)
2	14-ounce cans chicken or vegetable broth
1	15-ounce can tomato sauce
1	14.5-ounce can Mexican-style stewed tomatoes, undrained and cut up
¼	cup fresh-squeezed lime juice
1	to 2 fresh jalapeño or serrano chile peppers, seeded and finely chopped**
	Crushed lime tortilla chips (optional)
	Thinly sliced green onion (optional)
	Snipped fresh cilantro (optional)
	Shredded Monterey jack cheese (optional)
	Lime wedges (optional)

STEP 1 Thaw shrimp, if frozen. Remove bones from reserved turkey and discard; chop turkey.

STEP 2 In a large saucepan stir together broth, tomato sauce, undrained tomatoes, reserved turkey and sauce, the lime juice, and chile pepper. Bring to boiling; reduce heat. Simmer, covered, for 10 minutes. Stir in shrimp. Cook about 3 to 5 minutes more or until shrimp turn opaque.

STEP 3 Top each serving with crushed tortilla chips, green onion, cilantro, and cheese. If desired, serve with lime wedges.

* There should be 2 reserved turkey thighs and 1 cup reserved sauce.

** Because hot peppers, such as jalapeños, contain volatile oils that can burn your skin and eyes, avoid direct contact with chiles as much as possible. When working with chile peppers, wear plastic or rubber gloves. If your bare hands do touch the chile peppers, wash your hands well with soap and water.

NUTRITION FACTS PER SERVING
265 CAL., 5 G TOTAL FAT (1 G SAT. FAT), 167 MG CHOL., 1,383 MG SODIUM, 13 G CARBO., 1 G FIBER, 39 G PRO.

DAILY VALUES
6% VIT. A, 46% VIT. C, 6% CALCIUM, 22% IRON

EXCHANGES
1 VEGETABLE, ½ OTHER CARBO., 5 VERY LEAN MEAT, 1 FAT

creamy turkey bow ties & cheese

AS YOU'D EXPECT WITH TWO CUPS OF WHIPPING CREAM, THIS IS ONE OPULENTLY RICH DISH! A VINAIGRETTE-TOSSED SALAD STARRING LOTS OF CHOPPED VEGETABLES WILL PROVIDE A SPRIGHTLY CONTRAST TO THE DISH.

PREP
25 MINUTES

COOK
3 HOURS (LOW)

MAKES
6 SERVINGS + RESERVES

4	cups chopped cooked turkey (about 1¼ pounds)
2	cups chopped onion (4 medium)
2	cups whipping cream
8	ounces American cheese, cubed
8	ounces process Swiss cheese, torn
1	teaspoon dried sage, crushed
½	teaspoon black pepper
16	ounces dried bow tie pasta

STEP 1 In a 4 or 5-quart slow cooker stir together turkey, onion, cream, American cheese, Swiss cheese, sage, and pepper.

STEP 2 Cover and cook on low-heat setting for 3 to 4 hours. (Do not use high-heat setting.)

STEP 3 Meanwhile, cook pasta according to package directions; drain. Stir cheese mixture in cooker. Stir cooked pasta into the cheese mixture in cooker. Reserve 2½ cups of the pasta mixture; store as directed below. Serve remaining pasta mixture immediately.

TO STORE RESERVES Place pasta mixture in an airtight container. Seal and chill for up to 3 days. Use in Turkey & Asparagus Strata, page 139.

NUTRITION FACTS
PER SERVING
755 CAL., 43 G TOTAL FAT (25 G SAT. FAT), 186 MG CHOL., 886 MG SODIUM, 49 G CARBO., 2 G FIBER, 43 G PRO.

DAILY VALUES
27% VIT. A, 4% VIT. C, 45% CALCIUM, 18% IRON

EXCHANGES
3 STARCH, 5 LEAN MEAT, 5 FAT

turkey & asparagus strata

THIS CLEVER RENDITION OF THE CLASSIC BRUNCH DISH IS MADE EXTRA HEARTY, THANKS TO THE PASTA. HONEYDEW & APPLE SALAD, PAGE 218, WOULD PROVIDE A NICE ACCOMPANIMENT.

1 ½	cups seasoned croutons
	Reserved Creamy Turkey Bow Ties & Cheese* (see recipe, page 138)
1	10-ounce package frozen cut asparagus, thawed and well drained
4	eggs
1 ¼	cups milk
½	teaspoon onion powder
1	tablespoon dry mustard
⅛	teaspoon ground nutmeg

STEP 1 Spread croutons in a greased 2-quart square baking dish. In a medium bowl combine reserved pasta mixture and the asparagus. Spoon pasta mixture evenly over the croutons.

STEP 2 In the same bowl whisk together eggs. Whisk in milk, onion powder, dry mustard, and nutmeg. Pour evenly over pasta mixture in baking dish. Cover and chill for 2 to 24 hours.

STEP 3 Bake, covered, in a 325°F oven for 30 minutes. Uncover and bake for 30 to 45 minutes more or until the internal temperature registers 170°F on an instant-read thermometer. Let stand for 10 minutes before serving.

* There should be 2½ cups reserved pasta mixture.

PREP
25 MINUTES

CHILL
2 HOURS

BAKE
1 HOUR

STAND
10 MINUTES

OVEN
325°F

MAKES
6 SERVINGS

NUTRITION FACTS
PER SERVING
389 CAL., 21 G TOTAL FAT (11 G SAT. FAT), 208 MG CHOL., 490 MG SODIUM, 28 G CARBO., 2 G FIBER, 23 G PRO.

DAILY VALUES
23% VIT. A, 27% VIT. C, 25% CALCIUM, 13% IRON

EXCHANGES
½ VEGETABLE, 1½ STARCH, 3 LEAN MEAT, 2 FAT

MEAL 1

turkey pasta sauce with mixed olives

LOVE SAUSAGE AND OLIVES ON PIZZA? IMAGINE HOW MUCH YOU'LL LIKE THEM IN A PASTA SAUCE TOO! HINT: OLIVES PACK A GREAT DEAL OF FLAVOR, BUT THEY CAN BE SALTY. THAT'S WHY THE RECIPE CALLS FOR NO-SALT-ADDED DICED TOMATOES; IF DESIRED, YOU CAN USE NO-SALT-ADDED TOMATO PASTE TOO.

PREP
30 MINUTES

COOK
7 HOURS (LOW) OR
3½ HOURS (HIGH)

MAKES
6 SERVINGS + RESERVES

	Nonstick cooking spray
3	pounds bulk Italian turkey sausage
3	14.5-ounce cans no-salt-added diced tomatoes
2	6-ounce cans tomato paste
1	cup finely chopped onion (2 medium)
1	5-ounce jar (drained weight) sliced pimiento-stuffed green olives, drained
1	3.8-ounce can (drained weight) sliced, pitted ripe olives, drained
1	3.5-ounce jar capers, drained
4	teaspoons bottled minced garlic or 8 cloves garlic, minced
4	teaspoons dried Italian seasoning, crushed
12	ounces dried ziti or penne pasta
	Finely shredded or grated Parmesan cheese (optional)

NUTRITION FACTS
PER SERVING
663 CAL., 41 G TOTAL FAT
(12 G SAT. FAT), 69 MG
CHOL., 1,127 MG SODIUM,
56 G CARBO., 5 G FIBER,
27 G PRO.

DAILY VALUES
12% VIT. A, 28% VIT. C,
10% CALCIUM, 27% IRON

EXCHANGES
1½ VEGETABLE, 3 STARCH,
2 MEDIUM-FAT MEAT, 5½ FAT

STEP 1   Lightly coat the inside of a 6- or 7-quart slow cooker with cooking spray; set aside. In a very large skillet cook sausage, half at a time, over medium heat until brown, stirring to break meat into small pieces. Drain off fat. Transfer sausage to a very large bowl. Stir in undrained tomatoes, the tomato paste, onion, olives, capers, garlic, and Italian seasoning. Transfer mixture to prepared cooker.

STEP 2   Cover and cook on low-heat setting for 7 to 8 hours or on high-heat setting for 3½ to 4 hours.

STEP 3   To serve, cook pasta according to package directions; drain and keep warm. Reserve half of the pasta sauce (about 5½ cups); store as directed below. Serve remaining sauce over hot cooked pasta. If desired, sprinkle with Parmesan cheese.

TO STORE RESERVES Place sauce in an airtight container. Seal and chill for up to 3 days. Use in Italian-Style Stuffed Peppers, page 141.

italian-style stuffed peppers

IF YOU'RE CRAVING PIZZA BUT WANT SOMETHING A LITTLE MORE HEALTHFUL, CONSIDER THIS AN INSIDE-OUT PIZZA—WITH GREAT PIZZA FLAVORS TUCKED INSIDE THE GREEN PEPPER. IT HELPS, TOO, THAT IT'S TOPPED WITH ALL-TIME FAVORITE PIZZA CHEESES!

6	large green and/or red sweet peppers
	Reserved Turkey Pasta Sauce with Mixed Olives* (see recipe, page 140)
1	cup soft bread crumbs
½	cup shredded mozzarella cheese (2 ounces)
⅓	cup shredded Parmesan cheese (1 ½ ounces)

STEP 1 Cut tops off sweet peppers. Remove seeds and membranes. Place peppers, cut sides up, in a lightly greased 3-quart rectangular baking dish; set aside. In a large bowl stir together reserved sauce and the bread crumbs. Spoon about 1 cup sauce mixture into each pepper.

STEP 2 Bake, covered, in a 375°F oven about 1¼ hours or until filling is heated through and peppers are crisp-tender. Sprinkle mozzarella cheese and Parmesan cheese on top of peppers. Bake, uncovered, about 5 minutes more or until cheese melts.

* There should be about 5½ cups reserved sauce.

PREP
15 MINUTES

BAKE
1 HOUR 35 MINUTES

OVEN
375°F

MAKES
6 SERVINGS

NUTRITION FACTS
PER SERVING
558 CAL., 44 G TOTAL FAT (14 G SAT. FAT), 80 MG CHOL., 1,315 MG SODIUM, 27 G CARBO., 7 G FIBER, 25 G PRO.

DAILY VALUES
28% VIT. A, 255% VIT. C, 22% CALCIUM, 24% IRON

EXCHANGES
3 VEGETABLE, ½ STARCH, 2½ MEDIUM-FAT MEAT, 5½ FAT

cook once eat twice

meatless

good news

committed and once-in-a-while vegetarians alike: you, too, can take advantage of the fix-and-forget ease of the slow cooker in these unique vegetarian creations. you'll love the way the leftovers make terrific empanadas, pizza, pasta, and other satisfying meatless meals.

mu shu-style vegetables

FOR A MORE TRADITIONAL MU SHU DISH, COOK A PLAIN OMELET, CUT IT UP, AND TOSS WITH THE VEGETABLES BEFORE SERVING.

PREP
20 MINUTES

COOK
5 HOURS (LOW)
+ 30 MINUTES

MAKES
4 SERVINGS + RESERVES

4	cups packaged shredded cabbage with carrot (coleslaw mix)
3	cups sliced button mushrooms (8 ounces)
2	cups thinly sliced bok choy
1	cup bean sprouts, trimmed
1	cup chopped red sweet pepper (1 large)
1	8-ounce can bamboo shoots, drained and chopped
6	green onions, cut into 1-inch pieces
¼	cup reduced-sodium soy sauce
2	tablespoons dry sherry (optional)
1	tablespoon toasted sesame oil
1	teaspoon ground ginger
2	cloves garlic, minced
1	tablespoon water
1	tablespoon cornstarch
	Bottled hoisin sauce
8	frozen Chinese pancakes, thawed and warmed, or eight 6- to 7-inch flour tortillas, warmed

NUTRITION FACTS
PER SERVING
227 CAL., 4 G TOTAL FAT
(0 G SAT. FAT), 0 MG CHOL.,
725 MG SODIUM,
42 G CARBO., 3 G FIBER,
6 G PRO.

DAILY VALUES
44% VIT. A, 91% VIT. C,
9% CALCIUM, 6% IRON

EXCHANGES
2 VEGETABLE, 1 STARCH,
1 OTHER CARBO., 1 FAT

STEP 1 In a 4- or 5-quart slow cooker stir together coleslaw mix, mushrooms, bok choy, bean sprouts, sweet pepper, bamboo shoots, green onion, soy sauce, sherry (if desired), sesame oil, ginger, and garlic.

STEP 2 Cover and cook on low-heat setting for 5 to 6 hours. Turn to high-heat setting.

STEP 3 In a small bowl stir together the water and cornstarch; stir into vegetable mixture in cooker. Cover and cook for 30 minutes more. Reserve half of the vegetable mixture (about 2½ cups); store as directed below.

STEP 4 To serve, spread desired amount of hoisin sauce on each pancake. Use a slotted spoon to portion a heaping ⅓ cup vegetable mixture onto each pancake. Roll up pancakes.

TO STORE RESERVES Place vegetable mixture in an airtight container. Seal and chill for up to 3 days. Use in Asian Vegetable Soup, page 145.

asian
vegetable soup

LEAVE IT TO LEMON, CILANTRO, AND GREEN ONIONS TO
REALLY ENERGIZE LEFTOVERS! OF COURSE, STARTING WITH A
WINDFALL OF COLORFUL VEGETABLES FROM MEAL NUMBER ONE
HELPS TOO!

2	**14-ounce cans vegetable broth**
	Reserved Mu Shu-Style Vegetables* (see recipe, page 144)
½	**of a 16-ounce package firm tofu (fresh bean curd), cut into bite-size strips**
½	**teaspoon finely shredded lemon peel**
¼	**cup snipped fresh cilantro**
¼	**cup sliced green onion (2)**

STEP 1   In a large saucepan stir together broth, reserved vegetables, the
tofu, and lemon peel. Bring to boiling. Top each serving with cilantro and
green onion.

* There should be 2½ cups reserved vegetables.

START TO FINISH
10 MINUTES

MAKES
4 SERVINGS

NUTRITION FACTS
PER SERVING
111 CAL., 4 G TOTAL FAT
(1 G SAT. FAT), 0 MG CHOL.,
1,114 MG SODIUM,
12 G CARBO., 3 G FIBER,
7 G PRO.

DAILY VALUES
55% VIT. A, 96% VIT. C,
8% CALCIUM, 11% IRON

EXCHANGES
2 VEGETABLE, ½ MEDIUM-FAT
MEAT, ½ FAT

1

asian vegetable rice with coconut milk

IF YOU LOVE THE MULTIFACET APPEAL OF THAI COOKING, WITH ITS SPICY, NUTTY, SWEET, AND HOT FLAVORS, YOU'LL APPRECIATE THIS FASCINATING MEATLESS DISH.

PREP
35 MINUTES

COOK
6 HOURS (LOW) OR
3 HOURS (HIGH)
+ 30 MINUTES

MAKES
4 SERVINGS + RESERVES

1	pound carrots, cut diagonally into ¼-inch slices
2	medium onions, cut into thin wedges
2	large red sweet peppers, cut into ¼-inch strips
2	large green sweet peppers, cut into ¼-inch strips
1	8-ounce can sliced water chestnuts, drained
1	teaspoon ground ginger
1	teaspoon green curry paste
½	teaspoon garlic powder
¼	teaspoon crushed red pepper
2	tablespoons cornstarch
1	13.5- to 14-ounce can coconut milk
12	ounces firm tofu, cubed
2	cups hot cooked rice
⅓	cup sliced green onion (3)
¼	cup chopped fresh cilantro
¼	cup chopped peanuts

NUTRITION FACTS
PER SERVING
420 CAL., 19 G TOTAL FAT
(9 G SAT. FAT), 0 MG CHOL.,
419 MG SODIUM,
50 G CARBO., 5 G FIBER,
15 G PRO.

DAILY VALUES
155% VIT. A, 158% VIT. C,
25% CALCIUM, 19% IRON

EXCHANGES
1½ VEGETABLE, 3 STARCH,
3 FAT

STEP 1   In a 5- or 6-quart slow cooker stir together carrot, onion, sweet pepper, water chestnuts, ⅓ cup water, 1 teaspoon salt, ginger, curry paste, garlic powder, and crushed red pepper.

STEP 2   Cover and cook on low-heat setting for 6 to 7 hours or on high-heat setting for 3 to 3½ hours or until vegetables are tender.

STEP 3   If using low-heat setting, turn to high-heat setting. Stir together cornstarch and 2 tablespoons water. Add cornstarch mixture to slow cooker. Stir in coconut milk. Cover; cook about 30 minutes more or until thickened.

STEP 4   Remove half of the vegetables (about 3 cups); store as directed below. Stir tofu into remaining vegetable mixture in cooker. Serve tofu mixture over rice; top with green onion, cilantro, and peanuts.

TO STORE RESERVES Place vegetable mixture in an airtight container. Seal; chill for up to 3 days. Use in Creamy Carrot & White Bean Soup, page 147.

creamy carrot & white bean soup

PRESTO CHANGE-O! WITH THE ADDITION OF JUST A FEW WELL-CHOSEN INGREDIENTS, THE ASIAN VEGETABLE RICE WITH COCONUT MILK DISH BECOMES A SATISFYING SOUP FOR LUNCH OR A LIGHT SUPPER.

Reserved vegetable mixture from Asian Vegetable Rice with Coconut Milk*
  (see recipe, page 146)

2	15-ounce cans navy beans, rinsed and drained
2	14-ounce cans vegetable broth
1½	teaspoons ground cumin
¼	teaspoon salt
⅛	teaspoon cayenne pepper
1	cup half-and-half or light cream

STEP 1 In a large saucepan stir together the reserved vegetable mixture, the beans, broth, cumin, salt, and cayenne pepper. Bring to boiling over medium-high heat; reduce heat. Simmer, covered, for 10 minutes. Remove from heat; process in batches in blender or food processor until smooth.

STEP 2 Return processed mixture to the saucepan; stir in half-and-half. Heat through but do not boil.

* There should be 3 cups reserved vegetable mixture.

START TO FINISH
20 MINUTES

MAKES
4 SERVINGS

NUTRITION FACTS
PER SERVING
538 CAL., 19 G TOTAL FAT (13 G SAT. FAT), 22 MG CHOL., 2,362 MG SODIUM, 76 G CARBO., 15 G FIBER, 22 G PRO.

DAILY VALUES
161% VIT. A, 156% VIT. C, 30% CALCIUM, 33% IRON

EXCHANGES
1 VEGETABLE, 4½ STARCH, 1 VERY LEAN MEAT, 2½ FAT

winter squash ragôut

THE WORD "RAGÔUT" IS DERIVED FROM A FRENCH WORD THAT MEANS "TO STIMULATE THE APPETITE." WITH A TOOTHSOME MIX OF EARTHY AND SWEET MIXED VEGETABLES, PLUS A HEARTY HELPING OF WHITE BEANS AND JUST THE RIGHT HERBS, THIS RECIPE WILL DO JUST THAT.

PREP
30 MINUTES

COOK
7 HOURS (LOW) OR
3½ HOURS (HIGH)

MAKES
4 SERVINGS + RESERVES

2½	pounds butternut squash, peeled, seeded, and cut into ¾-inch pieces (about 5 cups)
1	19-ounce can cannellini beans, rinsed and drained
2	14.5-ounce cans fire-roasted diced tomatoes
1	large sweet onion, cut into thin wedges (2 cups)
3½	cups chopped peeled parsnip (4 medium)
1	14-ounce can vegetable broth
3	cloves garlic, minced
1	teaspoon salt
1	teaspoon dried thyme, crushed
½	teaspoon dried sage, crushed
½	teaspoon dried rosemary, crushed
½	teaspoon black pepper
	Packaged shredded Italian cheese blend (optional)

STEP 1 In a 5- or 6-quart slow cooker stir together squash, beans, undrained tomatoes, onion, parsnip, broth, garlic, salt, thyme, sage, rosemary, and pepper.

STEP 2 Cover and cook on low-heat setting for 7 to 8 hours or on high-heat setting for 3½ to 4 hours.

STEP 3 Using a slotted spoon, remove 4 cups of the vegetables; store as directed below. Serve remaining squash ragôut in shallow bowls. If desired, sprinkle with cheese.

TO STORE RESERVES Place vegetables in an airtight container. Seal and chill for up to 3 days. Use in Winter Squash Pasta Shells Alfredo, page 149.

NUTRITION FACTS
PER SERVING
210 CAL., 1 G TOTAL FAT
(0 G SAT. FAT), 0 MG CHOL.,
1,104 MG SODIUM,
49 G CARBO., 10 G FIBER,
9 G PRO.

DAILY VALUES
48% VIT. A, 72% VIT. C,
12% CALCIUM, 18% IRON

EXCHANGES
3 VEGETABLE, 2 STARCH,
½ VERY LEAN MEAT

winter squash pasta shells alfredo

THERE'S A LOT TO LOVE ABOUT THIS RECIPE. HEARTY, VEGETABLE-FILLED SHELLS GET ENRICHED WITH ALFREDO SAUCE AND ITALIAN CHEESE. THE CLINCHER, HOWEVER, IS THE NICELY CRUNCHY BREAD-CRUMB-AND-NUT TOPPING!

	Nonstick cooking spray
12	dried shell macaroni (jumbo)*
	Reserved vegetables from Winter Squash Ragôut** (see recipe, page 148)
1	10-ounce container refrigerated Alfredo pasta sauce
⅔	cup shredded Italian cheese blend
½	cup panko (Japanese-style) bread crumbs or soft bread crumbs
¼	cup chopped pecans, toasted
2	tablespoons butter, melted

STEP 1 Lightly coat a 2-quart rectangular baking dish with cooking spray; set aside. Cook shells according to package directions; drain. Spoon reserved vegetables into pasta shells. Arrange filled shells in prepared dish. Spoon any remaining vegetables around the shells in the dish.

STEP 2 Pour Alfredo sauce evenly over shells. Sprinkle with cheese. In a small bowl stir together bread crumbs, pecans, and butter. Sprinkle crumb mixture over top of shells.

STEP 3 Bake, uncovered, in a 375°F oven about 30 minutes or until heated through.

* Cook 2 or 3 extra shells in case any tear while cooking.

** There should be 4 cups reserved vegetables.

PREP
30 MINUTES

BAKE
30 MINUTES

OVEN
375°F

MAKES
4 SERVINGS

NUTRITION FACTS
PER SERVING
616 CAL., 38 G TOTAL FAT
(7 G SAT. FAT), 63 MG CHOL.,
985 MG SODIUM,
55 G CARBO., 7 G FIBER,
18 G PRO.

DAILY VALUES
27% VIT. A, 36% VIT. C,
17% CALCIUM, 15% IRON

EXCHANGES
2 VEGETABLE, 3 STARCH,
1 MEDIUM-FAT MEAT, 6 FAT

cowboy rice & beans

BEANS PACK A POWERFUL ONE-TWO PUNCH OF FIBER AND PROTEIN. WITH THREE KINDS OF BEANS AND BROWN RICE, THIS DISH MAKES FOR A HEALTHY MEATLESS DINNER. THANKS TO KICKY SEASONINGS, IT'S AN EXCITING ONE TOO!

PREP
10 MINUTES

COOK
5 HOURS (LOW) OR
2½ HOURS (HIGH)

MAKES
4 (1½-CUP) SERVINGS
+ RESERVES

2	15-ounce cans chili beans in chili gravy
1	15.5- to 16-ounce can butter beans, rinsed and drained
1	15-ounce can black beans, rinsed and drained
1	cup chopped onion (1 large)
¾	cup chopped green sweet pepper (1 medium)
¾	cup chopped red sweet pepper (1 medium)
1	fresh jalapeño chile pepper, seeded and finely chopped*
1	18-ounce bottle barbecue sauce
1	cup vegetable broth
1	cup instant brown rice

STEP 1 In a 5- or 6-quart slow cooker combine undrained chili beans, the butter beans, black beans, onion, sweet peppers, and jalapeño. Pour barbecue sauce and chicken broth over bean mixture in cooker.

STEP 2 Cover and cook on low-heat setting for 5 to 6 hours or on high-heat setting for 2½ to 3 hours.

NUTRITION FACTS
PER SERVING
365 CAL., 3 G TOTAL FAT
(0 G SAT. FAT), 0 MG CHOL.,
1,676 MG SODIUM,
68 G CARBO., 17 G FIBER,
19 G PRO.

STEP 3 If using low-heat setting, turn to high-heat setting. Stir in rice. Cover and cook about 30 minutes more or until rice is tender. Reserve 3 cups bean mixture; store as directed below.

TO STORE RESERVES Place bean mixture in an airtight container. Seal and chill for up to 3 days. Use in Baked Cowboy Chimichangas, page 151.

DAILY VALUES
16% VIT. A, 92% VIT. C,
12% CALCIUM, 24% IRON

* Because hot peppers, such as jalapeños, contain volatile oils that can burn your skin and eyes, avoid direct contact with chiles as much as possible. When working with chile peppers, wear plastic or rubber gloves. If your bare hands do touch the chile peppers, wash your hands well with soap and water.

EXCHANGES
½ VEGETABLE, 3 STARCH,
1½ OTHER CARBO.,
1 VERY LEAN MEAT

baked cowboy chimichangas

BAKING CHIMICHANGAS IS MUCH EASIER THAN FRYING THEM! ADD A SPOONFUL OF SOUR CREAM AND YOUR FAVORITE PURCHASED SALSA TO THIS MEXICAN STANDBY, AND YOU MAY NEVER WANT THE TRADITIONAL FRIED VERSION AGAIN.

Reserved Cowboy Rice & Beans* (see recipe, page 150)

8 8-inch flour tortillas
1 8-ounce package shredded Mexican cheese blend (2 cups)
   Dairy sour cream (optional)
   Bottled salsa (optional)

STEP 1 Place a scant ⅓ cup of the reserved bean mixture down center of each tortilla; top each with ¼ cup of the shredded cheese. Fold in sides of the tortilla and roll up. If necessary, secure with toothpicks. Place chimichangas, seam sides down, on a baking sheet.

STEP 2 Bake, uncovered, in a 350°F oven for 15 to 20 minutes or until crisp and browned. If desired, serve with sour cream and salsa.

* There should be 3 cups reserved bean mixture.

PREP
15 MINUTES

BAKE
15 MINUTES

OVEN
350°F

MAKES
4 SERVINGS

NUTRITION FACTS
PER SERVING
580 CAL., 24 G TOTAL FAT (11 G SAT. FAT), 50 MG CHOL., 1,558 MG SODIUM, 66 G CARBO., 9 G FIBER, 26 G PRO.

DAILY VALUES
8% VIT. A, 46% VIT. C, 44% CALCIUM, 23% IRON

EXCHANGES
3½ STARCH, 1 OTHER CARBO., 2 HIGH-FAT MEAT, 1 FAT

MEAL

slow cooker mushroom risotto

IF YOU'VE GIVEN RISOTTO RECIPES A PASS IN THE PAST BECAUSE THEY REQUIRE TOO MUCH HANDS-ON STIRRING, TAKE A LOOK AT THIS RECIPE! HERE THE RICE COOKS UP TO THE TRADITIONAL MOIST AND CREAMY RISOTTO CONSISTENCY WITHOUT ALL THAT STIRRING.

PREP
25 MINUTES

COOK
5 HOURS (LOW)

STAND
15 MINUTES

MAKES
6 SERVINGS + RESERVES

Nonstick cooking spray
1 ½ pounds fresh mushrooms (such as cremini, button, and/or shiitake),
   sliced (about 9 cups)
5 14-ounce cans vegetable broth
3 cups converted rice*
1 cup dry white wine or vegetable broth
¾ cup chopped shallot
5 cloves garlic, minced
1 teaspoon dried thyme, crushed
½ teaspoon salt
¼ teaspoon black pepper
1 ½ cups finely shredded Parmesan cheese (6 ounces)
½ cup finely shredded Asiago cheese (2 ounces)
½ cup butter, cut up

STEP 1 Lightly coat the inside of a 6-quart slow cooker with cooking spray. Place mushrooms, broth, rice, wine, shallot, garlic, thyme, salt, and pepper in prepared cooker. Cover and cook on low-heat setting for 5 to 6 hours.

STEP 2 Stir Parmesan and Asiago cheeses and the butter into rice mixture in cooker. Remove liner from cooker, if possible, or turn off cooker. Let stand, covered, for 15 minutes before serving. Reserve 6 cups risotto; store as directed below.

TO STORE RESERVES Place risotto in an airtight container. Seal and chill for up to 3 days. Use in Roquefort & Walnut-Stuffed Risotto Cakes, page 153.

* Do not substitute long grain rice for converted rice.

NUTRITION FACTS
PER SERVING
421 CAL., 16 G TOTAL FAT
(9 G SAT. FAT), 39 MG CHOL.,
1,230 MG SODIUM,
53 G CARBO., 1 G FIBER,
13 G PRO.

DAILY VALUES
19% VIT. A, 2% VIT. C,
24% CALCIUM, 18% IRON

EXCHANGES
3½ STARCH,
½ MEDIUM-FAT MEAT, 2 FAT

roquefort & walnut-stuffed risotto cakes

BREADED RISOTTO CAKES COOK UP SOFT INSIDE, CRISP OUTSIDE, WITH A DELICATE BLUE CHEESE FLAVOR THROUGHOUT. ENJOY TOPPED WITH YOUR FAVORITE ALFREDO OR MARINARA SAUCE. ROASTED ASPARAGUS WOULD GO SWIMMINGLY WITH THE DISH.

5	eggs
1¾	cups seasoned fine dry bread crumbs
½	cup chopped walnuts, toasted
1	cup crumbled Roquefort or other blue cheese, crumbled (4 ounces)
	Reserved Slow Cooker Mushroom Risotto* (see recipe, page 152)
3	tablespoons milk
¾	cup all-purpose flour
¼	cup cooking oil
1	10-ounce container refrigerated Alfredo sauce or one 15-ounce container marinara sauce

STEP 1 In a large bowl beat 2 eggs. Stir in ½ cup of the bread crumbs, the walnuts, and cheese. Stir in reserved risotto until combined. Shape rice mixture into 12 patties, about ⅔ cup each. Cover and chill about 2 hours or until the patties hold their shape when picked up.

STEP 2 In a shallow dish beat the remaining 3 eggs; stir in milk. Place flour in another shallow dish. Pace the remaining 1¼ cups bread crumbs in a third shallow dish.

STEP 3 Dip a risotto patty in the flour, dip in the milk mixture, then in the bread crumbs to coat. Repeat with remaining risotto patties.

STEP 4 In a very large skillet heat oil over medium heat. Add 4 to 6 of the risotto patties in a single layer, frying on one side until golden, about 4 minutes. Turn carefully; fry until second side is golden, about 4 minutes. Drain on paper towels. Repeat with remaining patties. Keep patties warm in a 300°F oven.

STEP 5 Meanwhile, in a small saucepan, bring Alfredo sauce to simmer. Serve risotto cakes with sauce.

* There should be 6 cups risotto.

PREP
30 MINUTES

CHILL
2 HOURS

COOK
8 MINUTES PER BATCH

OVEN
300°F

MAKES
6 SERVINGS

NUTRITION FACTS PER SERVING
884 CAL., 52 G TOTAL FAT (13 G SAT. FAT), 241 MG CHOL., 2,184 MG SODIUM, 75 G CARBO., 2 G FIBER, 29 G PRO.

DAILY VALUES
20% VIT. A, 3% VIT. C, 33% CALCIUM, 24% IRON

EXCHANGES
5 STARCH, 2 HIGH-FAT MEAT, 6 FAT

zesty vegetable pasta sauce

EGGPLANT STARS AS THE ROBUST, BEEFY HERO IN MANY A MEATLESS RECIPE. INDEED, THE BRAWNY VEGGIE CERTAINLY ADDS A NICE HEFT TO THIS CHUNKY SAUCE.

PREP
30 MINUTES

COOK
10 HOURS (LOW) OR
5 HOURS (HIGH)

MAKES
6 SERVINGS + RESERVES

2	small eggplants, peeled, if desired, and cut into 1-inch cubes (6 cups)
1	cup chopped onion (2 medium)
2	cups chopped green or red sweet pepper (3 medium)
4	teaspoons bottled minced garlic or 8 cloves garlic, minced
4	14.5-ounce cans Italian-style stewed tomatoes, cut up
1	6-ounce can Italian-style tomato paste
2	tablespoons packed brown sugar
2	tablespoons dried Italian seasoning, crushed
¼	to ½ teaspoon crushed red pepper
⅓	cup sliced, pitted kalamata olives or sliced, pitted ripe olives
12	ounces dried fettuccine or linguine
	Finely shredded or grated Parmesan or Romano cheese (optional)

STEP 1   In a 5- to 7-quart slow cooker stir together eggplant, onion, sweet pepper, garlic, undrained tomatoes, tomato paste, brown sugar, Italian seasoning, and red pepper.

STEP 2   Cover and cook on low-heat setting for 10 to 12 hours or on high-heat setting for 5 to 6 hours.

STEP 3   Meanwhile, cook fettuccine according to package directions; drain and keep warm. Reserve 5 cups sauce; store as directed below. Stir olives into remaining sauce. Serve with hot cooked fettuccine and, if desired, Parmesan cheese.

TO STORE RESERVES Place sauce in an airtight container. Seal and chill for up to 3 days. Use in Double-Sauced Vegetable Lasagna, page 155.

NUTRITION FACTS
PER SERVING
339 CAL., 4 G TOTAL FAT
(0 G SAT. FAT), 0 MG CHOL.,
548 MG SODIUM,
65 G CARBO., 5 G FIBER,
10 G PRO.

DAILY VALUES
3% VIT. A, 54% VIT. C,
9% CALCIUM, 20% IRON

EXCHANGES
3 VEGETABLE, 3 STARCH,
½ FAT

double-sauced vegetable lasagna

HERE'S AN UNEXPECTED BONUS—THIS LUSCIOUS RECIPE MAKES TWELVE SERVINGS. UNLESS YOU'RE SERVING A CROWD, THAT MEANS YOU'LL HAVE YET ANOTHER NIGHT'S DINNER READY WHEN YOU ARE!

1	16-ounce jar Alfredo sauce
1	10-ounce package frozen chopped broccoli, thawed and well drained
2	cups shredded mozzarella cheese (8 ounces)
¾	cup finely shredded Parmesan cheese (6 ounces)
	Reserved Zesty Vegetable Pasta Sauce* (see recipe, page 154)
1	9-ounce package no-boil lasagna noodles

STEP 1   In a large bowl stir together Alfredo sauce and broccoli; set aside. In a medium bowl combine the mozzarella cheese and Parmesan cheese. Spread 1 cup of the reserved sauce in the bottom of a greased 3-quart rectangular baking dish. Top with 4 lasagna noodles, overlapping and breaking noodles as necessary to fit the dish. Spread half of the broccoli mixture over the noodles. Sprinkle with ½ cup of the cheese mixture. Top with 4 more noodles. Spread 1 cup of the reserved sauce over the noodles. Sprinkle with ½ cup cheese mixture. Top with 4 more noodles. Spread the remaining broccoli mixture over the noodles. Sprinkle with ½ cup of the cheese mixture. Top with the remaining lasagna noodles, reserved sauce, and cheese mixture.

STEP 2   Bake, covered, in a 350°F oven for 40 minutes. Uncover and bake for 10 to 15 minutes more or until lasagna is heated through. Let stand 10 minutes before serving.

* There should be 5 cups reserved sauce.

PREP
35 MINUTES

BAKE
50 MINUTES

STAND
10 MINUTES

OVEN
350°F

MAKES
12 SERVINGS

NUTRITION FACTS
PER SERVING
329 CAL., 18 G TOTAL FAT (3 G SAT. FAT), 37 MG CHOL., 341 MG SODIUM, 28 G CARBO., 2 G FIBER, 13 G PRO.

DAILY VALUES
9% VIT. A, 45% VIT. C, 20% CALCIUM, 9% IRON

EXCHANGES
1½ VEGETABLE, 1½ STARCH, 1 MEDIUM-FAT MEAT, 2 FAT

marinara sauce

THIS VEGGIE-CHOCKED RED SAUCE CALLS FOR A NICE, CREAMY ACCOMPANIMENT. HOW ABOUT A GREEN SALAD TOSSED WITH A VINAIGRETTE AND TOPPED WITH GORGONZOLA CHEESE?

PREP
30 MINUTES

COOK
10 HOURS (LOW) OR
5 HOURS (HIGH)

MAKES
6 SERVINGS + RESERVES

2	28-ounce cans Italian-style whole peeled tomatoes in puree, cut up
3	cups shredded carrot* (6 medium)
2	cups thinly sliced celery (4 stalks)
2	cups chopped red and/or green sweet pepper (3 medium)
1½	cups finely chopped onion (3 medium)
2	6-ounce cans tomato paste
½	cup water
½	cup dry red wine
4	teaspoons bottled minced garlic or 8 cloves garlic, minced
5	teaspoons dried Italian seasoning, crushed
1	tablespoon sugar
2	teaspoons salt
¼	to ½ teaspoon black pepper
12	ounces dried penne pasta
⅓	cup grated Parmesan cheese

STEP 1 In a 6- or 7-quart slow cooker stir together undrained tomatoes, carrot, celery, sweet pepper, onion, tomato paste, water, wine, garlic, Italian seasoning, sugar, salt, and black pepper.

STEP 2 Cover and cook on low-heat setting for 10 to 12 hours or on high-heat setting for 5 to 6 hours.

STEP 3 Meanwhile, cook pasta according to package directions; drain and keep warm. Reserve half of the sauce (about 6 cups); store as directed below. Serve remaining sauce over hot cooked pasta; sprinkle with Parmesan cheese.

TO STORE RESERVES Place sauce in an airtight container. Seal and chill for up to 3 days. Use in Marinara-Sauced Shells, page 157.

* For quicker preparation, use purchased shredded carrot.

NUTRITION FACTS
PER SERVING
327 CAL., 3 G TOTAL FAT
(1 G SAT. FAT), 4 MG CHOL.,
844 MG SODIUM,
62 G CARBO., 5 G FIBER,
13 G PRO.

DAILY VALUES
100% VIT. A, 116% VIT. C,
10% CALCIUM, 17% IRON

EXCHANGES
2 VEGETABLE, 3½ STARCH

marinara-sauced shells

WHAT ARE YOU LOOKING FOR IN A BAKED PASTA DISH? SOMETHING CHEESY, SAUCY, AND ZESTY, OF COURSE! THIS RECIPE IS DEFINITELY ALL THAT!

18	dried shell macaroni (jumbo)*
1	15-ounce carton ricotta cheese
1	12.3-ounce package firm, silken-style tofu (fresh bean curd), patted dry with paper towels
⅓	cup finely shredded Parmesan cheese (1½ ounces)
1	egg, slightly beaten
1	teaspoon dried basil, crushed
⅛	teaspoon black pepper
	Reserved Marinara Sauce** (see recipe, page 156)
1	cup shredded mozzarella cheese (4 ounces)

STEP 1 Cook shells according to package directions; drain and set aside.

STEP 2 Meanwhile, in a medium bowl mash ricotta cheese and tofu together with a potato masher or fork. Stir in Parmesan cheese, egg, basil, and pepper. Spoon about 3 tablespoons of the tofu mixture into each cooked shell. Arrange the filled shells in a greased 3-quart rectangular baking dish. Top with reserved sauce, spreading sauce evenly over the shells.

STEP 3 Bake, covered, in a 350°F oven for 30 minutes. Uncover and bake for 30 to 35 minutes more or until heated through. Sprinkle with mozzarella cheese. Bake, uncovered, about 5 minutes more or until cheese melts. Let stand, uncovered, on a wire rack for 10 minutes before serving.

* Cook 2 or 3 extra shells in case any tear while cooking.

** There should be about 6 cups reserved sauce.

PREP
30 MINUTES

BAKE
65 MINUTES

STAND
10 MINUTES

OVEN
350°F

MAKES
6 SERVINGS

NUTRITION FACTS PER SERVING
444 CAL., 18 G TOTAL FAT (10 G SAT. FAT), 89 MG CHOL., 1,060 MG SODIUM, 44 G CARBO., 4 G FIBER, 26 G PRO.

DAILY VALUES
110% VIT A, 116% VIT. C, 37% CALCIUM, 19% IRON

EXCHANGES
2 VEGETABLE, 2½ STARCH, 2 MEDIUM-FAT MEAT, 1 FAT

ratatouille

A SPECIALTY IN THE SOUTH OF FRANCE, RATATOUILLE IS A VERSATILE DISH THAT CAN BE SERVED WARM OR AT ROOM TEMPERATURE AS A SIDE (TRY IT WITH BROILED CHICKEN OR BEEF) OR AS AN APPETIZER (SERVE WITH BREAD OR CRACKERS FOR SCOOPING).

PREP
20 MINUTES

COOK
6 HOURS (LOW) OR
3 HOURS (HIGH)
+ 30 MINUTES

MAKES
4 SERVINGS + RESERVES

4	cups peeled, cubed eggplant (1 small)
1	14.5-ounce can diced tomatoes with green pepper and onion
1	15-ounce can tomato puree
1	cup chopped red sweet pepper (1 large)
1	cup chopped yellow sweet pepper (1 large)
5	cloves garlic, minced
1	teaspoon salt
1	teaspoon dried oregano, crushed
1	teaspoon dried basil, crushed
¼	teaspoon black pepper
2	medium zucchini and/or summer squash, halved lengthwise and cut into ¼-inch slices
2	cups hot cooked couscous
¼	cup finely shredded Parmesan cheese (1 ounce)

NUTRITION FACTS
PER SERVING
206 CAL., 2 G TOTAL FAT
(1 G SAT. FAT), 4 MG CHOL.,
812 MG SODIUM,
40 G CARBO., 7 G FIBER,
8 G PRO.

DAILY VALUES
28% VIT. A, 236% VIT. C,
12% CALCIUM, 11% IRON

EXCHANGES
2½ VEGETABLE, 2 STARCH

STEP 1 In a 4- or 5-quart slow cooker stir together eggplant, undrained tomatoes, tomato puree, sweet pepper, garlic, salt, oregano, basil, and black pepper.

STEP 2 Cover and cook on low-heat setting for 6 to 7 hours or high-heat setting for 3 to 3½ hours.

STEP 3 If using low-heat setting, turn to high-heat setting. Add zucchini. Cover and cook about 30 minutes more or until vegetables are tender.

STEP 4 Reserve 2 cups ratatouille; store as directed below. Serve remaining ratatouille over hot cooked couscous; sprinkle with cheese.

TO STORE RESERVES Place ratatouille in an airtight container. Seal and chill for up to 3 days. (Do not freeze.) Use in Southwest Vegetable Empanadas, page 159.

southwest vegetable empanadas

ADD A FEW QUINTESSENTIAL SOUTHWESTERN FLAVORS TO THE TENDER RATATOUILLE VEGETABLE MIXTURE, THEN TUCK IT INSIDE PIECRUST EASILY MADE FROM A MIX. THE RESULT? SOMETHING COMPLETELY OUT OF THE ORDINARY IN LESS THAN HALF AN HOUR.

1	11-ounce package piecrust mix
	Reserved Ratatouille* (see recipe, page 158)
1	cup shredded Monterey Jack cheese with jalapeño peppers (4 ounces)
1	4-ounce can diced green chile peppers, drained
1	2.25-ounce can sliced ripe olives, drained
½	teaspoon ground cumin
	Milk
¼	to ½ teaspoon Ancho chile powder or chili powder
⅔	cup prepared guacamole
⅓	cup dairy sour cream
½	cup bottled salsa

STEP 1 Prepare piecrust according to package directions for double crust. Divide dough into 4 pieces.

STEP 2 Drain excess liquid from reserved Ratatouille. In a medium bowl stir together drained ratatouille, the cheese, green chiles, olives, and cumin; set aside.

STEP 3 On a lightly floured surface, roll one portion of dough into a 7-inch round. Spoon one-fourth of the ratatouille mixture onto the center of the round. Moisten edges with water. Fold in half and press with fork tines to seal. Place empanada on a foil-lined baking sheet; pierce top with fork. Repeat with remaining dough and ratatouille mixture.

STEP 4 Brush tops of empanadas with milk and sprinkle with chile powder. Bake, uncovered, in a 400°F oven for 20 to 25 minutes or until golden.

STEP 5 Meanwhile, stir together guacamole and sour cream; chill until serving time. Serve hot empanadas with guacamole mixture and salsa.

* There should be 2 cups reserved ratatouille.

PREP
25 MINUTES

BAKE
20 MINUTES

OVEN
400°F

MAKES
4 SERVINGS

NUTRITION FACTS PER SERVING
717 CAL., 48 G TOTAL FAT (16 G SAT. FAT), 32 MG CHOL., 1,407 MG SODIUM, 51 G CARBO., 6 G FIBER, 15 G PRO.

DAILY VALUES
26% VIT. A, 116% VIT. C, 31% CALCIUM, 20% IRON

EXCHANGES
1 VEGETABLE, 3 STARCH, 1 MEDIUM-FAT MEAT, 8 FAT

garbanzo bean stew

GARBANZO BEANS ARE ONE OF THOSE WONDERFULLY RICH AND HEARTY LEGUMES THAT MAKE IT EASY TO GO MEATLESS NOW AND THEN, ESPECIALLY WHEN YOU PAIR THEM WITH POTATOES AND JUST THE RIGHT SPICES.

PREP
25 MINUTES

COOK
9 HOURS (LOW) OR
4½ HOURS (HIGH)

MAKES
4 (1½ CUP) SERVINGS
+ RESERVES

3	15-ounce cans garbanzo beans (chickpeas), rinsed and drained
1	pound red-skin potatoes, cut into ¾-inch pieces
1	14.5-ounce can diced tomatoes
¾	cup chopped red sweet pepper (1 medium)
½	cup chopped onion (1 medium)
3	cloves garlic, minced
1	teaspoon ground cumin
½	teaspoon paprika
¼	teaspoon cayenne pepper
2	14-ounce cans vegetable broth

STEP 1 In a 5- or 6-quart slow cooker stir together garbanzo beans, potato, undrained tomatoes, sweet pepper, onion, garlic, cumin, paprika, and cayenne pepper. Pour vegetable broth over bean mixture in cooker.

STEP 2 Cover and cook on low-heat setting for 9 to 10 hours or on high-heat setting for 4¼ to 5 hours. Reserve 4 cups of the stew; store as directed below.

TO STORE RESERVES Place stew in an airtight container. Seal and chill for up to 3 days. Use in Falafel-Style Patties with Tahini Sauce, page 161.

NUTRITION FACTS
PER SERVING
245 CAL., 3 G TOTAL FAT
(0 G SAT. FAT), 0 MG CHOL.,
1,251 MG SODIUM,
46 G CARBO., 8 G FIBER,
10 G PRO.

DAILY VALUES
18% VIT. A, 79% VIT. C,
7% CALCIUM, 19% IRON

EXCHANGES
½ VEGETABLE, 3 STARCH

falafel-style patties with tahini sauce

MADE FROM GROUND SESAME SEEDS, TAHINI IS A DENSE PASTE OFTEN USED IN MIDDLE EASTERN COOKING. A LITTLE GOES A LONG WAY TO ADD NUTTY APPEAL TO THESE MEAT-FREE BURGERS. LOOK FOR IT IN THE SPECIALTY FOOD AISLE OF LARGER SUPERMARKETS.

PREP
30 MINUTES

COOK
8 MINUTES

MAKES
4 SERVINGS

Reserved Garbanzo Bean Stew* (see recipe, page 160)

½	cup soft bread crumbs
2	tablespoons olive oil
⅓	cup plain low-fat yogurt
1	tablespoon tahini
2	teaspoons lemon juice
¼	cup chopped seeded cucumber
	Salt and black pepper
2	pita bread rounds, halved crosswise
½	cup chopped tomato (1 medium)
1	cup shredded lettuce

STEP 1   Drain liquid from reserved stew; discard liquid. In a medium bowl mash stew with a potato masher. Stir in bread crumbs. Shape mixture into 8 patties, about ¾ inch thick.

STEP 2   In a large nonstick skillet cook patties, four at a time, in hot oil for 2 minutes per side or until golden brown. Drain patties on paper towels.

STEP 3   Meanwhile, in a small bowl stir together yogurt, tahini, and lemon juice. Stir in cucumber and season to taste with salt and pepper.

STEP 4   Serve patties with tahini sauce, pita bread, chopped tomato, and shredded lettuce.

* There should be 4 cups reserved stew.

NUTRITION FACTS
PER SERVING
364 CAL., 11 G TOTAL FAT (2 G SAT. FAT), 1 MG CHOL., 1,126 MG SODIUM, 54 G CARBO., 7 G FIBER, 12 G PRO.

DAILY VALUES
33% VIT. A, 68% VIT. C, 13% CALCIUM, 21% IRON

EXCHANGES
1 VEGETABLE, 3 STARCH, 2 FAT

italian eggplant stew

THIS CHUNKY VEGGIE-PACKED STEW WAS INSPIRED BY CAPONATA, AN ITALIAN DISH THAT TYPICALLY STARS EGGPLANT, ONIONS, OLIVES, AND TOMATOES. WHILE THE ITALIAN SPECIALTY IS OFTEN SERVED AS A SIDE DISH, HERE THE CONCEPT GETS SIMMERED INTO A STEW.

PREP
30 MINUTES

COOK
8 HOURS (LOW) OR
4 HOURS (HIGH)

MAKES
4 (1¾-CUP) SERVINGS
+ RESERVES

1	large eggplant, peeled and cut into 1-inch cubes
1	large red sweet pepper, cut into 1-inch pieces
1	cup coarsely chopped onion (1 large)
1	4-ounce can (drained weight) sliced mushrooms, drained
⅓	cup pimiento-stuffed green olives, halved
3	tablespoons tomato paste
1	teaspoon dried Italian seasoning, crushed
2	cloves garlic, minced
½	teaspoon salt
2	14-ounce cans vegetable broth
1	14.5-ounce can diced tomatoes
¼	cup finely shredded Parmesan cheese (1 ounce)

STEP 1 In a 5- or 6-quart slow cooker stir together eggplant, sweet pepper, onion, mushrooms, olives, tomato paste, Italian seasoning, garlic, and salt. Pour vegetable broth and undrained tomatoes over eggplant in cooker.

STEP 2 Cover and cook on low-heat setting for 8 to 10 hours or on high-heat setting for 4 to 5 hours.

STEP 3 Using a slotted spoon, remove 2 cups of vegetables; store as directed below. Divide remaining mixture among 4 soup plates. Top each serving of stew with Parmesan cheese.

TO STORE RESERVES Place vegetable mixture in an airtight container. Seal and chill for up to 3 days. Use in Individual Caponata Pizzas, page 163.

NUTRITION FACTS
PER SERVING
124 CAL., 3 G TOTAL FAT
(1 G SAT. FAT), 4 MG CHOL.,
1,310 MG SODIUM,
20 G CARBO., 6 G FIBER,
5 G PRO.

DAILY VALUES
28% VIT. A, 114% VIT. C,
13% CALCIUM, 9% IRON

EXCHANGES
4 VEGETABLE, ½ LEAN MEAT

individual caponata pizzas

THE TERRIFIC COMBINATION OF VEGETABLES IN THE ITALIAN EGGPLANT STEW GETS A LITTLE EXTRA BOOST FROM BALSAMIC VINEGAR AND RED PEPPER SAUCE FOR A CREATIVE PIZZA TOPPING. NO NEED TO PRETOAST THE PINE NUTS; THEY'LL TOAST WHEN THEY BAKE.

PREP
15 MINUTES

BAKE
12 MINUTES

OVEN
425°F

MAKES
4 SERVINGS

Reserved Italian Eggplant Stew* (see recipe, page 162)
⅓ cup bottled Italian salad dressing
1 tablespoon balsamic vinegar
Few dashes bottled hot pepper sauce
2 4-ounce packages 8-inch Italian bread shells
1 cup shredded provolone or mozzarella cheese (4 ounces)
¼ cup finely shredded Parmesan cheese (1 ounce)
¼ cup pine nuts

STEP 1 Lightly mash reserved vegetable mixture; drain in a colander. In a large bowl stir together vegetable mixture, dressing, vinegar, and hot pepper sauce.

STEP 2 Spread vegetable mixture evenly on Italian bread shells; arrange on baking sheet(s). Top with cheeses and pine nuts.

STEP 3 Bake in a 425°F oven about 12 minutes or until cheese melts and pizzas are heated through.

* There should be 2 cups reserved vegetable mixture.

NUTRITION FACTS
PER SERVING
634 CAL., 29 G TOTAL FAT
(7 G SAT. FAT), 29 MG CHOL.,
1,737 MG SODIUM,
72 G CARBO., 4 G FIBER,
29 G PRO.

DAILY VALUES
13% VIT. A, 28% VIT. C,
45% CALCIUM, 25% IRON

EXCHANGES
1 VEGETABLE, 4½ STARCH,
2 HIGH-FAT MEAT, 1 FAT

spicy vegetable chili

STIR TOGETHER A LITTLE BUTTER, HONEY, AND CINNAMON TO SPREAD ON A SLICE OF WARM CORN BREAD TO SERVE ALONGSIDE THIS RECIPE AND YOU'LL BE SET FOR A WARMING AND SURPRISINGLY "MEATY" MEATLESS DINNER.

PREP
30 MINUTES

COOK
9 HOURS (LOW) OR
4½ HOURS (HIGH)

MAKES
6 SERVINGS + RESERVES

2	cups chopped onion (2 large)
1½	cups chopped green sweet pepper (2 medium)
1	cup chopped celery (2 stalks)
8	cloves garlic, minced
2	28-ounce cans diced tomatoes
2	15- to 16-ounce cans dark red kidney beans, rinsed and drained
2	15- to 16-ounce cans pinto beans, rinsed and drained
1	15-ounce can whole kernel corn, drained
1	cup water
1	6-ounce can tomato paste
2	tablespoons chili powder
1	tablespoon Worcestershire sauce
1	teaspoon ground cumin
1	teaspoon dried oregano, crushed
¼	teaspoon cayenne pepper (optional)
1	teaspoon bottled hot pepper sauce
	Dairy sour cream (optional)

**NUTRITION FACTS
PER SERVING**
229 CAL., 1 G TOTAL FAT
(0 G SAT. FAT), 0 MG CHOL.,
733 MG SODIUM,
48 G CARBO., 11 G FIBER,
12 G PRO.

DAILY VALUES
12% VIT. A, 79% VIT. C,
14% CALCIUM, 22% IRON

EXCHANGES
2½ VEGETABLE, 2 STARCH

STEP 1   In a 6- or 7-quart slow cooker stir together onion, sweet pepper, celery, garlic, undrained tomatoes, kidney beans, pinto beans, corn, 1 cup water, the tomato paste, chili powder, Worcestershire sauce, cumin, oregano, cayenne pepper (if using), and hot pepper sauce.

STEP 2   Cover and cook on low-heat setting for 9 to 10 hours or on high-heat setting for 4½ to 5 hours.

STEP 3   Reserve 6 cups chili; store as directed below. If desired, serve remaining chili with sour cream.

TO STORE RESERVES Place chili in an airtight container. Seal and chill for up to 3 days. (Or freeze for up to 3 months. Thaw in refrigerator overnight before using.) Use in Cincinnati-Style Chili & Noodles, page 165.

cincinnati-style chili & noodles

CINCINNATI CHILI IS OFTEN SPICED WITH SWEET SPICES SUCH AS NUTMEG, CINNAMON, AND COCOA OR CHOCOLATE AND SERVED OVER SPAGHETTI. AMERICAN CHEESE AND CHOPPED ONION ARE CLASSIC TOPPERS FOR THIS REGIONAL DISH.

START TO FINISH
20 MINUTES

MAKES
6 SERVINGS

8	ounces dried spaghetti
	Reserved Spicy Vegetable Chili* (see recipe, page 164)
½	ounce unsweetened chocolate, chopped
½	teaspoon ground cinnamon
⅛	teaspoon ground allspice
⅛	teaspoon ground cloves
	Shredded American cheese
	Finely chopped onion

STEP 1 Cook spaghetti according to package directions; drain.

STEP 2 Meanwhile, in a large saucepan heat reserved chili over medium heat until bubbly. Stir in chocolate, cinnamon, allspice, and cloves. Cook and stir until chocolate melts. Serve chili over spaghetti. Sprinkle each serving with cheese and onion.

* There should be 6 cups reserved chili.

NUTRITION FACTS
PER SERVING
398 CAL., 8 G TOTAL FAT (4 G SAT. FAT), 16 MG CHOL., 813 MG SODIUM, 67 G CARBO., 10 G FIBER, 18 G PRO.

DAILY VALUES
13% VIT. A, 62% VIT. C, 22% CALCIUM, 25% IRON

EXCHANGES
2 VEGETABLE, 3½ STARCH, ½ HIGH-FAT MEAT

MEAL

rustic
italian stew

THIS DISH IS INSPIRED BY THE MUCH-LOVED CUISINE OF TUSCANY, ITALY, WHERE NATIVE DINERS ENJOY WHITE BEANS SO MUCH IN THEIR HEARTY AND SATISFYING CUISINE, THEY'VE EARNED THE NICKNAME "MANGIAFAGIOLI"—OR "BEAN EATERS."

PREP
20 MINUTES

COOK
7 HOURS (LOW) OR
3½ HOURS (HIGH)

MAKES
4 SERVINGS + RESERVES

Nonstick cooking spray

2   medium yellow summer squash, halved lengthwise and sliced

8   ounces button mushrooms, quartered

1   15-ounce can navy beans, rinsed and drained

2   medium green sweet peppers, cut into 1-inch pieces

1   medium zucchini, halved lengthwise and sliced

1   large onion, cut into thin wedges

1   tablespoon olive oil

1   teaspoon salt

1   teaspoon dried Italian seasoning, crushed

⅛   to ¼ teaspoon crushed red pepper (optional)

2   14.5-ounce cans undrained stewed tomatoes, cut up

1   cup shredded mozzarella cheese (4 ounces)

STEP 1   Lightly coat a 5- or 6-quart slow cooker with cooking spray. In prepared cooker stir together yellow squash, mushrooms, navy beans, sweet pepper, zucchini, onion, oil, salt, Italian seasoning, and, if desired, crushed red pepper. Top with undrained tomatoes.

STEP 2   Cover and cook on low-heat setting for 7 to 8 hours or on high-heat setting for 3½ to 4 hours.

STEP 3   Using a slotted spoon, remove 2 cups vegetables; store as directed below. Spoon remaining stew into soup bowls; sprinkle with mozzarella.

TO STORE RESERVES   Place drained vegetables in an airtight container. Seal and chill for up to 3 days. Use in Pasta Bowls, page 167.

NUTRITION FACTS
PER SERVING
433 CAL., 12 G TOTAL FAT
(4 G SAT. FAT), 22 MG CHOL.,
1,768 MG SODIUM,
60 G CARBO., 13 G FIBER,
25 G PRO.

DAILY VALUES
10% VIT. A, 83% VIT. C,
30% CALCIUM, 29% IRON

EXCHANGES
4 VEGETABLE, 2 STARCH,
1½ MEDIUM-FAT MEAT, 1 FAT

pasta bowls

A SIMPLE DISH WITH GREAT FLAVORS—THIS DESCRIBES SOME OF THE BEST RECIPES IN EVERYDAY ITALIAN COOKING, AND IT PERFECTLY DESCRIBES THIS DISH. SERVE WITH CRUSTY BREAD AND A GLASS OF INEXPENSIVE ITALIAN MERLOT—A GRAPE THAT ITALIAN WINEMAKERS HAVE RECENTLY COAXED INTO SOME VERY GOOD WINES.

START TO FINISH
15 MINUTES

MAKES
4 SERVINGS

Reserved vegetables from Rustic Italian Stew* (see recipe, page 166)
1   **26-ounce jar spaghetti sauce**
1   **teaspoon dried basil, crushed, or ¼ cup snipped fresh basil**
2   **9-ounce packages refrigerated cheese ravioli**
     Finely shredded Parmesan or Asiago cheese

STEP 1 In a medium saucepan stir together reserved vegetables, the spaghetti sauce, and dried basil, if using. Bring to boiling over medium heat; remove from heat. Stir in fresh basil, if using.

STEP 2 Meanwhile, prepare ravioli according to package directions; drain and divide evenly among bowls. Spoon the vegetable mixture over pasta and sprinkle generously with cheese.

* There should be 2 cups reserved vegetables.

NUTRITION FACTS
PER SERVING
531 CAL., 9 G TOTAL FAT
(4 G SAT. FAT), 55 MG CHOL.,
1,910 MG SODIUM,
91 G CARBO., 11 G FIBER,
27 G PRO.

DAILY VALUES
3% VIT. A, 43% VIT. C,
29% CALCIUM, 29% IRON

EXCHANGES
2 VEGETABLE, 4 STARCH,
1½ OTHER CARBO., 1½ FAT

cheesy cauliflower, broccoli & corn soup

POUR A FEW ITEMS INTO THE SLOW COOKER AND LET THE SOUP SIMMER TO CREAMY, VEGGIE-CHOCKED PERFECTION—IT'S RECIPES LIKE THIS THAT HAVE MADE THE SLOW COOKER A FAVORITE APPLIANCE.

PREP
20 MINUTES

COOK
6 HOURS (LOW) OR
3 HOURS (HIGH)
+ 30 MINUTES

MAKES
6 SERVINGS + RESERVES

2	10-ounce packages frozen cauliflower, thawed and well drained
2	10-ounce packages frozen cut broccoli, thawed and well drained
1	10-ounce package frozen whole kernel corn, thawed and well drained
3	14-ounce cans vegetable broth
2	teaspoons dried dillweed, crushed
16	ounces American cheese, cubed

STEP 1   In a 5- or 6-quart slow cooker stir together cauliflower, broccoli, corn, broth, and dillweed. Cover and cook on low-heat setting for 6 to 7 hours or on high-heat setting for 3 to 3½ hours.

STEP 2   If using the low-heat setting, turn to high-heat setting. Stir in cheese. Cover and cook about 30 minutes more or until cheese is melted. Using a slotted spoon, remove 4 cups of the vegetables. Reserve the strained vegetables and 1 cup of the liquid; store as directed below.

TO STORE RESERVES   Place vegetables and liquid in an airtight container. Seal and chill for up to 3 days. Use in Cheese & Vegetable Rice Casserole, page 169.

NUTRITION FACTS
PER SERVING
295 CAL., 20 G TOTAL FAT
(12 G SAT. FAT), 58 MG
CHOL., 1,609 MG SODIUM,
15 G CARBO., 4 G FIBER,
17 G PRO.

DAILY VALUES
32% VIT. A, 103% VIT. C,
39% CALCIUM, 8% IRON

EXCHANGES
2 VEGETABLE, ½ STARCH,
2 HIGH-FAT MEAT

cheese & vegetable rice casserole

A VEGGIE-STUDDED RICE-AND-BEAN CASSEROLE IS ONE OF THE MOST SATISFYING WAYS TO GO MEATLESS. HERE DICED GREEN CHILE PEPPERS AND ROASTED RED SWEET PEPPERS REALLY HELP THE FLAVORS BLAST OFF.

Nonstick cooking spray

Reserved vegetable mixture from Cheesy Cauliflower, Broccoli & Corn Soup* **(see recipe, page 168)**

4	**cups cooked rice**
1	**15-ounce can black beans, rinsed and drained**
2	**4-ounce cans diced green chile peppers, drained**
1	**12-ounce jar roasted red sweet peppers, drained and coarsely chopped (1 cup)**
1	**cup shredded cheddar cheese (4 ounces)**
½	**cup seasoned fine dry bread crumbs**
2	**tablespoons butter, melted**

STEP 1   Lightly coat a 3-quart rectangular baking dish with cooking spray; set aside. In a large bowl stir together reserved vegetable mixture, the rice, black beans, chile peppers, and sweet pepper; spread in the prepared baking dish. Sprinkle with cheese. In a small bowl stir together bread crumbs and butter. Sprinkle over cheese.

STEP 2   Bake, uncovered, in a 350°F oven for 35 to 40 minutes or until heated through and top is golden. Let stand for 10 minutes before serving.

*   There should be 4 cups reserved vegetables and 1 cup reserved liquid.

PREP
25 MINUTES

BAKE
35 MINUTES

STAND
10 MINUTES

OVEN
350°F

MAKES
6 SERVINGS

NUTRITION FACTS
PER SERVING
446 CAL., 17 G TOTAL FAT (10 G SAT. FAT), 47 MG CHOL., 1,080 MG SODIUM, 57 G CARBO., 7 G FIBER, 21 G PRO.

DAILY VALUES
20% VIT. A, 202% VIT. C, 36% CALCIUM, 19% IRON

EXCHANGES
1½ VEGETABLE, 3 STARCH, 1½ HIGH-FAT MEAT, ½ FAT

vegetarian black bean soup

MASHING THE BEANS HELPS GIVE THIS SOUP A RICHER, THICKER CONSISTENCY. FOR A CASUAL-YET-FESTIVE SOUP SUPPER, SERVE WITH TORTILLA CHIPS AND AN ARRAY OF ACCOMPANIMENTS, SUCH AS SALSA, MELTED CHEESE DIP, AND GUACAMOLE.

PREP
30 MINUTES

COOK
8 HOURS (LOW) OR
4 HOURS (HIGH)

MAKES
4 SERVINGS + RESERVES

4	15-ounce cans black beans, rinsed and drained
5	cups vegetable broth
1	cup finely chopped onion (1 large)
¾	cup chopped red sweet pepper (1 medium)
6	cloves garlic, minced (1 tablespoon)
1	tablespoon finely chopped canned chipotle peppers in adobo sauce
2	to 3 teaspoons ground cumin
1	teaspoon salt
¼	teaspoon black pepper
¼	cup snipped fresh cilantro
2	tablespoons lime juice
½	cup dairy sour cream or plain yogurt
½	cup finely chopped tomato (1 medium)
¼	cup sliced green onion (2)

STEP 1 In a 5- or 6-quart slow cooker stir together black beans, vegetable broth, onion, sweet pepper, garlic, chipotle pepper, cumin, salt, and black pepper.

STEP 2 Cover and cook on low-heat setting for 8 to 10 hours or high-heat setting for 4 to 5 hours.

STEP 3 Stir in cilantro and lime juice. Using a slotted spoon, reserve 3 cups bean mixture; store as directed below. Slightly mash remaining soup to thicken. Serve soup topped with sour cream, tomato, and green onion.

TO STORE RESERVES Place bean mixture in an airtight container. Seal and chill for up to 3 days. Use in Black Bean & Corn-Topped Avocados, page 171.

NUTRITION FACTS
PER SERVING
298 CAL., 6 G TOTAL FAT
(3 G SAT. FAT), 11 MG CHOL.,
2,074 MG SODIUM,
53 G CARBO., 16 G FIBER,
22 G PRO.

DAILY VALUES
35% VIT. A, 75% VIT. C,
16% CALCIUM, 24% IRON

EXCHANGES
3½ STARCH,
1½ VERY LEAN MEAT

black bean & corn-topped avocados

TRANSFORM LAST NIGHT'S HOT SOUP INTO TODAY'S LUNCH! A
CHILLED CORN-AND-BEAN SALAD SPOONED OVER AVOCADOS
MAKES FOR A REFRESHING BREAK IN THE DAY.

Reserved bean mixture from Vegetarian Black Bean Soup* (see recipe, page 170)

1	10-ounce package frozen whole kernel corn, thawed
1	4.5-ounce can diced green chile peppers, drained
⅓	cup finely chopped red sweet pepper
⅓	cup bottled mild fire-roasted tomato salsa
6	cups shredded lettuce (1 small head)
2	medium avocados, halved, seeded, peeled, and sliced
½	cup crumbled queso fresco cheese or shredded Monterey Jack cheese (2 ounces)
¼	cup dairy sour cream
¼	cup bottled mild fire-roasted tomato salsa

STEP 1 In a medium bowl stir together reserved bean mixture, the corn, chile peppers, sweet pepper, and ⅓ cup salsa.

STEP 2 Place lettuce on serving plates. Arrange avocado slices over lettuce; top with bean mixture. Sprinkle cheese over top. Serve with sour cream and additional salsa.

* There should be 3 cups reserved bean mixture.

START TO FINISH
20 MINUTES

MAKES
4 SERVINGS

NUTRITION FACTS
PER SERVING
393 CAL., 20 G TOTAL FAT
(5 G SAT. FAT), 15 MG CHOL.,
1,025 MG SODIUM,
49 G CARBO., 16 G FIBER,
18 G PRO.

DAILY VALUES
126% VIT. A, 128% VIT. C,
23% CALCIUM, 20% IRON

EXCHANGES
2 VEGETABLE, 2½ STARCH,
1 LEAN MEAT, 3 FAT

cook once eat twice

5-ingredient slow cooker

when you just don't have time to shop, chop, and measure a lot of ingredients, turn here. you can count the number of ingredients needed for these recipes on one hand. yet each brings all the satisfaction you seek in a home-cooked supper.

pot roast with mushroom sauce

TAKE 15 MINUTES IN THE MORNING TO BROWN THE ROAST,
CUT UP THE POTATOES, AND LAYER THE INGREDIENTS IN YOUR
COOKER. AT THE END OF THE DAY, GATHER THE FAMILY FOR A
COMPLETE POT ROAST DINNER.

PREP
15 MINUTES

COOK
10 HOURS (LOW) OR
5 HOURS (HIGH)

MAKES
5 SERVINGS

1	1½-pound boneless beef eye round roast or rump roast
	Nonstick cooking spray
4	medium potatoes, quartered
1	16-ounce package peeled baby carrots
1	10.75-ounce can condensed golden mushroom soup
½	teaspoon dried tarragon or basil, crushed

STEP 1 Trim fat from roast. Lightly coat a large skillet with cooking spray; heat skillet over medium heat. Brown roast on all sides in hot skillet.

STEP 2 In a 3½- or 4-quart slow cooker place potato and carrots. Place roast on vegetables. In a small bowl stir together soup and tarragon. Spoon over roast and vegetables in cooker.

STEP 3 Cover and cook on low-heat setting for 10 to 12 hours or on high-heat setting for 5 to 6 hours. Transfer roast and vegetables to a serving platter. Stir sauce; spoon over roast and vegetables.

NUTRITION FACTS
PER SERVING
391 CAL., 13 G TOTAL FAT
(5 G SAT. FAT), 79 MG CHOL.,
567 MG SODIUM,
33 G CARBO., 5 G FIBER,
33 G PRO.

DAILY VALUES
237% VIT. A, 38% VIT. C,
4% CALCIUM, 19% IRON

EXCHANGES
1 VEGETABLE, 1½ STARCH,
½ FAT, 4 LEAN MEAT

cola pot roast

DIFFERENT AND DELICIOUS, THIS CHUCK ROAST WITH VEGGIES AND BROWN GRAVY GETS ITS SWEET KICK FROM A CAN OF COLA. THE ROAST IS TENDER; THE GRAVY IS THICK.

1	2½- to 3-pound boneless beef chuck pot roast
	Nonstick cooking spray
2	16-ounce packages frozen stew vegetables
1	12-ounce can cola
½	of a 2-ounce package onion soup mix (1 envelope)
2	tablespoons quick-cooking tapioca

STEP 1 Trim fat from roast. Lightly coat a large skillet with nonstick cooking spray; heat skillet over medium heat. Brown roast on all sides in hot skillet. Drain off fat.

STEP 2 Place roast in a 4½- or 5-quart slow cooker. Top with frozen vegetables. In a small bowl stir together cola, soup mix, and tapioca. Pour cola mixture over roast and vegetables in cooker.

STEP 3 Cover and cook on low-heat setting for 7 to 8 hours or on high-heat setting for 3½ to 4 hours.

PREP
15 MINUTES

COOK
7 HOURS (LOW) OR
3½ HOURS (HIGH)

MAKES
6 SERVINGS

NUTRITION FACTS
PER SERVING
278 CAL., 5 G TOTAL FAT
(2 G SAT. FAT), 75 MG CHOL.,
582 MG SODIUM,
28 G CARBO., 2 G FIBER,
29 G PRO.

DAILY VALUES
148% VIT. A, 3% VIT. C,
1% CALCIUM, 17% IRON

EXCHANGES
1 VEGETABLE, 1½ OTHER
CARBO., 4 VERY LEAN MEAT,
½ FAT

oriental beef
& noodles

SESAME-GINGER STIR-FRY SAUCE INFUSES JUST THE RIGHT AMOUNT OF NUTTY ZING. ADD CRUSHED RED PEPPER IF YOU OPT FOR EXTRA HEAT.

PREP
10 MINUTES

COOK
9 HOURS (LOW) OR
4½ HOURS (HIGH)

STAND
10 MINUTES

MAKES
4 TO 6 SERVINGS

1   16-ounce package frozen broccoli stir-fry vegetables (broccoli, carrots, onions, red peppers, celery, water chestnuts, mushrooms)

2   pounds beef stew meat, cut into ¾- to 1-inch cubes

1   12-ounce bottle sesame-ginger stir-fry sauce

½   cup water

¼   teaspoon crushed red pepper (optional)

1   3-ounce package ramen noodles, broken

STEP 1   Place frozen vegetables in a 3½- or 4-quart slow cooker. Top with stew meat. In a medium bowl stir together stir-fry sauce, water, and, if desired, crushed red pepper. Pour over stew meat and vegetables in cooker.

STEP 2   Cover and cook on low-heat setting for 9 to 10 hours or on high-heat setting for 4½ to 5 hours. Discard spice packet from ramen noodles. Stir noodles into meat mixture in slow cooker. Cover and let stand for 10 minutes. Stir before serving.

NUTRITION FACTS
PER SERVING
494 CAL., 11 G TOTAL FAT
(2 G SAT. FAT), 135 MG
CHOL., 1,889 MG SODIUM,
37 G CARBO., 2 G FIBER,
53 G PRO.

DAILY VALUES
30% VIT. A, 43% VIT. C,
2% CALCIUM, 32% IRON

EXCHANGES
1 VEGETABLE, 1 STARCH,
1 OTHER CARBO., 6 LEAN MEAT

beef burgundy

WITH THE SOPHISTICATION OF BURGUNDY, THIS STEW HAS A DEEP WOODY TASTE, MELLOWED WITH MUSHROOMS AND STEW VEGETABLES. HOT COOKED NOODLES OR MASHED POTATOES ARE A MUST.

	Nonstick cooking spray
2	pounds beef stew meat, cut into ¾- to 1-inch cubes
1	16-ounce package frozen stew vegetables
1	10.75-ounce can condensed golden mushroom soup
⅔	cup Burgundy wine
⅓	cup water
1	tablespoon quick-cooking tapioca

STEP 1 Lightly coat a large skillet with cooking spray; heat skillet over medium heat. Brown stew meat, half at a time, in hot skillet. Drain off fat. Set aside.

STEP 2 Place frozen vegetables in a 3½- or 4-quart slow cooker. Top with stew meat. In a medium bowl stir together soup, wine, water, and tapioca. Pour soup mixture over stew meat and vegetables in cooker.

STEP 3 Cover and cook on low-heat setting for 7 to 9 hours or on high-heat setting for 3½ to 4½ hours.

PREP
20 MINUTES

COOK
7 HOURS (LOW) OR
3½ HOURS (HIGH)

MAKES
6 SERVINGS

NUTRITION FACTS
PER SERVING
291 CAL., 8 G TOTAL FAT
(3 G SAT. FAT), 91 MG CHOL.,
535 MG SODIUM,
14 G CARBO., 1 G FIBER,
34 G PRO.

DAILY VALUES
80% VIT. A, 2% VIT. C,
1% CALCIUM, 23% IRON

EXCHANGES
½ VEGETABLE, ½ STARCH,
4½ LEAN MEAT

old-fashioned
beef stew

PURCHASE PRECUT STEW MEAT FROM THE MEAT COUNTER. OR SELECT A BEEF CHUCK OR SHOULDER ROAST AND CUT IT INTO $^{3}/_{4}$- TO 1-INCH PIECES YOURSELF.

PREP
15 MINUTES

COOK
8 HOURS (LOW) OR
4 HOURS (HIGH)

MAKES
4 MAIN-DISH SERVINGS
(6 CUPS)

1	pound beef stew meat, cut into ¾- to 1-inch cubes
12	ounces small potatoes, peeled and quartered (about 2 cups)
4	medium carrots, cut into ½-inch pieces (2 cups)
1	10.75-ounce can condensed cream of potato soup
½	cup water
1	envelope (½ of a 2.2-ounce package) beefy onion soup mix

STEP 1   In a 3½- or 4-quart slow cooker stir together meat, potato, and carrot. In a bowl stir together condensed soup, water, and soup mix. Pour soup mixture over meat and vegetables in cooker.

STEP 2   Cover and cook on low-heat setting for 8 to 9 hours or on high-heat setting for 4 to 4½ hours.

NUTRITION FACTS
PER SERVING
298 CAL., 7 G TOTAL FAT
(2 G SAT. FAT), 73 MG CHOL.,
1,262 MG SODIUM,
31 G CARBO., 3 G FIBER,
28 G PRO.

DAILY VALUES
309% VIT. A, 23% VIT. C,
4% CALCIUM, 23% IRON

EXCHANGES
1 VEGETABLE, 1½ STARCH,
3 LEAN MEAT

southwestern steak roll-ups

FLANK STEAK, SWEET PEPPERS, ONIONS, AND TOMATOES SPIKED
WITH CHILI POWDER SIMMER INTO A STEW THAT TASTES GREAT
WRAPPED IN A WARMED TORTILLA.

1   16-ounce package frozen pepper stir-fry vegetables (yellow, green,
       and red peppers and onions)
1   pound beef flank steak
1   14.5-ounce can Mexican-style stewed tomatoes
1   small jalapeño pepper, seeded and finely chopped* (optional)
2   teaspoons chili powder
4   9- to 10-inch flour tortillas, warmed**

STEP 1   Place frozen vegetables in a 3½- or 4-quart slow cooker. Trim fat
from steak. If necessary, cut steak to fit in cooker. Place steak on vegetables
in cooker. In a medium bowl stir together undrained tomatoes, jalapeño
pepper, if desired, and chili powder. Pour over steak in cooker.

STEP 2   Cover and cook on low-heat setting for 7 to 8 hours or on high-heat
setting for 3½ to 4 hours. Remove steak from cooker; slice against the grain.
Using a slotted spoon, remove vegetables from cooker. Divide steak and
vegetables among warm tortillas; roll up.

*   Because hot peppers, such as jalapeños, contain volatile oils that can
burn your skin and eyes, avoid direct contact with chiles as much as
possible. When working with chile peppers, wear plastic or rubber gloves.
If your bare hands do touch the chile peppers, wash your hands well with
soap and water.

**   To warm tortillas, stack tortillas and wrap tightly in foil. Heat in a 350°F
oven about 10 minutes or until heated through.

PREP
15 MINUTES

COOK
7 HOURS (LOW) OR
3½ HOURS (HIGH)

BAKE
10 MINUTES

OVEN
350°F

MAKES
4 SERVINGS

NUTRITION FACTS
PER SERVING
389 CAL., 12 G TOTAL FAT
(5 G SAT. FAT), 46 MG CHOL.,
647 MG SODIUM,
36 G CARBO., 4 G FIBER,
32 G PRO.

DAILY VALUES
29% VIT. A, 54% VIT. C,
10% CALCIUM, 24% IRON

EXCHANGES
1½ VEGETABLE, 2 STARCH,
3½ LEAN MEAT

thai beef

THOSE WHO LOVE PAD THAI'S SIGNATURE PEANUT SAUCE WILL ADORE THIS EASY-TO-PREPARE DISH OF TENDER FLANK STEAK AND CARROTS. SERVE WITH HOT COOKED RICE TO SOP UP THE NUTTY SAUCE.

PREP
15 MINUTES

COOK
8 HOURS (LOW) OR
4 HOURS (HIGH)

MAKES
6 SERVINGS

1	1½- to 2-pound beef flank steak
1	16-ounce package peeled baby carrots
1	11.5-ounce bottle Thai peanut sauce
1	cup unsweetened coconut milk
¼	cup chopped dry-roasted peanuts

STEP 1 Trim fat from steak. Cut steak into thin bite-size strips. In a 3½- or 4-quart slow cooker place steak and carrots. Pour peanut sauce over all.

STEP 2 Cover and cook on low-heat setting for 8 to 10 hours or on high-heat setting for 4 to 5 hours. Stir in coconut milk. Top each serving with peanuts.

NUTRITION FACTS
PER SERVING
449 CAL., 25 G TOTAL FAT
(12 G SAT. FAT), 46 MG
CHOL., 814 MG SODIUM,
23 G CARBO., 6 G FIBER,
31 G PRO.

DAILY VALUES
384% VIT. A, 11% VIT. C,
4% CALCIUM, 18% IRON

EXCHANGES
1 VEGETABLE, 3 FAT,
1 OTHER CARBO., 4 LEAN MEAT

taco soup

TACO IN A BOWL! YOU'LL NEED A SPOON TO EAT THIS MEAL TOPPED WITH CRUNCHY TORTILLA CHIPS AND SHREDDED CHEESE. IT'S A REFRESHING TWIST ON THE TRADITIONAL PRESENTATION.

1	pound lean ground beef
3	cups water
1	15- to 16-ounce can red kidney beans, rinsed and drained
1	14.5-ounce can Mexican-style stewed tomatoes
1	10.75-ounce can condensed tomato soup
1	1.25-ounce package taco seasoning mix
	Crushed tortilla chips (optional)
	Shredded Monterey Jack cheese (optional)

STEP 1 In a large skillet cook the ground beef over medium heat until brown. Drain off fat.

STEP 2 In a 3½- or 4-quart slow cooker stir together beef, water, beans, undrained tomatoes, tomato soup, and taco seasoning mix.

STEP 3 Cover and cook on low heat setting for 6 to 8 hours or on high-heat setting for 3 to 4 hours. If desired, top each serving with tortilla chips and cheese.

PREP
15 MINUTES

COOK
6 HOURS (LOW) OR
3 HOURS (HIGH)

MAKES
4 TO 6 MAIN-DISH SERVINGS
(ABOUT 8 CUPS)

NUTRITION FACTS
PER SERVING
456 CAL., 23 G TOTAL FAT
(8 G SAT. FAT), 78 MG CHOL.,
2,092 MG SODIUM,
36 G CARBO., 6 G FIBER,
31 G PRO.

DAILY VALUES
8% VIT. A, 82% VIT. C,
6% CALCIUM, 27% IRON

EXCHANGES
1 VEGETABLE, 2 STARCH,
3½ MEDIUM-FAT MEAT

tostadas

TURN TO THIS SOFT, CHUNKY MEXICAN CLASSIC WHEN YOU WANT THE CONVENIENCE OF LEAVING A SLOW-COOKING MEAL UNATTENDED BUT NEED IT FINISHED IN A SHORT TIME. IT'S IDEAL WHEN COMPANY POPS IN ON SHORT NOTICE.

PREP
15 MINUTES

COOK
3 HOURS (LOW) OR
1½ HOURS (HIGH)

MAKES
10 SERVINGS

2	pounds lean ground beef
2	1.25-ounce envelopes taco seasoning mix
1	16-ounce can refried beans
1	10.75-ounce can condensed fiesta nacho cheese soup
1	4.8-ounce package tostada shells (10)
	Shredded lettuce, chopped tomato, dairy sour cream, and/or bottled salsa (optional)

STEP 1 In a large skillet cook the ground beef over medium heat until brown. Drain off fat. Add taco seasoning mix to beef and continue according to package directions.

STEP 2 Transfer seasoned meat mixture to a 3½- or 4-quart slow cooker. Stir in beans and soup.

STEP 3 Cover and cook on low-heat setting for 3 to 4 hours or on high-heat setting for 1½ to 2 hours. Serve on tostada shells. If desired, top with lettuce, tomatoes, sour cream, and/or salsa.

NUTRITION FACTS
PER SERVING
347 CAL., 20 G TOTAL FAT
(6 G SAT. FAT), 65 MG CHOL.,
1,198 MG SODIUM,
21 G CARBO., 4 G FIBER,
24 G PRO.

DAILY VALUES
6% VIT. A, 5% VIT. C,
6% CALCIUM, 15% IRON

EXCHANGES
1½ STARCH, 1 FAT,
2 MEDIUM-FAT MEAT

beefy mexican potatoes

CHEESY BEAN AND BEEF CHILI FLOODS BAKED POTATOES FOR A
RIB-STICKING MEAL. THE CHILI TOPPER ALSO MAKES A HEARTY
DIP FOR CORN CHIPS OR A MEATY ADDITION TO A TACO SALAD.

Nonstick cooking spray

1 20-ounce package refrigerated seasoned cooked ground beef for tacos

2 15- to 16-ounce cans red kidney and/or black beans, rinsed and drained

1 10-ounce can enchilada sauce

2 cups shredded American cheese (8 ounces)

6 medium russet potatoes

STEP 1 Coat the inside of a 3½- or 4-quart slow cooker with cooking spray. In the prepared cooker stir together the beef for tacos, beans, enchilada sauce, and 1½ cups of the cheese.

STEP 2 Cover and cook on low-heat setting for 3 to 4 hours.

STEP 3 Meanwhile, prick potatoes all over with a fork. Arrange potatoes in spoke-fashion on a microwave-safe plate. Microwave, uncovered, on 100 percent power (high) for 15 to 18 minutes or until tender, rearranging potatoes every 5 minutes. (Or bake pricked potatoes in a 450°F oven for 40 to 60 minutes.) Carefully cut an x in the top of each potato. Push in both sides to open potato. Stir beef mixture in cooker. Spoon beef mixture over baked potatoes. Top with remaining ¼ cup cheese.

PREP
15 MINUTES

COOK
3 HOURS (LOW)

MAKES
6 SERVINGS

NUTRITION FACTS
PER SERVING
553 CAL., 22 G TOTAL FAT
(11 G SAT. FAT),
61 MG CHOL., 1,560 MG
SODIUM, 64 G CARBO.,
11 G FIBER, 32 G PRO.

DAILY VALUES
17% VIT. A, 22% VIT. C,
32% CALCIUM, 25% IRON

EXCHANGES
4 STARCH, 3 MEDIUM-FAT MEAT

lamb curry

CURRY POWDER IMPARTS A SUNNY COLOR AND A SPICY TASTE TO LAMB AND VEGGIES. SPRINKLE EACH SERVING WITH COCONUT, RAISINS, AND SUNFLOWER SEEDS FOR A TRUE INDIAN CLASSIC.

PREP
10 MINUTES

COOK
7 HOURS (LOW) OR
3½ HOURS (HIGH)

MAKES
10 SERVINGS

2   pounds lamb stew meat, cut into ¾- to 1-inch cubes

1   16-ounce package frozen broccoli, cauliflower, and carrots

2   10.75-ounce cans condensed cream of onion soup

½   cup water

2   to 3 teaspoons curry powder

5   cups hot cooked rice

STEP 1 In a 3½- or 4-quart slow cooker stir together lamb, frozen vegetables, soup, water, and curry powder.

STEP 2 Cover and cook on low-heat setting for 7 to 8 hours or on high-heat setting for 3½ to 4 hours. Serve over hot cooked rice.

NUTRITION FACTS
PER SERVING
295 CAL., 7 G TOTAL FAT
(2 G SAT. FAT), 68 MG CHOL.,
727 MG SODIUM,
33 G CARBO., 2 G FIBER,
23 G PRO.

DAILY VALUES
22% VIT. A, 9% VIT. C,
5% CALCIUM, 18% IRON

EXCHANGES
½ VEGETABLE, 2 STARCH,
2½ LEAN MEAT

plum good meatballs

ALTHOUGH THIS RECIPE CALLS FOR A PACKAGE OF 16 FROZEN
MEATBALLS, DIFFERENT BRANDS CONTAIN DIFFERENT NUMBERS.
YOU CAN EASILY SUBSTITUTE A PACKAGE THAT CONTAINS
35 SMALLER MEATBALLS.

1   18-ounce bottle (1⅔ cups) barbecue sauce

1   10- or 12-ounce jar plum jam or preserves

1   pound cooked smoked jalapeño sausage or smoked sausage links,
     cut into bite-size pieces

1   16- to 18-ounce package Italian-style or plain frozen cooked meatballs, thawed

STEP 1   In a 3½- or 4-quart slow cooker stir together barbecue sauce and
jam. Add sausage and thawed meatballs, stirring to coat with sauce mixture.

STEP 2   Cover and cook on low-heat setting for 5 to 6 hours or on high-heat
setting for 2½ to 3 hours. Serve with decorative toothpicks. To serve at a
buffet, keep warm on low-heat setting for up to 2 hours.

PREP
10 MINUTES

COOK
5 HOURS (LOW) OR
2½ HOURS (HIGH)

MAKES
16 SERVINGS

NUTRITION FACTS
PER SERVING
267 CAL., 16 G TOTAL FAT
(6 G SAT. FAT), 38 MG CHOL.,
898 MG SODIUM,
19 G CARBO., 2 G FIBER,
12 G PRO.

DAILY VALUES
6% VIT. A, 7% VIT. C,
3% CALCIUM, 7% IRON

EXCHANGES
1 OTHER CARBO.,
2 HIGH-FAT MEAT

pizza by the yard

TOASTED ITALIAN BREAD MAKES AN EASY CRUST FOR YOUR PIZZA. SERVE IT WITH SALAD FOR SUPPER OR AS A HEARTY PARTY APPETIZER. ADD SLICED OLIVES FOR EXTRA FLAVOR.

PREP
25 MINUTES

COOK
5 HOURS (LOW) OR
2½ HOURS (HIGH)

MAKES
8 SERVINGS

2	pounds bulk Italian sausage
1	26-ounce jar garlic and mushroom pasta sauce
2	cups chopped green and/or red sweet pepper (2 large)
1	1-pound loaf Italian bread, split lengthwise and toasted*
1	8-ounce package shredded pizza cheese (2 cups)

STEP 1   In a large skillet cook the sausage over medium heat until brown. Drain off fat. In a 3½- or 4-quart slow cooker stir together sausage, pasta sauce, and sweet pepper.

STEP 2   Cover and cook on low-heat setting for 5 to 6 hours or on high-heat setting for 2½ to 3 hours. Spoon sausage mixture over toasted bread. Sprinkle with cheese.

* To toast bread, place bread, cut sides up, on a baking sheet. Broil 3 to 4 inches from heat for 3 to 4 minutes or until toasted.

NUTRITION FACTS
PER SERVING
699 CAL., 46 G TOTAL FAT
(17 G SAT. FAT), 106 MG
CHOL., 1,935 MG SODIUM,
38 G CARBO., 4 G FIBER,
30 G PRO.

DAILY VALUES
16% VIT. A, 57% VIT. C,
30% CALCIUM, 22% IRON

EXCHANGES
½ VEGETABLE, 1½ STARCH,
1 OTHER CARBO., 3½ HIGH-FAT
MEAT, 3½ FAT

mexican lasagna

THE LAYERS ARE TENDER; THE FLAVOR IS FULL AND ZESTY. BEST OF ALL, THERE'S NO SCOOPING NECESSARY—AFTER STANDING, THIS LASAGNA HOLDS A SOFT-CUT EDGE.

Nonstick cooking spray

1 ½ pounds bulk pork sausage

9 6-inch corn tortillas

1 11-ounce can whole kernel corn with sweet peppers, drained

1 8-ounce package shredded taco cheese (2 cups)

1 19-ounce can enchilada sauce

STEP 1 Lightly coat a 3½- or 4-quart slow cooker with cooking spray; set aside. In a large skillet cook the sausage over medium heat until brown. Drain off fat.

STEP 2 Place 3 of the tortillas in the bottom of the prepared cooker, overlapping as necessary. Top with half of the corn and half of the sausage. Sprinkle with ¼ cup of the cheese. Pour ¾ cup of the enchilada sauce over layers in cooker. Repeat with 3 more tortillas, remaining corn, and remaining sausage. Sprinkle with ¼ cup of the cheese. Pour ¾ cup enchilada sauce over cheese. Top with remaining 3 tortillas, remaining 1 cup cheese, and remaining enchilada sauce.

STEP 3 Cover and cook on low-heat setting for 3 to 4 hours. Remove liner from cooker, if possible, or turn off cooker. Let stand, covered, for 15 minutes before serving.

PREP
25 MINUTES

COOK
3 HOURS (LOW)

STAND
15 MINUTES

MAKES
8 SERVINGS

NUTRITION FACTS
PER SERVING
512 CAL., 34 G TOTAL FAT (15 G SAT. FAT), 71 MG CHOL., 1,082 MG SODIUM, 27 G CARBO., 3 G FIBER, 18 G PRO.

DAILY VALUES
17% VIT. A, 2% VIT. C, 22% CALCIUM, 5% IRON

EXCHANGES
2 STARCH, 3½ FAT, 2 HIGH-FAT MEAT

pork, lentil & apple soup

PUT AUTUMN'S APPLE HARVEST TO GOOD USE. HERE THE APPLES DISSOLVE TO THICKEN AND SWEETEN THE BROTH. IT'S A NICE WAY TO REWARD YOURSELF AFTER A DAY OF RAKING LEAVES.

PREP
20 MINUTES

COOK
6 HOURS (LOW) OR
3 HOURS (HIGH)

MAKES
4 MAIN-DISH SERVINGS
(6 CUPS)

Nonstick cooking spray

1   **pound lean boneless pork, cut into ½-inch cubes**

1   **cup dry lentils, rinsed and drained**

3   **cooking apples, peeled, cored, and cut up**

1   **teaspoon dried marjoram, crushed**

2   **14-ounce cans beef broth (3½ cups)**

STEP 1   Lightly coat a large skillet with cooking spray; heat skillet over medium heat. Brown pork on all sides in hot skillet. Drain off fat.

STEP 2   Place pork in a 3½-quart slow cooker. Add lentils, apple, and marjoram. Add beef broth; stir to mix.

STEP 3   Cover and cook on low-heat setting for 6 to 8 hours or on high-heat setting for 3 to 4 hours.

NUTRITION FACTS
PER SERVING
384 CAL., 6 G TOTAL FAT
(2 G SAT. FAT), 71 MG CHOL.,
741 MG SODIUM,
44 G CARBO., 17 G FIBER,
39 G PRO.

DAILY VALUES
2% VIT. A, 12% VIT. C,
5% CALCIUM, 29% IRON

EXCHANGES
1 FRUIT, 2 STARCH,
4½ VERY LEAN MEAT

slow-cooked asian-style pork

WHY PICK UP TAKEOUT ON A WEEKNIGHT WHEN SLOW COOKING AT HOME IS SO EASY? THIS DISH, WITH ITS LONG COOKING TIME, IS IDEAL FOR THOSE WHO HEAD OUT TO WORK IN THE MORNING. PIECES OF PORK COOK WITH STIR-FRY VEGETABLES IN A SWEET-AND-SOUR SAUCE. TOP IT WITH CASHEW HALVES OR PIECES, IF DESIRED.

Nonstick cooking spray

3 pounds boneless pork shoulder roast, cut into 1-inch cubes

2 tablespoons quick-cooking tapioca

1 10-ounce jar sweet-and-sour sauce

1 16-ounce package frozen broccoli stir-fry vegetables (broccoli, carrots, onions, red peppers, celery, water chestnuts, mushrooms)

3 cups hot cooked rice or rice noodles

STEP 1   Lightly coat a large skillet with cooking spray; heat skillet over medium heat. Brown pork, half at a time, in hot skillet. Drain off fat.

STEP 2   Place pork in a 3½- or 4-quart slow cooker. Sprinkle with tapioca; pour sweet-and-sour sauce over pork in cooker.

STEP 3   Cover and cook on low-heat setting for 7 to 8 hours or on high-heat setting for 3½ to 4 hours. If using low-heat setting, turn to high-heat setting. Stir in frozen vegetables. Cover and cook for 30 to 60 minutes more or until vegetables are tender. Serve over hot cooked rice.

PREP
20 MINUTES

COOK
7 HOURS (LOW)
OR 3½ HOURS (HIGH)
+ 30 MINUTES

MAKES
6 TO 8 SERVINGS

NUTRITION FACTS PER SERVING
484 CAL., 19 G TOTAL FAT
(6 G SAT. FAT), 153 MG
CHOL., 342 MG SODIUM,
40 G CARBO., 2 G FIBER,
48 G PRO.

DAILY VALUES
20% VIT. A, 30% VIT. C,
6% CALCIUM, 21% IRON

EXCHANGES
½ VEGETABLE, 1½ STARCH,
1 OTHER CARBO.,
5½ LEAN MEAT

pork roast with apricot glaze

ENOUGH TO MAKE ANY MOUTH WATER, THESE SUCCULENT PORK SLICES ARE DRIPPING IN A SPICY APRICOT SAUCE. SERVE RICE AS A SIDE DISH TO SOAK UP SOME OF THE FLAVORFUL SAUCE.

PREP
15 MINUTES

COOK
10 HOURS (LOW) OR
5 HOURS (HIGH)

MAKES
6 TO 8 SERVINGS

1	3- to 3½-pound boneless pork shoulder roast
1	18-ounce jar apricot preserves
1	cup chopped onion (1 large)
¼	cup chicken broth
2	tablespoons Dijon-style mustard

STEP 1 Trim fat from roast. If necessary, cut roast to fit into a 3½- to 6-quart slow cooker. Place roast in cooker. In a small bowl combine preserves, onion, broth, and mustard; pour over roast in cooker.

STEP 2 Cover and cook on low-heat setting for 10 to 12 hours or on high-heat setting for 5 to 6 hours. Transfer roast to a serving plate. Skim fat from sauce. Spoon some of the sauce onto the roast; discard any remaining sauce.

NUTRITION FACTS
PER SERVING
456 CAL., 10 G TOTAL FAT
(3 G SAT. FAT), 93 MG CHOL.,
184 MG SODIUM,
61 G CARBO., 2 G FIBER,
29 G PRO.

DAILY VALUES
17% VIT. C, 5% CALCIUM,
13% IRON

EXCHANGES
4 OTHER CARBO.,
4 LEAN MEAT

ranch pork roast

THIS IS NO ORDINARY ROAST WITH POTATOES. MADE WITH A TANGY, CREAMY SAUCE OF CREAM CHEESE SEASONED WITH RANCH DRESSING, THIS ONE-DISH MEAL STANDS IN A CATEGORY ALL ITS OWN.

1	2½- to 3-pound boneless pork shoulder roast
	Nonstick cooking spray
1	pound new red-skin potatoes, halved
1	10.75-ounce can condensed cream of chicken soup
1	8-ounce package cream cheese, softened and cut up
1	0.4-ounce envelope dry ranch salad dressing mix

STEP 1 Trim fat from roast. Lightly coat a large skillet with cooking spray; heat skillet over medium heat. Brown roast on all sides in hot skillet. Remove from heat.

STEP 2 Place potato halves in a 3½- or 4-quart slow cooker. Place roast on potato. In a medium bowl whisk together soup, cream cheese, and dressing mix. Spoon over roast and potato in cooker.

STEP 3 Cover and cook on low-heat setting for 9 to 10 hours or on high-heat setting for 4½ to 5 hours.

PREP
15 MINUTES

COOK
9 HOURS (LOW) OR
4½ HOURS (HIGH)

MAKES
6 SERVINGS

NUTRITION FACTS
PER SERVING
521 CAL., 31 G TOTAL FAT
(15 G SAT. FAT),
173 MG CHOL., 757 MG
SODIUM, 16 G CARBO.,
1 G FIBER, 42 G PRO.

DAILY VALUES
15% VIT. A, 17% VIT. C,
9% CALCIUM, 21% IRON

EXCHANGES
1 STARCH, 3 FAT,
5½ LEAN MEAT

ham & black bean
salsa soup with lime

TOP THIS ZESTY, MEATY SOUP WITH BIG SPOONFULS OF SOUR
CREAM AND PASS LIME WEDGES TO SQUEEZE OVER THE TOP.

2 ¼   cups dry black beans (about 1 pound)

2   cups chopped cooked smoked ham (10 ounces)

1   cup chopped yellow and/or red sweet pepper (1 large)

3 ½   cups water

1   16-ounce jar lime-garlic salsa

      Dairy sour cream (optional)

      Lime wedges (optional)

PREP
20 MINUTES

COOK
11 HOURS (LOW) OR
5½ HOURS (HIGH)

STAND
1 HOUR

MAKES
6 SERVINGS
(10 CUPS)

STEP 1   Rinse beans; place in a large saucepan. Add enough water to cover beans by 2 inches. Bring to boiling; reduce heat. Simmer, uncovered, for 10 minutes. Remove from heat. Cover; let stand about 1 hour. Drain and rinse beans.

STEP 2   In a 3½- or 4-quart slow cooker stir together beans, ham, sweet pepper, and the 3½ cups water.

STEP 3   Cover and cook on low-heat setting for 11 to 13 hours or on high-heat setting for 5½ to 6½ hours or until beans are tender. If desired, use a potato masher to mash beans slightly in the slow cooker. Stir salsa into soup. If desired, serve soup with sour cream and lime wedges.

NUTRITION FACTS
PER SERVING
341 CAL., 4 G TOTAL FAT
(1 G SAT. FAT), 28 MG CHOL.,
1,176 MG SODIUM,
49 G CARBO., 12 G FIBER,
29 G PRO.

DAILY VALUES
6% VIT. A, 93% VIT. C,
12% CALCIUM, 24% IRON

EXCHANGES
½ VEGETABLE, 3 STARCH,
2½ VERY LEAN MEAT

pork chops & corn bread stuffing

TRY THIS RECIPE WHEN YOU GET A CRAVING FOR THANKSGIVING FARE. BROWNED CHOPS SLOW COOK OVER VEGETABLES, MUSHROOM SOUP, AND CORN BREAD STUFFING MIX, YIELDING A TENDER AUTUMN-STYLE MEAL.

	Nonstick cooking spray
4	pork rib chops, cut ¾ inch thick
1	10.75-ounce can condensed golden mushroom or cream of mushroom soup
¼	cup butter or margarine, melted
1	16-ounce package frozen broccoli, cauliflower, and carrots
½	of a 16-ounce package corn bread stuffing mix (about 3 cups)

STEP 1 Lightly coat the inside of a 5½- or 6-quart slow cooker with cooking spray; set aside. Lightly coat a medium skillet with cooking spray; heat skillet over medium heat. Brown chops, half at a time, in hot skillet. Remove chops from skillet; set aside.

STEP 2 In a very large bowl stir together soup and melted butter. Add frozen vegetables and stuffing mix; stir to combine. Transfer stuffing mixture to prepared cooker. Arrange chops on top of stuffing mixture.

STEP 3 Cover and cook on low-heat setting for 5 to 6 hours or on high-heat setting for 2½ to 3 hours.

PREP
20 MINUTES

COOK
5 HOURS (LOW) OR
2½ HOURS (HIGH)

MAKES
4 SERVINGS

NUTRITION FACTS
PER SERVING
558 CAL., 22 G TOTAL FAT
(10 G SAT. FAT),
89 MG CHOL., 1,533 MG
SODIUM, 56 G CARBO.,
7 G FIBER, 30 G PRO.

DAILY VALUES
66% VIT. A, 47% VIT. C,
9% CALCIUM, 20% IRON

EXCHANGES
1 VEGETABLE, 3 STARCH,
2½ FAT, 3 LEAN MEAT

apple-sauced pork chops

THE SAUCE RESEMBLES CHUNKY SPICED APPLESAUCE, THE BEST PARTNER FOR SMOKED PORK CHOPS. SERVE ON TOP OF HOT COOKED COUSCOUS.

PREP
10 MINUTES

COOK
6 HOURS (LOW) OR
3 HOURS (HIGH)

MAKES
6 SERVINGS

6   boneless smoked pork chops (about 1 pound)

1   cup apple butter

1   teaspoon quick-cooking tapioca

½   teaspoon dried sage, crushed

2   large red cooking apples

3   cups hot cooked couscous (optional)

STEP 1 Place pork chops in a 3½- or 4-quart slow cooker. For sauce, in a small bowl combine apple butter, tapioca, and sage. Pour sauce over chops in cooker. If desired, peel the apples. Core apples and cut into quarters; place on top of chops.

STEP 2 Cover and cook on low-heat setting for 6 to 7 hours or on high-heat setting for 3 to 3½ hours. If desired, serve pork chops and sauce over hot cooked couscous.

NUTRITION FACTS
PER SERVING
427 CAL., 12 G TOTAL FAT
(4 G SAT. FAT), 40 MG CHOL.,
653 MG SODIUM,
68 G CARBO., 3 G FIBER,
13 G PRO.

DAILY VALUES
1% VIT. A, 5% VIT. C,
2% CALCIUM, 5% IRON

EXCHANGES
½ FRUIT, 1 FAT,
4 OTHER CARBO., 2 LEAN MEAT

honey-mustard barbecue pork ribs

THE SIMPLE PLEASURE OF EATING RIBS STARTS WITH A SIMPLE BLEND OF SEASONINGS, BARBECUE SAUCE, AND A JAR OF HONEY MUSTARD.

3 ½   pounds boneless pork country-style ribs
1   cup bottled barbecue sauce
1   8-ounce jar honey mustard
2   teaspoons zesty herb marinade mix

STEP 1   Place ribs in a 3½- or 4-quart slow cooker. In a small bowl stir together barbecue sauce, honey mustard, and seasoning blend. Pour over ribs in cooker. Stir to coat.

STEP 2   Cover and cook on low-heat setting for 8 to 10 hours or on high-heat setting for 4 to 5 hours. Transfer ribs to a serving platter. Strain sauce; skim off fat. Drizzle ribs with some of the strained sauce. Pass remaining sauce.

PREP
15 MINUTES

COOK
8 HOURS (LOW) OR
4 HOURS (HIGH)

MAKES
6 TO 8 SERVINGS

NUTRITION FACTS
PER SERVING
322 CAL., 12 G TOTAL FAT
(4 G SAT. FAT), 94 MG CHOL.,
497 MG SODIUM,
18 G CARBO., 1 G FIBER,
29 G PRO.

DAILY VALUES
7% VIT. A, 6% VIT. C,
4% CALCIUM, 10% IRON

EXCHANGES
1 FAT, 1 OTHER CARBO.,
4 LEAN MEAT

mediterranean chicken

FOR A ONE-DISH MEAL, SERVE THIS TENDER CHICKEN DISH OVER POLENTA OR COUSCOUS. WHO CAN RESIST A SECOND HELPING?

PREP
20 MINUTES

COOK
6 HOURS (LOW) OR
3 HOURS (HIGH)

MAKES
6 SERVINGS

Nonstick cooking spray

2 ½	pounds chicken thighs and/or drumsticks, skinned
1	8- or 9-ounce package frozen artichoke hearts
¾	cup pitted kalamata olives
1	28-ounce jar roasted garlic pasta sauce
1	cup crumbled feta cheese (4 ounces)

STEP 1 Lightly coat the inside of a 3½- or 4-quart slow cooker with cooking spray. Place chicken pieces in the prepared cooker. Top with artichoke hearts and olives. Pour pasta sauce over artichokes and olives in cooker.

STEP 2 Cover and cook on low-heat setting for 6 to 7 hours or on high-heat setting for 3 to 3½ hours. Sprinkle each serving with feta cheese.

NUTRITION FACTS
PER SERVING
296 CAL., 13 G TOTAL FAT
(5 G SAT. FAT), 111 MG
CHOL., 971 MG SODIUM,
16 G CARBO., 4 G FIBER,
28 G PRO.

DAILY VALUES
13% VIT. A, 18% VIT. C,
22% CALCIUM, 12% IRON

EXCHANGES
1 VEGETABLE, 1 FAT,
½ OTHER CARBO.,
3½ LEAN MEAT

chicken stroganoff

MOIST CHICKEN, EARTHY MUSHROOMS, AND SAVORY SOUR CREAM SPREAD ACROSS SOFT NOODLES: STROGANOFF IS CLASSIC COMFORT FOOD.

2	pounds skinless, boneless chicken breast halves and/or thighs
1	cup chopped onion (1 large)
2	10.75-ounce cans condensed cream of mushroom soup with roasted garlic
⅓	cup water
12	ounces dried wide egg noodles
1	8-ounce carton dairy sour cream
	Freshly ground black pepper (optional)

STEP 1 Cut chicken into 1-inch pieces. In a 3½- or 4-quart slow cooker combine the chicken pieces and onion. In a medium bowl stir together soup and water. Pour soup mixture over chicken and onion in cooker.

STEP 2 Cover and cook on low-heat setting for 6 to 7 hours or on high-heat setting for 3 to 3½ hours.

STEP 3 Cook noodles according to package directions; drain. Just before serving, stir sour cream into chicken mixture in cooker. To serve, spoon chicken mixture over hot cooked noodles. If desired, sprinkle with pepper.

PREP
20 MINUTES

COOK
6 HOURS (LOW) OR
3 HOURS (HIGH)

MAKES
6 TO 8 SERVINGS

NUTRITION FACTS
PER SERVING
532 CAL., 14 G TOTAL FAT
(6 G SAT. FAT), 162 MG
CHOL., 775 MG SODIUM,
54 G CARBO., 3 G FIBER,
46 G PRO.

DAILY VALUES
7% VIT. A, 6% VIT. C,
10% CALCIUM, 17% IRON

EXCHANGES
1½ FAT, 3½ STARCH,
5 VERY LEAN MEAT

saucy tex-mex
chicken over red beans & rice

DRESSED UP WITH BRIGHT SWEET PEPPERS, THIS FULL-FLAVOR
DISH SATISFIES THE DESIRE FOR FOOD THAT LOOKS GOOD TOO.

1	pound skinless, boneless chicken breasts and/or thighs
1	16-ounce package frozen pepper stir-fry vegetables (yellow, green, and red sweet peppers, and onions)
1	12-ounce jar chicken gravy
1	cup bottled chipotle salsa
1	7-ounce package red beans and rice mix

PREP
15 MINUTES

COOK
4 HOURS (LOW) OR
2 HOURS (HIGH)

MAKES
4 SERVINGS

STEP 1 Cut chicken into bite-size strips. In a 3½- or 4-quart slow cooker stir together the frozen vegetables, chicken strips, gravy, and salsa.

STEP 2 Cover and cook on low-heat setting for 4 to 5 hours or on high-heat setting for 2 to 2½ hours.

STEP 3 Cook red beans and rice according to package directions. To serve, divide red beans and rice into 4 shallow bowls. Using a slotted spoon, spoon chicken and vegetable mixture over the rice and beans.

NUTRITION FACTS
PER SERVING
399 CAL., 7 G TOTAL FAT
(2 G SAT. FAT), 68 MG CHOL.,
1,480 MG SODIUM,
49 G CARBO., 6 G FIBER,
35 G PRO.

DAILY VALUES
27% VIT. A, 93% VIT. C,
8% CALCIUM, 20% IRON

EXCHANGES
1 VEGETABLE, 2½ STARCH,
1 FAT, 3½ VERY LEAN MEAT

chicken
tortilla soup

BOTH CREAMY AND CRUNCHY, CHICKEN TORTILLA SOUP IS
ALWAYS SURPRISINGLY GOOD. OLÉ!

2   14-ounce cans chicken broth with roasted garlic
1   14.5-ounce can Mexican-style stewed tomatoes
2   cups chopped cooked chicken
2   cups frozen pepper stir-fry vegetables (yellow, green, and
     red sweet peppers and onions)
1   cup crushed tortilla chips
     Sour cream, fresh cilantro, and/or sliced avocado (optional)

STEP 1   In a 3½- or 4-quart slow cooker stir together broth, undrained
tomatoes, chicken, and frozen vegetables.

STEP 2   Cover and cook on low heat setting for 6 to 7 hours or on high-heat
setting for 3 to 3½ hours.

STEP 3   To serve, ladle soup into warm soup bowls and sprinkle with crushed
tortilla chips. If desired, top with sour cream, cilantro, and/or avocado.

PREP
15 MINUTES

COOK
6 HOURS (LOW) OR
3 HOURS (HIGH)

MAKES
4 SERVINGS

NUTRITION FACTS
PER SERVING
189 CAL., 5 G TOTAL FAT
(0 G SAT. FAT), 36 MG CHOL.,
1,258 MG SODIUM,
19 G CARBO., 1 G FIBER,
18 G PRO.

DAILY VALUES
14% VIT. A, 40% VIT. C,
6% CALCIUM, 9% IRON

EXCHANGES
1 VEGETABLE, 1 STARCH,
2½ VERY LEAN MEAT, 1 FAT

turkey
shepherd's pie

TRADITIONALLY MADE WITH LAMB OR MUTTON, SHEPHERD'S PIE
WORKS EQUALLY WELL SLOW COOKED WITH TURKEY AND FROZEN
VEGETABLES. DRIED THYME INFUSES AN HERBAL NOTE.

PREP
20 MINUTES

COOK
6 HOURS (LOW) OR
3 HOURS (HIGH)
+ 10 MINUTES

MAKES
4 SERVINGS

12   ounces turkey breast tenderloins or skinless, boneless chicken breast halves

1   10-ounce package frozen mixed vegetables

1   12-ounce jar turkey or chicken gravy

1   teaspoon dried thyme, crushed

1   20-ounce package refrigerated mashed potatoes

STEP 1   Cut turkey into ½-inch strips. In a 3½- or 4-quart slow cooker place frozen vegetables. Top with turkey strips. In a small bowl stir together gravy and thyme; pour over turkey in cooker.

STEP 2   Cover and cook on low-heat setting for 6 to 7 hours or on high-heat setting for 3 to 3½ hours.

STEP 3   If using low-heat setting, turn to high-heat setting. Drop mashed potatoes by spoonfuls into 8 small mounds on top of turkey mixture. Cover and cook for 10 minutes more. To serve, in each of 4 shallow bowls spoon some of the turkey mixture and two of the potato mounds.

NUTRITION FACTS

PER SERVING
297 CAL., 5 G TOTAL FAT
(1 G SAT. FAT), 51 MG CHOL.,
781 MG SODIUM,
33 G CARBO., 4 G FIBER,
27 G PRO.

DAILY VALUES
74% VIT. A, 54% VIT. C,
5% CALCIUM, 15% IRON

EXCHANGES
½ VEGETABLE, 2 STARCH,
½ FAT, 3 VERY LEAN MEAT

turkey & pasta primavera

GREAT FOR THE FAMILY, THIS RECIPE SERVES MANY AND DOESN'T TAKE LONG TO MAKE. SERVE IT WITH A SPRINKLING OF PARMESAN CHEESE, A SHARP NOTE IN A CREAMY BLEND.

2 pounds turkey breast tenderloins or skinless, boneless chicken breast halves

1 16-ounce package frozen sugar snap stir-fry vegetables
   (sugar snap peas, carrots, onions, mushrooms)

2 teaspoons dried basil, oregano, or Italian seasoning, crushed

1 16-ounce jar Alfredo pasta sauce

12 ounces dried spaghetti or linguine, broken
   Shredded Parmesan cheese (optional)

STEP 1 Cut turkey into 1-inch pieces. In a 4½- to 6-quart slow cooker stir together turkey and frozen vegetables. Sprinkle with dried basil. Stir in Alfredo sauce.

STEP 2 Cover and cook on low-heat setting for 4 to 5 hours or on high-heat setting for 2 to 2½ hours.

STEP 3 Cook pasta according to package directions. Drain. Stir pasta into chicken mixture in slow cooker. If desired, sprinkle each serving with Parmesan cheese.

PREP
15 MINUTES

COOK
4 HOURS (LOW) OR
2 HOURS (HIGH)

MAKES
8 SERVINGS

NUTRITION FACTS
PER SERVING
407 CAL., 11 G TOTAL FAT
(5 G SAT. FAT), 103 MG
CHOL., 447 MG SODIUM,
39 G CARBO., 2 G FIBER,
36 G PRO.

DAILY VALUES
77% VIT. A, 10% VIT. C,
9% CALCIUM, 19% IRON

EXCHANGES
½ VEGETABLE, 2½ STARCH,
1 FAT, 4 VERY LEAN MEAT

taco-style black beans & hominy

TACO SEASONING IS THE KEY TO REVVING UP THE RICH AND VELVETY BEAN-GRAIN MIX. SERVE IT IN TACO SHELLS FOR DINNER OR MINI TACO SHELLS FOR A PARTY APPETIZER OR SNACK.

PREP
15 MINUTES

COOK
7 HOURS (LOW) OR
3½ HOURS (HIGH)

MAKES
9 SERVINGS

	Nonstick cooking spray
2	15- to 15.5-ounce cans black beans, rinsed and drained
2	14½- to 15½-ounce cans golden hominy, drained
1¼	cups water
1	10.75-ounce can condensed cream of mushroom soup
½	of a 1.25-ounce package (1½ tablespoons) taco seasoning mix
18	taco shells
	Sliced green onion, chopped tomato, and/or shredded lettuce (optional)

STEP 1 Coat the inside of a 3½- or 4-quart slow cooker with cooking spray. In the prepared cooker stir together beans, hominy, water, soup, and taco seasoning.

STEP 2 Cover and cook on low-heat setting for 7 to 8 hours or on high-heat setting for 3½ to 4 hours.

STEP 3 To serve, spoon bean mixture into taco shells. If desired, sprinkle with green onion, tomato, and/or lettuce.

NUTRITION FACTS
PER SERVING
317 CAL., 10 G TOTAL FAT
(2 G SAT. FAT), 0 MG CHOL.,
1,001 MG SODIUM,
52 G CARBO., 11 G FIBER,
12 G PRO.

DAILY VALUES
2% VIT. A, 1% VIT. C,
11% CALCIUM, 16% IRON

EXCHANGES
3½ STARCH, 1 FAT

sweet & sour tofu

CUBES OF TERIYAKI-FLAVOR TOFU ARE SOFT AND PRETTY IN A SWEET-AND-SOUR SAUCE WITH CRUNCHY SWEET PEPPERS AND WATER CHESTNUTS. SERVE THIS COLORFUL DISH OVER HOT COOKED RICE.

PREP
15 MINUTES

COOK
4 HOURS (LOW) OR
2 HOURS (HIGH)

MAKES
4 TO 6 SERVINGS

2   16-ounce packages frozen pepper stir-fry vegetables (yellow, green, and red sweet peppers and onions)

1   9-ounce jar sweet-and-sour sauce

1   8-ounce can sliced water chestnuts, drained

1   6½- to 7-ounce package baked or smoked teriyaki-flavor tofu, drained and cut into ½-inch pieces

2   cups hot cooked rice

STEP 1   In a 3½- or 4-quart slow cooker stir together frozen vegetables, sweet-and-sour sauce, and water chestnuts.

STEP 2   Cover and cook on low-heat setting for 4 to 4½ hours or on high-heat setting for 2 to 2¼ hours. Stir in tofu. Serve over hot cooked rice.

NUTRITION FACTS
PER SERVING
318 CAL., 7 G TOTAL FAT
(1 G SAT. FAT), 0 MG CHOL.,
597 MG SODIUM,
73 G CARBO., 4 G FIBER,
13 G PRO.

DAILY VALUES
27% VIT. A, 142% VIT. C,
22% CALCIUM, 18% IRON

EXCHANGES
1½ VEGETABLE, 2 STARCH,
2 OTHER CARBO., ½ FAT

creamy tomato & broccoli sauce with pasta

BEARING THE RED, WHITE, AND GREEN OF THE ITALIAN FLAG, THIS PASTA DISH GETS A LIVELY EDGE FROM PARMA ROSA SAUCE MIX. THE SAUCE IS CREAMY AND THE BROCCOLI CHUNKS ARE CRISP-TENDER.

PREP
15 MINUTES

COOK
6 HOURS (LOW) OR
3 HOURS (HIGH)
+ 15 MINUTES

MAKES
8 TO 10 SERVINGS

	Nonstick cooking spray
2	14.5-ounce cans diced tomatoes with basil, oregano, and garlic
2	10.75-ounce cans condensed cream of mushroom soup
1	1.3-ounce envelope parma rosa pasta sauce mix
1	cup water
1	16-ounce package frozen cut broccoli
16	ounces dried penne or mostaccioli pasta

STEP 1   Coat the inside of a 3½- or 4-quart slow cooker with cooking spray. In the prepared cooker stir together the undrained tomatoes, soup, sauce mix, and water.

STEP 2   Cover and cook on low-heat setting for 6 to 8 hours or on high-heat setting for 3 to 4 hours. If using low-heat setting, turn to high-heat setting. Stir in broccoli; cover and cook on high-heat setting for 15 minutes or until broccoli is crisp-tender.

STEP 3   Meanwhile, cook pasta according to package directions; drain. Toss pasta with sauce.

NUTRITION FACTS
PER SERVING
365 CAL., 7 G TOTAL FAT
(2 G SAT. FAT), 1 MG CHOL.,
1,270 MG SODIUM,
62 G CARBO., 4 G FIBER,
12 G PRO.

DAILY VALUES
26% VIT. A, 54% VIT. C,
12% CALCIUM, 21% IRON

EXCHANGES
1½ VEGETABLE, 3½ STARCH,
1 FAT

pasta
with edamame

ROSEMARY'S GARDEN SCENT REIGNS OVER THIS SWEET EDAMAME
ALFREDO SAUCE MIXTURE SERVED OVER LINGUINE.

1   12-ounce package frozen edamame (green soybeans), thawed (2¾ cups)

2   cups shredded carrot (4 medium)

1   16-ounce jar Alfredo pasta sauce

1   teaspoon dried rosemary, crushed

8   ounces dried linguine

    Finely shredded Parmesan cheese (optional)

STEP 1   In a 3½- or 4-quart slow cooker stir together edamame, carrot, pasta sauce, and rosemary.

STEP 2   Cover and cook on low-heat setting for 4 to 5 hours or on high-heat setting for 2 to 2½ hours. Cook pasta according to package directions; drain. Serve bean mixture over hot cooked pasta. If desired, sprinkle with Parmesan cheese.

PREP
15 MINUTES

COOK
4 HOURS (LOW) OR
2 HOURS (HIGH)

MAKES
4 SERVINGS

NUTRITION FACTS
PER SERVING
720 CAL., 42 G TOTAL FAT
(1 G SAT. FAT), 57 MG CHOL.,
448 MG SODIUM,
64 G CARBO., 7 G FIBER,
25 G PRO.

DAILY VALUES
312% VIT. A, 36% VIT. C,
17% CALCIUM, 28% IRON

EXCHANGES
½ VEGETABLE, 4 STARCH,
7 FAT, 1½ VERY LEAN MEAT

stuffed
cabbage rolls

YOUR CHOICE OF BLACK OR RED BEANS AND PROTEIN-RICH
BROWN RICE STAND IN FOR THE GROUND BEEF AND RICE
FILLING THAT'S TYPICAL OF THIS CLASSIC.

PREP
25 MINUTES

COOK
6 HOURS (LOW) OR
3 HOURS (HIGH)

MAKES
4 SERVINGS

½   cup instant brown rice
1   large head green cabbage (about 2 pounds)
1   15- to 16-ounce can black beans or red kidney beans, rinsed and drained
½   cup chopped onion (1 medium)
1   26- or 28-ounce jar chunky tomato pasta sauce or meatless spaghetti sauce
     Shredded cheddar cheese (optional)

STEP 1   In a small saucepan bring ½ cup water to boiling. Stir in uncooked rice. Reduce heat; cover and simmer for 10 minutes or until water is absorbed. Remove from heat; set aside.

STEP 2   Meanwhile, remove 8 large outer leaves from the cabbage.* In a 4-quart Dutch oven cook cabbage leaves, covered, in boiling water for 4 to 5 minutes or just until leaves are limp. Drain cabbage leaves. Trim the thick rib in the center of each leaf. Set leaves aside. Shred 4 cups of the remaining cabbage; place shredded cabbage in a 3½- or 4-quart slow cooker. (Wrap and chill remaining cabbage for another use.)

STEP 3   In a medium bowl stir together beans, cooked rice, onion, and ¼ cup of the pasta sauce. Evenly divide the bean mixture among the 8 cabbage leaves (about ⅓ cup per leaf). Fold sides of leaf over filling and roll up. Pour about half of the remaining pasta sauce over shredded cabbage in cooker; stir to combine. Place cabbage rolls on the shredded cabbage. Top with remaining pasta sauce.

STEP 4   Cover and cook on low-heat setting for 6 to 7 hours or on high-heat setting for 3 to 3½ hours. Carefully remove the cooked cabbage rolls and serve with the shredded cabbage mixture. If desired, sprinkle with cheddar cheese.

*   To easily remove the cabbage leaves, place the cabbage head in boiling water for 2 to 3 minutes to loosen the outer leaves.

NUTRITION FACTS
PER SERVING
332 CAL., 6 G TOTAL FAT
(1 G SAT. FAT), 0 MG CHOL.,
1,042 MG SODIUM,
64 G CARBO., 15 G FIBER,
15 G PRO.

DAILY VALUES
41% VIT. A, 112% VIT. C,
17% CALCIUM, 22% IRON

EXCHANGES
2 VEGETABLE, 2½ STARCH,
1 OTHER CARBO., ½ FAT

white beans with dried tomatoes

SOFT WHITE BEANS IN VEGETABLE BROTH ABSORB THE FLAVORS
OF GARLIC, DRIED TOMATOES, AND SHAVED ASIAGO CHEESE.
PARTNER WITH TOASTED, BUTTERED BAGUETTE SLICES FOR A
COMPLEMENTARY CRUNCH.

3	15- to 19-ounce cans white kidney beans (cannellini beans), rinsed and drained
1	14-ounce can vegetable broth
3	cloves garlic, minced
1	7-ounce jar oil-packed dried tomatoes, drained and chopped
1	cup shaved Asiago or Parmesan cheese (4 ounces)
⅓	cup pine nuts, toasted (optional)

STEP 1 In a 3½- or 4-quart slow cooker stir together beans, vegetable broth, and garlic.

STEP 2 Cover and cook on low-heat setting for 6 to 8 hours or on high-heat setting for 3 to 4 hours.

STEP 3 If using low-heat setting, turn to high-heat setting. Stir in tomato. Cover and cook about 15 minutes more or until tomato is heated through. To serve, top each serving with cheese. If desired, top with toasted pine nuts.

PREP
15 MINUTES

COOK
6 HOURS (LOW) OR
3 HOURS (HIGH)
+ 15 MINUTES

MAKES
6 SERVINGS

NUTRITION FACTS
PER SERVING
285 CAL., 13 G TOTAL FAT
(5 G SAT. FAT), 20 MG CHOL.,
901 MG SODIUM,
38 G CARBO., 12 G FIBER,
19 G PRO.

DAILY VALUES
10% VIT. A, 57% VIT. C,
23% CALCIUM, 18% IRON

EXCHANGES
½ VEGETABLE, 2 STARCH,
1 FAT, 1½ LEAN MEAT

vegetarian chili

LOTS OF BEANS AND CRUMBLED MEAT SUBSTITUTE MINGLE WITH
ONIONS, MEXICAN-STYLE TOMATOES, AND CHILI POWDER. IF
YOU NEED TO STRETCH THE NUMBER OF SERVINGS, SPOON IT
OVER COUSCOUS OR CORN BREAD WEDGES. DELICIOUS!

PREP
10 MINUTES

COOK
6 HOURS (LOW) OR
3 HOURS (HIGH)

MAKES
6 SERVINGS

Nonstick cooking spray

2   15-ounce cans chili beans with chili gravy

2   14.5-ounce cans Mexican-style stewed tomatoes

2   cups frozen cooked and crumbled ground meat substitute (soy protein)

1   cup chopped onion (1 large)

1   tablespoon chili powder

STEP 1   Lightly coat the inside of a 3½- or 4-quart slow cooker with cooking spray. In the prepared cooker stir together the undrained beans, undrained tomatoes, ground meat substitute, onion, and chili powder.

STEP 2   Cover and cook on low-heat setting for 6 to 7 hours or on high-heat setting for 3 to 3½ hours.

NUTRITION FACTS

PER SERVING
230 CAL., 2 G TOTAL FAT
(0 G SAT. FAT), 0 MG CHOL.,
959 MG SODIUM,
40 G CARBO., 13 G FIBER,
17 G PRO.

DAILY VALUES
9% VIT. A, 23% VIT. C,
12% CALCIUM, 17% IRON

EXCHANGES
1 VEGETABLE, 2 STARCH,
1½ LEAN MEAT

alfredo
tortellini soup

WHAT DO YOU EAT WHEN COMFORT FOOD SOUNDS TOO HEAVY AND
SOUP SOUNDS TOO LIGHT? THIS SOUP, WITH ITS SUBSTANTIAL PASTA
AND CREAMY SAUCE, IS AN ATTRACTIVE IN-BETWEEN SOLUTION.

1	28-ounce jar or two 16-ounce jars Alfredo pasta sauce
2	14-ounce cans vegetable broth
½	cup chopped onion (1 medium)
1	2-ounce jar sliced pimientos, drained and chopped
1	6- to 8-ounce package dried cheese-filled tortellini

STEP 1   In a 3½ or 4 quart slow cooker stir together pasta sauce, vegetable broth, onion, and pimiento.

STEP 2   Cover and cook on low-heat setting for 5 to 6 hours or on high-heat setting for 2½ to 3 hours.

STEP 3   If using low-heat setting, turn to high-heat setting. Stir in tortellini. Cover and cook for 1 hour more.

PREP
15 MINUTES

COOK
5 HOURS (LOW) OR
2½ HOURS (HIGH)
+ 1 HOUR

MAKES
4 SERVINGS
(7½ CUPS)

NUTRITION FACTS
PER SERVING
544 CAL., 34 G TOTAL FAT
(16 G SAT. FAT),
114 MG CHOL.,
2,247 MG SODIUM,
47 G CARBO., 2 G FIBER,
14 G PRO.

DAILY VALUES
31% VIT. A, 22% VIT. C,
14% CALCIUM, 11% IRON

EXCHANGES
4½ FAT, 3 STARCH,
1 HIGH FAT MEAT

cook once eat twice

swift sides
& desserts

it's amazing what
a bright salad, a zesty side,
a hearty bread, or
a sweet and simple dessert
can do to transform
a very good meal into
a great one. you'll also
love how effortlessly
the recipes come together.

mediterranean salad

OPEN A JAR, A CAN, AND A BOTTLE, ADD A FEW FRESH TOUCHES, AND VOILÀ—A SATISFYING SALAD THAT'S READY IN 10 MINUTES. TO TRANSFORM THIS SIDE DISH INTO A MAIN-DISH, ADD CANNED OR PACKAGED TUNA.

START TO FINISH
10 MINUTES

MAKES
6 SERVINGS

1   6.5-ounce jar marinated artichoke hearts, drained
1   15-ounce can three-bean salad, drained
¾   cup chopped, seeded tomato (1 large)
1   tablespoon snipped fresh basil or ½ teaspoon dried basil, crushed
¼   cup bottled Italian salad dressing
     Lettuce leaves (optional)

STEP 1 Halve any large artichoke hearts. In a medium bowl combine artichoke hearts, three-bean salad, tomato, and basil. Drizzle Italian dressing over bean mixture; toss gently to coat. If desired, serve on plates lined with lettuce leaves.

NUTRITION FACTS
PER SERVING
109 CAL., 5 G TOTAL FAT
(0 G SAT. FAT), 0 MG CHOL.,
538 MG SODIUM,
16 G CARBO., 3 G FIBER,
3 G PRO.

DAILY VALUES
10% VIT. A, 17% VIT. C,
5% CALCIUM, 7% IRON

EXCHANGES
½ VEGETABLE, 1 STARCH,
½ FAT

greens with dill dressing

CHOCK-FULL OF A SPECTRUM OF VEGETABLES AND TOPPED WITH A CREAMY DILL-SPIKED DRESSING, THIS IS THE RECIPE TO CHOOSE WHEN YOU WANT A SUBSTANTIAL SALAD TO TRANSFORM A LIGHT SOUP OR STEW INTO A FULL MEAL DEAL.

⅓	cup mayonnaise or salad dressing
¼	cup plain yogurt
1	tablespoon milk
½	teaspoon dried dillweed
¼	teaspoon lemon-pepper seasoning
	Dash garlic powder
4	cups mesclun, or 2 cups torn mixed salad greens plus 2 cups torn curly endive
1	cup fresh mushrooms, quartered
1	small yellow summer squash, thinly bias-sliced (1 cup)
1	small zucchini, thinly bias-sliced (1 cup)
1	cup fresh pea pods, trimmed and halved crosswise
	Fresh dillweed (optional)

START TO FINISH
25 MINUTES

MAKES
4 SERVINGS

STEP 1   For dressing, in a small bowl stir together mayonnaise, yogurt, milk, dillweed, lemon-pepper seasoning, and garlic powder.

STEP 2   In a salad bowl combine mesclun, mushrooms, yellow squash, zucchini, and pea pods. Drizzle dressing over salad; toss to coat. If desired, garnish with fresh dillweed.

NUTRITION FACTS
PER SERVING
180 CAL., 15 G TOTAL FAT (2 G SAT. FAT), 8 MG CHOL., 190 MG SODIUM, 7 G CARBO., 2 G FIBER, 3 G PRO.

DAILY VALUES
8% VIT. A, 17% VIT. C, 7% CALCIUM, 5% IRON

EXCHANGES
1½ VEGETABLE, 3 FAT

cranberry-walnut
cabbage slaw

THIS ISN'T JUST ANY ORDINARY SIDE DISH! TOASTED WALNUTS, RED SWEET PEPPER, AND DRIED CRANBERRIES HELP ELEVATE COLESLAW FROM "GOOD" TO "WOW!"

START TO FINISH
15 MINUTES

MAKES
8 TO 10 SERVINGS

¼	cup mayonnaise or salad dressing
1	tablespoon sweet pickle relish
1	tablespoon honey mustard
1	tablespoon honey
¼	teaspoon white or black pepper
⅛	teaspoon salt
⅛	teaspoon celery seeds
5	cups shredded green cabbage (1 small)
⅓	cup chopped walnuts, toasted if desired
¼	cup finely chopped celery
¼	cup finely chopped red sweet pepper
¼	cup dried cranberries

STEP 1   For dressing, in small bowl stir together mayonnaise, pickle relish, honey mustard, honey, white pepper, salt, and celery seeds.

STEP 2   In large bowl combine cabbage, walnuts, celery, sweet pepper, and dried cranberries. Add dressing to cabbage mixture; toss to coat. Serve immediately or cover and chill up to 6 hours.

NUTRITION FACTS
PER SERVING
118 CAL., 9 G TOTAL FAT
(1 G SAT. FAT), 5 MG CHOL.,
112 MG SODIUM, 9 G CARBO.,
2 G FIBER, 1 G PRO.

DAILY VALUES
4% VIT. A, 55% VIT. C,
3% CALCIUM, 4% IRON

EXCHANGES
1 VEGETABLE, 2 FAT

pear & endive salad

ALWAYS ELEGANT, THIS ENDIVE AND PEAR SALAD—AND ITS BOLD VINAIGRETTE—IS WORTHY OF YOUR MOST IMPRESSIVE COMPANY. IF YOU HAVE WALNUT OIL ON YOUR SHELF, SUBSTITUTE IT FOR THE OLIVE OIL FOR A NUTTIER FLAVOR.

3	ripe red Bartlett pears, Bosc pears, and/or apples, cored and thinly sliced
2	tablespoons water
1	tablespoon lemon juice
12	ounces Belgian endive, leaves separated (3 medium heads)
2	tablespoons coarsely chopped walnuts, toasted
	Dash salt
	Dash black pepper
2	tablespoons olive oil or salad oil
2	tablespoons sherry vinegar or white wine vinegar
1	shallot, finely chopped, or 1 tablespoon finely chopped onion
1	tablespoon honey
1	teaspoon Dijon-style mustard
	Freshly cracked black pepper (optional)

STEP 1 In a medium bowl gently toss pear and/or apple slices with 1 tablespoon of the water and the lemon juice. Arrange endive leaves on 6 salad plates. Using a slotted spoon, spoon the sliced fruit onto the endive. Sprinkle with walnuts, salt, and pepper.

STEP 2 For vinaigrette, in a small bowl combine the remaining 1 tablespoon water, the oil, vinegar, shallot, honey, and mustard. Whisk until thoroughly mixed.

STEP 3 Drizzle the vinaigrette over the salads. If desired, top salads with cracked pepper.

START TO FINISH
20 MINUTES

MAKES
6 SIDE-DISH SERVINGS

NUTRITION FACTS
PER SERVING
129 CAL., 7 G TOTAL FAT (1 G SAT. FAT), 0 MG CHOL., 48 MG SODIUM, 18 G CARBO., 2 G FIBER, 1 G PRO.

DAILY VALUES
1% VIT. A, 17% VIT. C, 1% CALCIUM, 4% IRON

EXCHANGES
1 VEGETABLE, 1 FRUIT, 1 FAT

salad with mango dressing

PEPPERY WATERCRESS AND ARUGULA ARE GIVEN THE TROPICAL TOUCH WITH THE ADDITION OF JUICY, SWEET-TART MANGO BOTH ON THE PLATE AND IN THE DRESSING. WHEN BUYING MANGOES, CHOOSE RIPE FRUIT THAT HAS A YELLOW SKIN BLUSHED WITH RED PATCHES.

START TO FINISH
30 MINUTES

MAKES
8 TO 10 SERVINGS

1	head red or green leaf lettuce, torn into bite-size pieces (about 10 cups)
3	ounces arugula, trimmed and torn into bite-size pieces (about 2½ cups)
½	cup watercress leaves
3	tablespoons snipped fresh basil
3	mangoes
¼	cup rice vinegar
3	tablespoons salad oil
2	tablespoons honey
1	teaspoon snipped fresh mint
1	teaspoon snipped fresh chives
	Salt
	Black pepper

STEP 1 In a large salad bowl toss together lettuce, arugula, watercress, and basil; set aside. Pit, peel, and slice mangoes. Chop enough of the sliced mango to make ½ cup; set remaining sliced mango aside.

STEP 2 For dressing, in a blender or food processor place the ½ cup chopped mango, the rice vinegar, oil, honey, mint, and chives. Cover and blend or process until smooth. Season to taste with salt and pepper.

STEP 3 Drizzle about half of the dressing over lettuce mixture; toss gently to coat. Arrange salad on salad plates. Top with mango slices and drizzle with remaining dressing. Sprinkle with additional pepper.

NUTRITION FACTS
PER SERVING
130 CAL., 6 G TOTAL FAT (0 G SAT. FAT), 0 MG CHOL., 29 MG SODIUM, 21 G CARBO., 3 G FIBER, 2 G PRO.

DAILY VALUES
124% VIT. A, 62% VIT. C, 5% CALCIUM, 6% IRON

EXCHANGES
2 VEGETABLE, ½ FRUIT, 1 FAT

orange dream
fruit salad

SOMETIMES THE BEST THING TO SERVE WITH A HEARTY WINTER STEW IS SOMETHING BRIGHT, LIGHT, AND COLORFUL. WITH A RAINBOW OF SWEET, REFRESHING FRUITS, THIS SALAD FILLS THE BILL. TIP: USE BOTTLED MANGO SLICES FOR A SHORTCUT.

1   mango, pitted, peeled, and chopped (1 cup)
1   11-ounce can mandarin orange sections, drained
1   cup seedless red and/or green grapes, halved
½   cup orange-flavor yogurt
¼   teaspoon poppy seeds

STEP 1   In a medium bowl combine mango, orange sections, and grapes. Stir together yogurt and poppy seeds; fold into fruit mixture until combined.

START TO FINISH
15 MINUTES

MAKES
4 TO 6 SERVINGS

NUTRITION FACTS
PER SERVING
136 CAL., 1 G TOTAL FAT
(0 G SAT. FAT), 2 MG CHOL.,
26 MG SODIUM, 32 G CARBO.,
2 G FIBER, 2 G PRO.

DAILY VALUES
46% VIT. A, 52% VIT. C,
7% CALCIUM, 3% IRON

EXCHANGES
1 FRUIT, 1 OTHER CARBO.

honeydew
& apple salad

WHEN SUMMER FRUITS AREN'T IN SEASON, TRY THE REFRESHING
THREE-INGREDIENT YOGURT DRESSING ON A COMBINATION OF
ORANGE SECTIONS AND BANANA SLICES.

START TO FINISH
15 MINUTES

MAKES
6 SERVINGS

½   medium honeydew melon, peeled, seeded, and cut into bite-size pieces (2 cups)

2   medium tart apples, cored, halved lengthwise, and cut into bite-size pieces
     (1 ⅓ cups)

2   medium nectarines or peaches, pitted and thinly sliced (1 cup)

¼   cup vanilla low-fat yogurt

3   tablespoons apricot jam

¼   teaspoon ground ginger or nutmeg

1   cup fresh red raspberries

STEP 1   In a large bowl combine melon, apple, and nectarine. For dressing, in a small bowl stir together yogurt, jam, and ginger.

STEP 2   Add dressing to fruit mixture; toss to coat. Top with raspberries. Serve immediately.

NUTRITION FACTS

PER SERVING
109 CAL., 1 G TOTAL FAT
(0 G SAT. FAT), 1 MG CHOL.,
16 MG SODIUM, 27 G CARBO.,
3 G FIBER, 1 G PRO.

DAILY VALUES
5% VIT. A, 42% VIT. C,
3% CALCIUM, 2% IRON

EXCHANGES
2 FRUIT

fruit & nut
couscous

THE TERM "COUSCOUS" REFERS TO BOTH THE GRAIN—A TYPE OF
TINY PASTA—AND TO THE FINISHED DISH. COUSCOUS DERIVES
FROM THE FRENCH PRONUNCIATION OF THE NORTH AFRICAN
WORD "SUKSOO," WHICH IN THEORY DESCRIBES THE SOUND
VAPOR MAKES AS IT PASSES THROUGH THE STEAMING GRAINS.
TOP IT WITH BEEF OR CHICKEN, OR MIX IT WITH DRIED FRUITS
AND NUTS AND SERVE IT AS AN ACCOMPANIMENT TO STEW.

START TO FINISH
15 MINUTES

MAKES
4 SERVINGS

1	cup couscous
¼	teaspoon salt
1	cup boiling water
1	teaspoon butter or margarine
¼	cup slivered almonds
¼	cup snipped dried apricots
½	teaspoon finely shredded orange peel

STEP 1   In a medium bowl combine couscous and salt. Gradually add boiling
water. Let stand about 5 minutes or until liquid is absorbed.

STEP 2   Meanwhile, in a small skillet melt butter over medium heat. Add
almonds; cook and stir until almonds are light golden brown. Remove from
heat. Fluff couscous with a fork; stir in almonds, apricots, and orange peel.
Fluff again. Serve immediately.

NUTRITION FACTS
PER SERVING
250 CAL., 5 G TOTAL FAT
(1 G SAT. FAT), 2 MG CHOL.,
163 MG SODIUM,
42 G CARBO., 4 G FIBER,
8 G PRO.

DAILY VALUES
13% VIT. A, 1% VIT. C,
4% CALCIUM, 7% IRON

EXCHANGES
2½ STARCH, 1 FAT

asian pea pod salad

WITH A CRISP, CRUNCHY TEXTURE AND INTRIGUING SPICY, SWEET, AND TANGY FLAVOR FROM THE HOISIN SAUCE, THIS IS THE SALAD TO CHOOSE WHEN YOU WANT A SIDE DISH THAT'S WELL OFF THE BEATEN PATH! HINT: LOOK FOR PLUMP, CRISP PODS WITH A BRIGHT GREEN COLOR.

START TO FINISH
20 MINUTES

MAKES
6 SERVINGS

6	cups torn romaine lettuce
2	cups fresh snow pea pods, trimmed and halved lengthwise
⅓	cup bottled Italian salad dressing
1	tablespoon hoisin sauce
4	radishes, coarsely shredded
1	tablespoon sesame seeds, toasted

STEP 1 In a large salad bowl toss together romaine lettuce and pea pods. In a small bowl stir together dressing and hoisin sauce.

STEP 2 Pour dressing mixture over lettuce mixture; toss gently to coat. Sprinkle with shredded radish and sesame seeds.

NUTRITION FACTS

PER SERVING
98 CAL., 7 G TOTAL FAT
(1 G SAT. FAT), 0 MG CHOL.,
153 MG SODIUM, 6 G CARBO.,
2 G FIBER, 2 G PRO.

DAILY VALUES
31% VIT. A, 25% VIT. C,
4% CALCIUM, 6% IRON

EXCHANGES
1½ VEGETABLE, 1½ FAT

green beans
& carrots with bacon

GREEN BEANS AND BACON ARE A CLASSIC COMBO. NOW RAMP
THE RECIPE UP A BIT WITH A FEW CARROTS FOR ADDED COLOR
AND CRUNCH.

4	slices bacon
12	ounces green beans, cut into 1-inch pieces (2½ cups)
1	cup thinly sliced carrot (2 medium)
1	clove garlic, minced
⅛	to ¼ teaspoon black pepper

START TO FINISH
25 MINUTES

MAKES
4 TO 5 SERVINGS

STEP 1 In a large skillet cook bacon over medium heat until crisp. Remove bacon, reserving 2 tablespoons drippings in skillet. Drain and crumble bacon; set aside.

STEP 2 Meanwhile, in a saucepan cook green beans in a small amount of boiling salted water for 7 minutes; drain.

STEP 3 Add green beans, carrot, and garlic to drippings in skillet. Cook and stir over medium heat about 5 minutes or until vegetables are crisp-tender. Sprinkle vegetables with pepper; stir in bacon.

NUTRITION FACTS
PER SERVING
140 CAL., 10 G TOTAL FAT
(4 G SAT. FAT), 13 MG CHOL.,
142 MG SODIUM, 9 G CARBO.,
3 G FIBER, 4 G PRO.

DAILY VALUES
163% VIT. A, 19% VIT. C,
4% CALCIUM, 6% IRON

EXCHANGES
1½ VEGETABLE, 2 FAT

lemon broccoli

YOU CAN USUALLY COUNT ON BROCCOLI TO ADD A LITTLE COLOR AND SPARKLE TO THE TABLE, BUT SOMETIMES THE VEGGIE NEEDS A LITTLE JAZZING UP. HERE JUST A FEW INGREDIENTS THAT YOU WILL LIKELY HAVE ON HAND DO THE TRICK.

START TO FINISH
20 MINUTES

MAKES
6 SERVINGS

6	cups broccoli florets
2	tablespoons olive oil
½	teaspoon finely shredded lemon peel
4	teaspoons lemon juice
¼	teaspoon salt
⅛	teaspoon black pepper
1	clove garlic, minced

STEP 1 Place a steamer basket in a large saucepan. Add water to just below the bottom of the basket. Bring water to boiling. Add broccoli to steamer basket. Cover and reduce heat. Steam for 8 to 10 minutes or until crisp-tender.

STEP 2 Meanwhile, in a small bowl stir together oil, lemon peel, lemon juice, salt, pepper, and garlic. Drizzle over hot broccoli; toss to coat.

NUTRITION FACTS
PER SERVING
66 CAL., 5 G TOTAL FAT
(1 G SAT. FAT), 0 MG CHOL.,
121 MG SODIUM, 5 G CARBO.,
3 G FIBER, 3 G PRO.

DAILY VALUES
26% VIT. A, 119% VIT. C,
4% CALCIUM, 5% IRON

EXCHANGES
1 VEGETABLE, 1 FAT

smoky gouda-
sauced broccoli

THE KIDS WILL WANT TO EAT THEIR BROCCOLI WHEN THEY
TASTE THIS SIDE DISH, MADE IRRESISTIBLE WITH GOUDA
CHEESE. SERVE IT WITH SOMETHING SIMPLE IN FLAVOR, SUCH
AS A PORK ROAST OR PORK CHOPS.

1 ¼	pounds broccoli, cut into spears
½	cup chopped onion (1 medium)
2	cloves garlic, minced
1	tablespoon butter
2	tablespoons all-purpose flour
¼	teaspoon salt
⅛	teaspoon black pepper
1 ½	cups low-fat milk (1%)
¾	cup shredded smoked Gouda cheese (3 ounces)
¾	cup soft bread crumbs (1 slice bread)
2	teaspoons butter, melted

STEP 1 Place a steamer basket in a large saucepan. Add water to just below the bottom of the basket. Bring water to boiling. Add broccoli to steamer basket. Cover and reduce heat. Steam for 6 to 8 minutes or until just tender.

STEP 2 Meanwhile, for sauce, in a medium saucepan cook onion and garlic in 1 tablespoon hot butter until tender. Stir in flour, salt, and pepper. Stir in milk. Cook and stir until thickened and bubbly. Gradually add cheese, stirring until cheese melts.

STEP 3 Transfer broccoli to a 1½-quart au gratin dish or 2-quart square baking dish. Pour sauce over broccoli. Combine bread crumbs and 2 teaspoons melted butter; sprinkle over sauce. Bake, uncovered, in 425°F oven about 15 minutes or until crumbs are lightly browned.

PREP
20 MINUTES

BAKE
15 MINUTES

OVEN
425°F

MAKES
6 SERVINGS

**NUTRITION FACTS
PER SERVING**
145 CAL., 8 G TOTAL FAT
(5 G SAT. FAT), 23 MG CHOL.,
429 MG SODIUM,
13 G CARBO., 2 G FIBER,
7 G PRO.

DAILY VALUES
22% VIT. A, 79% VIT. C,
20% CALCIUM, 5% IRON

EXCHANGES
½ MILK, 1 VEGETABLE,
½ MEDIUM-FAT MEAT, ½ FAT

curried carrots

KEEP A SUPPLY OF FROZEN VEGGIES ON HAND FOR DAYS WHEN YOU
NEED SPEEDY SIDE DISHES SUCH AS THESE SPICY CARROTS.

START TO FINISH
15 MINUTES

MAKES
6 SERVINGS

1	16-ounce package crinkle-cut carrots
¼	cup chopped onion
2	tablespoons butter or margarine
1	teaspoon sugar
1	teaspoon curry powder
½	teaspoon salt
⅛	teaspoon cayenne pepper
	Dash ground allspice or nutmeg

STEP 1   In a covered medium saucepan cook carrots and onion in a small
amount of boiling salted water for 5 to 7 minutes or until crisp-tender.
Drain; set aside.

STEP 2   In the same saucepan melt butter over medium heat. Stir in
sugar, curry powder, salt, cayenne pepper, and allspice. Stir in carrot
mixture; heat through.

NUTRITION FACTS
PER SERVING
73 CAL., 4 G TOTAL FAT
(2 G SAT. FAT), 11 MG CHOL.,
275 MG SODIUM, 9 G CARBO.,
2 G FIBER, 1 G PRO.

DAILY VALUES
257% VIT. A, 8% VIT. C,
3% CALCIUM, 2% IRON

EXCHANGES
1½ VEGETABLE, 1 FAT

spiced cauliflower with tomatoes

CAULIFLOWER GETS THE SPICE TREATMENT WITH FRAGRANT
CORIANDER, CUMIN, AND CRUSHED RED PEPPER.

5	cups cauliflower florets
1	tablespoon butter or margarine
1	teaspoon ground coriander
½	teaspoon ground cumin
¼	teaspoon salt
⅛	teaspoon crushed red pepper
2	roma tomatoes, chopped

START TO FINISH
20 MINUTES

MAKES
6 SERVINGS

STEP 1   In a covered saucepan cook cauliflower in a small amount of boiling salted water for 8 to 10 minutes or until crisp-tender. Drain; remove cauliflower from pan and set aside.

STEP 2   In the same saucepan melt butter over medium heat. Stir in coriander, cumin, salt, and crushed red pepper. Cook and stir for 1 minute. Remove from heat. Stir in tomatoes and cauliflower.

NUTRITION FACTS
PER SERVING
46 CAL., 2 G TOTAL FAT
(1 G SAT. FAT), 5 MG CHOL.,
138 MG SODIUM, 6 G CARBO.,
3 G FIBER, 2 G PRO.

DAILY VALUES
6% VIT. A, 70% VIT. C,
3% CALCIUM, 3% IRON

EXCHANGES
1 VEGETABLE, ½ FAT

skillet mushrooms

BUTTER, GARLIC, WHITE WINE, AND HERBS GIVE THE MILD-TASTING MUSHROOMS LOTS OF INTENSE FLAVOR.

START TO FINISH
15 MINUTES

MAKES
6 SERVINGS

1	tablespoon butter or margarine
1	tablespoon olive oil
2	cloves garlic, minced
2	8-ounce packages fresh mushrooms, quartered
¼	cup dry white wine or chicken broth
½	teaspoon dried oregano or marjoram, crushed
¼	teaspoon salt
⅛	teaspoon black pepper

STEP 1   In a large skillet heat butter and olive oil over medium heat. Add garlic; cook and stir for 1 minute. Increase heat to medium-high. Add mushrooms to skillet. Cook for 6 to 8 minutes or until almost tender, stirring occasionally.

STEP 2   Carefully add wine and oregano to skillet. Cook about 2 minutes more or until mushrooms are tender and the liquid has evaporated. Stir in salt and pepper.

NUTRITION FACTS
PER SERVING
67 CAL., 6 G TOTAL FAT
(2 G SAT. FAT), 5 MG CHOL.,
115 MG SODIUM,
3 G CARBO.,
1 G FIBER, 2 G PRO.

DAILY VALUES
1% VIT. A, 1% VIT. C,
1% CALCIUM, 3% IRON

EXCHANGES
1 VEGETABLE, 1 FAT

glazed parsnips & apples

PARSNIPS AND APPLES ARE AT THEIR BEST IN THE FALL.
CONVENIENTLY, THAT'S EXACTLY WHEN YOU'RE GOING TO CRAVE
THIS SWEETLY GLAZED DISH.

1   pound small parsnips, sliced ¼ inch thick
¾   cup apple cider or apple juice
2   tablespoons butter
2   tablespoons brown sugar
2   medium cooking apples, cored and thinly sliced

STEP 1   In a large covered skillet cook parsnip in simmering apple cider for 7 to 8 minutes or until crisp-tender. Remove parsnip and any liquid from skillet.

STEP 2   In the same skillet combine butter and brown sugar. Cook, uncovered, over medium-high heat about 1 minute or until mixture begins to thicken. Add apple and undrained parsnip; cook, uncovered, about 2 minutes or until glazed, stirring frequently.

PREP
10 MINUTES

COOK
10 MINUTES

MAKES
4 TO 5 SERVINGS

NUTRITION FACTS
PER SERVING
206 CAL., 7 G TOTAL FAT
(4 G SAT. FAT), 16 MG CHOL.,
74 MG SODIUM, 38 G CARBO.,
7 G FIBER, 1 G PRO.

DAILY VALUES
5% VIT. A, 26% VIT. C,
5% CALCIUM, 5% IRON

EXCHANGES
2 VEGETABLE, 1 FRUIT,
1½ FAT, ½ OTHER CARBO.

peas & onions

THERE IS VERY LITTLE PREPARATION INVOLVED HERE—JUST ASSEMBLE, COOK, SIMMER, AND SERVE!

START TO FINISH
15 MINUTES

MAKES
6 SERVINGS

½	cup coarsely chopped onion (1 medium)
2	cloves garlic, minced
1	tablespoon olive oil
1	16-ounce package frozen tiny peas
½	cup chicken broth
½	teaspoon fennel seeds or dried basil, crushed
¼	teaspoon salt
⅛	teaspoon black pepper

STEP 1 In a large skillet cook onion and garlic in hot oil over medium heat for 3 minutes. Add peas, broth, fennel seeds, salt, and pepper.

STEP 2 Bring to boiling; reduce heat. Simmer, uncovered, about 5 minutes or until peas are tender and most of the liquid has evaporated.

NUTRITION FACTS
PER SERVING
87 CAL., 3 G TOTAL FAT
(0 G SAT. FAT), 0 MG CHOL.,
264 MG SODIUM,
12 G CARBO., 3 G FIBER,
4 G PRO.

DAILY VALUES
31% VIT. A, 24% VIT. C,
2% CALCIUM, 7% IRON

EXCHANGES
1 STARCH, ½ FAT

sesame zucchini

THESE SESAME- AND SOY-ACCENTED ZUCCHINI STRIPS ARE PARTICULARLY TASTY IN SUMMER WHEN YOUR GARDEN IS OVERFLOWING WITH THE POPULAR GREEN SQUASH.

2	shallots, halved lengthwise and thinly sliced
2	cloves garlic, minced
1	tablespoon cooking oil
2	medium zucchini, cut into bite-size strips
1	tablespoon sesame seeds, toasted
1	tablespoon soy sauce
1	teaspoon toasted sesame oil (optional)
⅛	teaspoon crushed red pepper

STEP 1 In a large skillet cook shallot and garlic in hot oil over medium heat for 30 seconds. Add zucchini; cook for 5 to 7 minutes more or just until vegetables are tender, stirring occasionally.

STEP 2 Add sesame seeds, soy sauce, sesame oil (if desired), and crushed red pepper. Cook and stir for 1 minute more.

START TO FINISH
15 MINUTES

MAKES
4 SERVINGS

NUTRITION FACTS PER SERVING
70 CAL., 5 G TOTAL FAT (1 G SAT. FAT), 0 MG CHOL., 239 MG SODIUM, 6 G CARBO., 1 G FIBER, 2 G PRO.

DAILY VALUES
6% VIT. A, 18% VIT. C, 4% CALCIUM, 5% IRON

EXCHANGES
1 VEGETABLE, 1 FAT

veggie mash

DO YOU HAVE KIDS WHO WON'T EAT THEIR VEGETABLES? HERE'S A BRILLIANT SOLUTION—DISGUISE THEM! WHIPPED UP WITH RICH AND CREAMY FRENCH ONION DIP, THIS MASH IS SO GOOD YOUR KIDS WILL BE ASKING FOR SECONDS.

PREP
15 MINUTES

COOK
15 MINUTES

MAKES
6 SERVINGS

3   cups sliced carrot (6 medium)
4   cups cubed peeled red potato (4 medium)
½   teaspoon salt
1   cup coarsely chopped broccoli
½   cup dairy sour cream French onion dip
½   teaspoon seasoned pepper

STEP 1   In a Dutch oven or large saucepan cook carrot, potato, and salt, covered, in enough boiling water to cover, about 15 minutes or until tender, adding broccoli the last 3 minutes of cooking.

STEP 2   Drain vegetables; return to pan. Mash vegetable mixture with a potato masher or beat with an electric mixer on low speed. Add dip and pepper; beat until light and fluffy.

NUTRITION FACTS
PER SERVING
137 CAL., 3 G TOTAL FAT
(2 G SAT. FAT), 0 MG CHOL.,
196 MG SODIUM, 25 G
CARBO., 4 G FIBER, 4 G PRO.

DAILY VALUES
313% VIT. A, 50% VIT. C,
4% CALCIUM, 9% IRON

EXCHANGES
1 VEGETABLE, 1 STARCH,
½ FAT

seeded dinner rolls

SPIFF UP PLAIN WHITE DINNER ROLLS BY GIVING THEM A COATING OF SESAME, POPPY, DILL, OR CARAWAY SEEDS.

2 tablespoons butter, melted
1 to 2 tablespoons mixed seeds (such as sesame seeds, poppy seeds, dill seeds, and caraway seeds)
6 frozen baked soft white dinner rolls
   Purchased garlic butter (optional)

STEP 1 Place melted butter in a small shallow dish. Place mixed seeds in another small shallow dish or spread on waxed paper. Dip tops of rolls into melted butter; dip into mixed seeds. Place rolls on a baking sheet.

STEP 2 Bake in a 375°F oven for 7 to 9 minutes or until hot. Serve warm. If desired, serve with garlic butter.

PREP
10 MINUTES

BAKE
7 MINUTES

OVEN
375°F

MAKES
6 ROLLS

NUTRITION FACTS
PER ROLL
154 CAL., 7 G TOTAL FAT
(2 G SAT. FAT), 11 MG CHOL.,
299 MG SODIUM,
18 G CARBO., 1 G FIBER,
4 G PRO.

DAILY VALUES
2% VIT. A, 6% IRON

EXCHANGES
1 STARCH, 1½ FAT

old-fashioned corn bread

THE NEXT TIME YOU SERVE STEW OR CHILI, BAKE A PAN OF THIS GOLDEN DOWN-HOME DELIGHT TO USE AS SCOOPERS AND DIPPERS. FOR THOSE WHO DON'T SCOOP OR DIP, PASS SOME HONEY TO DRIZZLE ON TOP.

PREP
10 MINUTES

BAKE
20 MINUTES

OVEN
425°F

MAKES
10 SERVINGS

	Nonstick cooking spray
1	cup yellow cornmeal
¾	cup all-purpose flour
2	tablespoons sugar
1½	teaspoons baking powder
¼	teaspoon baking soda
¼	teaspoon salt
¾	cup buttermilk or sour milk*
½	cup refrigerated or frozen egg product, thawed, or 2 beaten eggs
2	tablespoons cooking oil
	Yellow cornmeal (optional)

STEP 1 Coat a 9×1½-inch round baking pan or oven-going skillet with cooking spray. Set aside.

STEP 2 In a large bowl stir together 1 cup cornmeal, the flour, sugar, baking powder, baking soda, and salt. In a medium bowl stir together buttermilk, egg product, and oil.

STEP 3 Add buttermilk mixture all at once to flour mixture. Stir just until moistened. Spread batter in prepared pan. If desired, sprinkle with additional cornmeal.

STEP 4 Bake in a 425°F oven about 20 minutes or until golden. Cut into wedges and serve warm.

* To make ¾ cup sour milk, place 2¼ teaspoons lemon juice or vinegar in a glass measuring cup. Add enough milk to make ¾ cup total liquid; stir. Let mixture stand for 5 minutes before using.

NUTRITION FACTS PER SERVING
129 CAL., 3 G TOTAL FAT (1 G SAT. FAT), 1 MG CHOL., 190 MG SODIUM, 21 G CARBO., 1 G FIBER, 4 G PRO.

DAILY VALUES
2% VIT. A, 6% CALCIUM, 7% IRON

EXCHANGES
1 STARCH, ½ FAT

garlic & cheese foccacia

KEEP FROZEN BREAD DOUGH AND A FEW EXTRA INGREDIENTS ON HAND SO YOU CAN ENJOY A FRESHLY MADE ROUND OF FOCCACIA IN MINUTES—WITHOUT AN EXTRA TRIP TO THE BAKERY.

1   **16-ounce loaf frozen bread dough, thawed according to package directions**
1   **tablespoon olive oil**
1½   **teaspoons dried Italian seasoning, crushed**
4   **cloves garlic, minced**
1   **cup shredded pizza cheese (4 ounces)**

STEP 1   Lightly grease a 12- to 13-inch pizza pan; set aside. On a lightly floured surface, roll thawed bread dough into a 12- to 13-inch circle. Transfer dough to prepared pizza pan. With 2 fingers, make ½-inch-deep indentations all over the dough.

STEP 2   In a small bowl stir together oil, Italian seasoning, and garlic; brush over top of dough. Sprinkle with cheese. Bake in a 375°F oven for 18 to 20 minutes or until golden. Transfer to a wire rack; let cool. Cut into wedges to serve.

PREP
10 MINUTES

BAKE
18 MINUTES

OVEN
375°F

MAKES
8 SERVINGS

NUTRITION FACTS
PER SERVING
197 CAL., 5 G TOTAL FAT (2 G SAT. FAT), 10 MG CHOL., 95 MG SODIUM, 25 G CARBO., 0 G FIBER, 8 G PRO.

DAILY VALUES
3% VIT. A, 1% VIT. C, 16% CALCIUM, 2% IRON

EXCHANGES
2 STARCH, ½ HIGH-FAT MEAT

easy parmesan breadsticks

A NICE TOASTED-CHEESE FLAVOR MAKES THESE AN IRRESISTIBLE APPETIZER, ESPECIALLY IF YOU SERVE THEM WITH DIPPING SAUCE. FREEZE LEFTOVER BREADSTICKS—THAT WAY YOU'LL HAVE SOMETHING TO SERVE NEXT TIME HUNGER PANGS HIT BEFORE DINNER IS READY.

PREP
15 MINUTES

BAKE
10 MINUTES PER BATCH

OVEN
375°F

MAKES
12 TO 15 BREADSTICKS

1   12-ounce loaf baguette-style French bread
      Nonstick cooking spray
½   cup olive oil
¾   cup grated or finely shredded Parmesan cheese
      Dipping sauces, such as Red Pepper Sauce (see below) or marinara sauce
      Flavored oils, such as lemon, basil, or garlic (optional)

STEP 1 Cut bread crosswise in half or into quarters. Cut each piece in half lengthwise, then into ¼- to ½-inch strips. (It is helpful to cut bread so there is crust on each strip.)

STEP 2 Line a 15×10×1-inch baking pan with foil; lightly coat foil with cooking spray. Arrange half of the breadsticks in a single layer on prepared pan; drizzle with half of the oil. Using a spatula or tongs, carefully turn breadsticks to coat with oil. Sprinkle with half of the Parmesan cheese.

STEP 3 Bake in a 375°F oven for 10 to 12 minutes or until brown and crisp. Repeat with remaining breadsticks, oil, and cheese. Transfer to a large serving bowl or platter. Serve with dipping sauce and/or flavored oils, if desired.

TO STORE LEFTOVER BREADSTICKS Place breadsticks in a covered container and store at room temperature for 2 days or in the freezer for up to 1 month.

RED PEPPER SAUCE In a large skillet cook 4 red sweet peppers, coarsely chopped, and 2 shallots, chopped, in ¼ cup olive oil over medium heat about 10 minutes or until tender, stirring occasionally. Stir in ½ cup dry white wine; 4 cloves garlic, minced; 2 tablespoons snipped fresh Italian parsley; ½ teaspoon salt; and ¼ teaspoon black pepper. Bring mixture to boiling; reduce heat. Cover and simmer for 10 to 15 minutes or until peppers are very tender. Cool slightly. Transfer to a food processor. Add 2 tablespoons snipped fresh Italian parsley and 2 tablespoons olive oil; cover and process until almost smooth. Makes about 1¼ cups.

NUTRITION FACTS

PER BREADSTICK
179 CAL., 11 G TOTAL FAT
(2 G SAT. FAT), 4 MG CHOL.,
249 MG SODIUM,
15 G CARBO., 1 G FIBER,
4 G PRO.

DAILY VALUES
8% CALCIUM, 5% IRON

EXCHANGES
1 STARCH, 1½ FAT,
½ LEAN MEAT

currant & cream scones

THESE CLASSIC SCONES ARE EVERYTHING THEY SHOULD BE—RICH, FLAKY, AND TENDER. AND SINCE THEY'RE NOT TOO SWEET, THEY'RE VERSATILE. SWEETEN THEM WITH JAM FOR A TEATIME TREAT OR CUT THEM IN HALF, APPLY BUTTER, AND FILL WITH BAKED HAM FOR A LIGHT SANDWICH TO SERVE WITH SOUP.

PREP
15 MINUTES

BAKE
12 MINUTES

OVEN
350°F

MAKES
16 SCONES

2	cups all-purpose flour
½	cup granulated sugar
2½	teaspoons baking powder
¼	teaspoon salt
½	cup butter
½	cup dried currants or coarsely chopped dried tart cherries
½	cup half-and-half or light cream
1	tablespoon half-and-half or light cream
	Coarse sugar

STEP 1 In a large bowl stir together flour, ¼ cup sugar, the baking powder, and salt. Using a pastry blender, cut in butter until mixture resembles coarse crumbs. Stir in currants. Add ½ cup half-and-half, stirring just until flour mixture is moistened.

STEP 2 Turn dough out onto a lightly floured surface. Knead dough by folding and gently pressing for 6 to 8 strokes or just until dough holds together. Divide dough in half. Pat each half into a 6-inch circle. Cut each circle into 8 wedges.

STEP 3 Place wedges 1 inch apart on an ungreased baking sheet. Brush tops with 1 tablespoon half-and-half; sprinkle with coarse sugar.

STEP 4 Bake in a 350°F oven for 12 to 15 minutes or until bottoms are golden. Remove from baking sheet. Cool on a wire rack for 5 minutes. Serve warm.

NUTRITION FACTS
PER SCONE
158 CAL., 7 G TOTAL FAT
(4 G SAT. FAT), 18 MG CHOL.,
119 MG SODIUM,
22 G CARBO., 1 G FIBER,
2 G PRO.

DAILY VALUES
4% VIT. A, 3% CALCIUM,
5% IRON

EXCHANGES
1½ OTHER CARBO., 1½ FAT

buttermilk biscuits

THESE IRRESISTIBLE BISCUITS ARE GREAT FOR DIPPING INTO A CREAMY CHOWDER OR MOPPING UP THE LAST OF THE GRAVY. IF YOU HAVE ANY LEFT OVER AT THE END OF DINNER, THEY ALSO MAKE A DELECTABLE BREAKFAST TREAT WHEN SMEARED WITH HONEY OR JAM. IN FACT, YOU MAY WANT TO HIDE A COUPLE BEFORE DINNER, JUST SO YOU'LL BE SURE TO HAVE SOME THE NEXT MORNING.

PREP
10 MINUTES

BAKE
12 MINUTES

OVEN
425°F

MAKES
8 BISCUITS

2	cups all-purpose flour
2	teaspoons baking powder
1	teaspoon sugar
½	teaspoon baking soda
½	teaspoon salt
6	tablespoons butter, cut up
¾	cup buttermilk

STEP 1 In a large bowl stir together flour, baking powder, sugar, baking soda, and salt. Using a pastry blender, cut in butter until mixture resembles coarse crumbs. Make a well in the center of flour mixture. Add buttermilk all at once. Using a fork, stir just until moistened.

STEP 2 Turn dough out onto a lightly floured surface. Knead dough by folding and gently pressing for 3 to 4 strokes until smooth. Roll dough until ¾ inch thick. Cut with a floured 2½-inch biscuit cutter. If necessary, reroll scraps. Place biscuits 1 inch apart on an ungreased baking sheet.

STEP 3 Bake in a 425°F oven for 12 to 14 minutes or until golden. Remove biscuits from baking sheet and serve warm.

NUTRITION FACTS
PER BISCUIT
196 CAL., 10 G TOTAL FAT (5 G SAT. FAT), 25 MG CHOL., 373 MG SODIUM, 24 G CARBO., 1 G FIBER, 4 G PRO.

DAILY VALUES
6% VIT. A, 5% CALCIUM, 7% IRON

EXCHANGES
1½ STARCH, 1½ FAT

fudge cookies in chocolate cream

THIS IS THE BEST FAST-FIXIN' CHOCOLATE DESSERT YOU'LL EVER TASTE!

½	of an 8-ounce package cream cheese, softened
¼	cup chocolate-flavor syrup
1	teaspoon vanilla
½	cup whipping cream
6	fudge-covered chocolate sandwich cookies, chopped
2	fudge-covered chocolate sandwich cookies, halved

STEP 1 In a medium bowl beat cream cheese with an electric mixer on medium to high speed for 30 seconds. Beat in chocolate-flavor syrup and vanilla until well mixed. Add whipping cream; beat until fluffy. Fold in chopped cookies. Spoon into dessert dishes. Top with half-cookies.

START TO FINISH
10 MINUTES

MAKES
4 SERVINGS

NUTRITION FACTS
PER SERVING
426 CAL., 31 G TOTAL FAT
(15 G SAT. FAT), 72 MG
CHOL., 253 MG SODIUM,
39 G CARBO., 2 G FIBER,
5 G PRO.

DAILY VALUES
17% VIT. A, 4% CALCIUM,
12% IRON

EXCHANGES
2½ OTHER CARBO., 6 FAT

easy peanut butter bars

DESSERT ON A WEEKNIGHT? YOU BET! YOU'RE JUST A FEW MINUTES FROM POPPING THESE YUMMY BARS INTO THE OVEN FOR A SWEET AFTER-DINNER SURPRISE THAT WILL DELIGHT EVERYONE.

START TO FINISH
30 MINUTES

BAKE
20 MINUTES

OVEN
350°F

MAKES
32 BARS

1	cup packed brown sugar
½	cup peanut butter
¼	cup cooking oil
2	eggs
1	teaspoon baking powder
½	teaspoon baking soda
¼	teaspoon salt
¼	cup milk
1 ½	cups all-purpose flour
1 ¼	cups peanut butter-flavor pieces and/or semisweet chocolate pieces
½	cup coarsely chopped peanuts

STEP 1   Lightly grease a 13×9×2-inch baking pan; set aside. In a large bowl combine brown sugar, peanut butter, oil, eggs, baking powder, baking soda, and salt. Beat with a wooden spoon until combined. Stir in milk. Add flour, stirring until combined. Stir in about half of the peanut butter-flavor pieces. Spread dough in prepared pan. Sprinkle remaining pieces and peanuts over the top.

STEP 2   Bake in a 350°F oven for 20 to 25 minutes or until a wooden toothpick inserted near the center comes out clean. Cool in pan on a wire rack; cut into bars.

NUTRITION FACTS
PER BAR
155 CAL., 8 G TOTAL FAT
(3 G SAT. FAT), 13 MG CHOL.,
108 MG SODIUM,
17 G CARBO., 1 G FIBER,
5 G PRO.

DAILY VALUES
4% CALCIUM, 3% IRON

EXCHANGES
1 OTHER CARBO., 1½ FAT

chocolate-chocolate chip cookies

HOW CAN YOU IMPROVE THE EVER-POPULAR CHOCOLATE CHIP COOKIE? ADD COCOA POWDER TO THE COOKIE DOUGH FOR A RICH, FUDGY BASE THAT'S STUDDED WITH CHOCOLATE CHIPS FOR A CHOCOLATE LOVER'S BLOWOUT!

¾	cup all-purpose flour
⅓	cup unsweetened cocoa powder
½	teaspoon baking soda
¼	teaspoon salt
½	cup butter
3	ounces unsweetened chocolate, coarsely chopped
1	cup sugar
2	eggs
½	teaspoon vanilla
1	cup semisweet chocolate pieces
2	tablespoons toffee pieces (optional)

STEP 1 Stir together flour, cocoa powder, baking soda, and salt; set aside. Place butter and unsweetened chocolate in a medium microwave-safe bowl. Microwave, uncovered, on 100 percent power (high) for 1 minute; stir. Microwave 15 to 45 seconds more until chocolate is melted, stirring every 15 seconds.

STEP 2 Stir sugar into melted chocolate mixture. Add eggs, one at a time, beating with a wooden spoon just until combined. Stir in vanilla. Add flour mixture, stirring just until combined. Stir in chocolate pieces and, if desired, toffee pieces.

STEP 3 Drop dough by rounded teaspoons 2 inches apart onto an ungreased cookie sheet. Bake in a 350°F oven for 9 to 10 minutes or until tops look dull, not shiny. Transfer to a wire rack; let cool.

PREP
15 MINUTES

BAKE
9 MINUTES PER BATCH

OVEN
350°F

MAKES
ABOUT 30 COOKIES

NUTRITION FACTS
PER COOKIE
112 CAL., 7 G TOTAL FAT
(4 G SAT. FAT), 23 MG CHOL.,
120 MG SODIUM,
13 G CARBO., 1 G FIBER,
2 G PRO.

DAILY VALUES
3% VIT. A, 2% CALCIUM,
4% IRON

EXCHANGES
1 OTHER CARBO., 1 FAT

cherry trifles

ALTHOUGH YOU CAN PREPARE THEM IN A FLASH, THESE CHERRY TRIFLES ALSO ARE A GREAT MAKE-AHEAD CHOICE FOR DAYS WHEN YOU KNOW YOU'LL BE PRESSED FOR TIME DURING THE DINNER HOUR.

START TO FINISH
10 MINUTES

MAKES
4 SERVINGS

1   cup plain lowfat yogurt
2   tablespoons cherry preserves
½   teaspoon vanilla
2   cups angel food cake cubes (about 4 ounces purchased cake)
1   15-ounce can pitted dark sweet cherries, drained
¼   cup purchased glazed walnuts, chopped

STEP 1   In a small bowl stir together yogurt, cherry preserves, and vanilla; set aside.

STEP 2   Divide 1 cup of the cake cubes among four parfait glasses or dessert dishes. Top cake cubes in parfait glasses with half of the dark sweet cherries, then spoon half of the yogurt mixture over top. Sprinkle with half of the nuts. Repeat layers. Serve immediately or cover and chill for up to 4 hours.

NUTRITION FACTS
PER SERVING
280 CAL., 7 G TOTAL FAT
(2 G SAT. FAT), 5 MG CHOL.,
198 MG SODIUM,
51 G CARBO., 2 G FIBER,
7 G PRO.

DAILY VALUES
5% VIT. A, 9% VIT. C,
15% CALCIUM, 4% IRON

EXCHANGES
3 OTHER CARBO., 1½ FAT,
½ FRUIT

sticky lemon pinwheels

CREAMY, LUSCIOUS LEMON CURD IS A WONDERFULLY VERSATILE INGREDIENT TO HAVE ON HAND. IT BRINGS A TOUCH OF THE SUN TO THESE PINWHEELS WITH ITS CHEERFUL YELLOW COLOR AND ITS RICH AND TANGY FLAVOR. SERVE THESE PINWHEELS AT HOLIDAY BREAKFASTS, SPECIAL BRUNCHES, AND SUMMER TEA PARTIES.

⅓   cup purchased lemon curd or orange curd
¼   cup sliced almonds, toasted
1   11-ounce package (12) refrigerated breadsticks

STEP 1   Grease an 8×1½-inch round baking pan; set aside. In a small bowl stir together lemon curd and almonds. Spread mixture evenly over bottom of prepared baking pan.

STEP 2   Separate, but do not uncoil, the breadsticks. Arrange coiled dough over lemon mixture in baking pan.

STEP 3   Bake in a 375°F oven for 15 to 18 minutes or until golden brown. Immediately invert pan onto a platter. Spread any remaining lemon mixture in the pan over the pinwheels. Serve warm.

PREP
10 MINUTES

BAKE
15 MINUTES

OVEN
375°F

MAKES
12 PINWHEELS

NUTRITION FACTS
PER PINWHEEL
118 CAL., 4 G TOTAL FAT
(1 G SAT. FAT), 7 MG CHOL.,
200 MG SODIUM,
19 G CARBO., 2 G FIBER,
3 G PRO.

DAILY VALUES
1% CALCIUM, 5% IRON

EXCHANGES
1 STARCH, 1 FAT

lemon meringue cookie tarts

REFRESHING LEMON PUDDING IS THE QUICK AND EASY BASE FOR
THESE DARLING AND DELICIOUS MERINGUE COOKIE TARTS.

2	3.5- to 4-ounce containers lemon pudding (prepared pudding cups), chilled
1	teaspoon finely shredded lemon peel (optional)
¼	of an 8-ounce container frozen whipped dessert topping, thawed
12	vanilla-flavor bite-size meringue cookies
6	3½-inch graham cracker crumb tart shells (one 4-ounce package)

STEP 1   In a small bowl stir together pudding and, if desired, lemon peel. Fold in whipped topping. Coarsely crush six of the cookies. Spoon half of the pudding mixture into tart shells; sprinkle with crushed cookies. Top with remaining pudding mixture and whole cookies.

lemon cheesecake mousse

FOR A FANCY PRESENTATION, LAYER THE MOUSSE WITH CRUSHED GINGERSNAPS IN PRETTY PARFAIT GLASSES.

1   8-ounce package cream cheese, softened
½   cup frozen lemonade concentrate, thawed
½   teaspoon vanilla
1   8-ounce container frozen whipped dessert topping, thawed
       Purchased gingersnaps (optional)

STEP 1   In a medium bowl beat cream cheese with an electric mixer on medium to high speed for 30 seconds. Beat in lemonade concentrate and vanilla. Fold in whipped topping. Divide among dessert dishes. If desired, serve with gingersnaps.

START TO FINISH
10 MINUTES

MAKES
6 SERVINGS

NUTRITION FACTS
PER SERVING
282 CAL., 20 G TOTAL FAT
(15 G SAT. FAT), 42 MG
CHOL., 113 MG SODIUM,
21 G CARBO., 0 G FIBER,
3 G PRO.

DAILY VALUES
10% VIT. A, 7% VIT. C,
3% CALCIUM, 3% IRON

EXCHANGES
1½ OTHER CARBO., 4 FAT

crepes with maple-pear sauce

SWEET AND TENDER SLICES OF JUICY PEAR SIMMERED WITH
MAPLE SYRUP MAKE A GLORIOUS FILLING FOR CREPES. TOASTED
PECANS SPRINKLED ON TOP ADD A CRUNCHY FINAL TOUCH.

START TO FINISH
10 MINUTES

MAKES
5 (2-CREPE) SERVINGS

1   15.25-ounce can pear slices, drained

1   cup pure maple syrup or maple-flavor syrup

1   4- to 4.5-ounce package (10 crepes) ready-to-use crepes

½   cup chopped pecans, toasted

STEP 1   In a small saucepan combine pear slices and maple syrup; heat through over medium-low heat.

STEP 2   Meanwhile, fold crepes into quarters; arrange on a serving platter. Spoon hot pear mixture over crepes. Sprinkle with pecans.

NUTRITION FACTS

PER SERVING

344 CAL., 10 G TOTAL FAT
(1 G SAT. FAT), 36 MG CHOL.,
77 MG SODIUM, 63 G CARBO.,
2 G FIBER, 3 G PRO.

DAILY VALUES

2% VIT. A, 1% VIT. C,
7% CALCIUM, 9% IRON

EXCHANGES

3½ OTHER CARBO., 2½ FAT,
½ FRUIT

quick rice pudding

NOTHING SAYS "COMFORT FOOD" BETTER THAN A WARM AND CREAMY RICE PUDDING. AND NOTHING SAYS "SIMPLE" BETTER THAN STARTING WITH A CONVENIENT MIX. ADD JUST A FEW WELL-CHOSEN STIR-INS FOR A LOT MORE PLEASURE!

1	4.1-ounce box French vanilla rice pudding mix
2	cups milk
½	teaspoon ground ginger
½	cup tropical dried fruit bits or dried fruit bits
¼	cup chopped macadamia nuts

STEP 1   In a 2-quart saucepan stir together rice pudding mix with seasoning packet, milk, and ginger. Cook according to package directions. Remove from heat; stir in dried fruit. Cover; let stand for 5 minutes. Stir again. Divide among dessert bowls. Top each serving with nuts.

PREP
25 MINUTES

STAND
5 MINUTES

MAKES
4 SERVINGS

NUTRITION FACTS
PER SERVING
294 CAL., 9 G TOTAL FAT
(3 G SAT. FAT), 10 MG CHOL.,
181 MG SODIUM,
47 G CARBO., 3 G FIBER,
6 G PRO.

DAILY VALUES
8% VIT. A, 1% VIT. C,
19% CALCIUM, 4% IRON

EXCHANGES
2½ OTHER CARBO., 2 FAT,
½ MILK

quick apple crisp

THIS SIMPLE VERSION OF AN ALL-TIME FAVORITE WILL APPEAL TO BUSY COOKS WHO WANT TO SERVE DELICIOUS DESSERTS WITHOUT A LOT OF PREPARATION.

START TO FINISH
15 MINUTES

MAKES
4 SERVINGS

1	21-ounce can apple pie filling
¼	cup dried cranberries
¼	teaspoon ground ginger or cinnamon
¼	teaspoon vanilla
1	cup granola
1	pint vanilla ice cream

STEP 1 In a medium saucepan stir together pie filling, dried cranberries, and ginger. Heat through over medium-low heat, stirring occasionally. Remove from heat; stir in vanilla. Spoon into bowls. Top each serving with granola. Serve with ice cream.

NUTRITION FACTS
PER SERVING
507 CAL., 15 G TOTAL FAT
(8 G SAT. FAT), 68 MG CHOL.,
113 MG SODIUM,
88 G CARBO., 6 G FIBER,
9 G PRO.

DAILY VALUES
10% VIT. A, 2% VIT. C,
11% CALCIUM, 14% IRON

EXCHANGES
5 OTHER CARBO., 3 FAT,
1 FRUIT

peach-coconut mousse

AS AN ALTERNATIVE TO THE COCONUT TOPPING, SPRINKLE FINELY CHOPPED CRYSTALLIZED GINGER ON TOP.

2	tablespoons sugar
1 ½	teaspoons unflavored gelatin
¼	cup cold water
1	16-ounce package frozen unsweetened peach slices, completely thawed and drained
½	teaspoon vanilla
½	of an 8-ounce container frozen fat-free whipped dessert topping, thawed
2	tablespoons coconut, toasted
	Fresh mint sprigs (optional)

STEP 1 In a small saucepan stir together sugar and gelatin. Stir in cold water. Cook and stir over low heat until gelatin and sugar dissolve. Remove from heat.

STEP 2 Place peaches in a blender container; add gelatin mixture and vanilla. Cover and blend until smooth. Pour peach mixture into a large bowl. Cover and chill for 1 hour. Fold whipped topping into fruit mixture. Spoon into dessert dishes.

STEP 3 Cover and chill about 3 hours or until set. To serve, sprinkle with coconut. If desired, garnish with fresh mint.

PREP
25 MINUTES

CHILL
1 HOUR + 3 HOURS

MAKES
6 SERVINGS

NUTRITION FACTS
PER SERVING
94 CAL., 1 G TOTAL FAT
(1 G SAT. FAT), 0 MG CHOL.,
20 MG SODIUM, 20 G CARBO.,
2 G FIBER, 1 G PRO.

DAILY VALUES
8% VIT. A, 8% VIT. C,
1% IRON

EXCHANGES
1½ FRUIT

hot taffy apple pita pizza

IF YOU LOVE CARAMEL APPLES, YOU WILL ADORE THIS CREATIVE VARIATION OF THE SWEET FRUIT TREAT ON A STICK. IT'S ALSO MUCH EASIER TO EAT!

PREP
15 MINUTES

BAKE
10 MINUTES

OVEN
400°F

MAKES
8 SERVINGS

2	pita bread rounds
½	cup purchased caramel dip for apples
¼	cup dairy sour cream
1	20-ounce can sliced apples, well drained
1	tablespoon butter, melted
2	tablespoons sugar
¼	teaspoon ground cinnamon
⅓	cup chopped pecans
	Vanilla or cinnamon ice cream (optional)

STEP 1   Place pita bread rounds on an ungreased baking sheet. In a small bowl combine ¼ cup of the caramel dip and the sour cream; spread over pitas. Top with drained apples. Drizzle with melted butter. In a small bowl stir together sugar and cinnamon; sprinkle over apples. Drizzle with remaining ¼ cup caramel dip;* sprinkle with pecans.

STEP 2   Bake in a 400°F oven about 10 minutes or until heated through. Cut each round into quarters. Serve warm. If desired, serve with ice cream.

*TEST KITCHEN TIP If the caramel dip is too thick to drizzle, heat it in a saucepan or microwave oven just until it thins slightly. An easy way to drizzle the dip is to spoon it into a plastic bag, snip off one corner, and squeeze the bag.

NUTRITION FACTS
PER SERVING
233 CAL., 10 G TOTAL FAT (3 G SAT. FAT), 9 MG CHOL., 142 MG SODIUM, 36 G CARBO., 2 G FIBER, 3 G PRO.

DAILY VALUES
2% VIT. A, 1% VIT. C, 4% CALCIUM, 4% IRON

EXCHANGES
2 OTHER CARBO., 1½ FAT, 1 STARCH

banana & caramel cream pies

A DRIZZLE OF GOLDEN CARAMEL ADDS A CREAMY RICHNESS TO
THESE IRRESISTIBLE MINIATURE CREAM PIES.

1   medium banana, sliced

6   3½-inch graham cracker tart shells (one 4-ounce package)

2   tablespoons caramel ice cream topping

2   3.5- to 4-ounce containers vanilla pudding (prepared pudding cups), chilled

¼   of an 8-ounce container frozen whipped dessert topping, thawed

STEP 1 Divide banana slices among tart shells; drizzle with caramel
topping. Spoon chilled pudding into tart shells. Top with whipped topping.
Serve immediately or cover and chill for up to 8 hours.

START TO FINISH
15 MINUTES

MAKES
6 SERVINGS

NUTRITION FACTS
PER SERVING
229 CAL., 9 G TOTAL FAT
(3 G SAT. FAT), 0 MG CHOL.,
215 MG SODIUM,
34 G CARBO., 1 G FIBER,
2 G PRO.

DAILY VALUES
1% VIT. A, 3% VIT. C,
3% CALCIUM, 3% IRON

EXCHANGES
2 OTHER CARBO., 2 FAT

Metric Information

The charts on this page provide a guide for converting measurements from the U.S. customary system, used throughout this book, to the metric system.

Product Differences

Most of the ingredients called for in the recipes in this book are available in most countries. However, some are known by different names. Here are some common American ingredients and their possible counterparts:

- Sugar (white) is granulated, fine granulated, or castor sugar.
- Powdered sugar is icing sugar.
- All-purpose flour is enriched, bleached or unbleached white household flour. When self-rising flour is used in place of all-purpose flour in a recipe that calls for leavening, omit the leavening agent (baking soda or baking powder) and salt.
- Light-colored corn syrup is golden syrup.
- Cornstarch is cornflour.
- Baking soda is bicarbonate of soda.
- Vanilla or vanilla extract is vanilla essence.
- Bell peppers are capsicums.
- Golden raisins are sultanas.

Volume & Weight

The United States traditionally uses cup measures for liquid and solid ingredients. The chart below shows the approximate imperial and metric equivalents. If you are accustomed to weighing solid ingredients, the following approximate equivalents will be helpful.

- 1 cup butter, castor sugar, or rice = 8 ounces = ½ pound = 250 grams
- 1 cup flour = 4 ounces = ¼ pound = 125 grams
- 1 cup icing sugar = 5 ounces = 150 grams

Canadian and U.S. volume for a cup measure is 8 fluid ounces (237 ml), but the standard metric equivalent is 250 ml.

1 British imperial cup is 10 fluid ounces.

In Australia, 1 tablespoon equals 20 ml, and there are 4 teaspoons in the Australian tablespoon.

Spoon measures are used for smaller amounts of ingredients. Although the size of the tablespoon varies slightly in different countries, for practical purposes and for recipes in this book, a straight substitution is all that's necessary. Measurements made using cups or spoons should be level unless stated otherwise.

Common Weight Range Replacements

Imperial / U.S.	Metric
½ ounce	15 g
1 ounce	25 g or 30 g
4 ounces (¼ pound)	115 g or 125 g
8 ounces (½ pound)	225 g or 250 g
16 ounces (1 pound)	450 g or 500 g
1¼ pounds	625 g
1½ pounds	750 g
2 pounds or 2¼ pounds	1,000 g or 1 Kg

Oven Temperature Equivalents

Fahrenheit Setting	Celsius Setting*	Gas Setting
300°F	150°C	Gas Mark 2 (very low)
325°F	160°C	Gas Mark 3 (low)
350°F	180°C	Gas Mark 4 (moderate)
375°F	190°C	Gas Mark 5 (moderate)
400°F	200°C	Gas Mark 6 (hot)
425°F	220°C	Gas Mark 7 (hot)
450°F	230°C	Gas Mark 8 (very hot)
475°F	240°C	Gas Mark 9 (very hot)
500°F	260°C	Gas Mark 10 (extremely hot)
Broil	Broil	Grill

*Electric and gas ovens may be calibrated using celsius. However, for an electric oven, increase celsius setting 10 to 20 degrees when cooking above 160°C. For convection or forced air ovens (gas or electric) lower the temperature setting 25°F/10°C when

Baking Pan Sizes

Imperial / U.S.	Metric
9×1½-inch round cake pan	22- or 23×4-cm (1.5 L)
9×1½-inch pie plate	22- or 23×4-cm (1 L)
8×8×2-inch square cake pan	20×5-cm (2 L)
9×9×2-inch square cake pan	22- or 23×4.5-cm (2.5 L)
11×7×1½-inch baking pan	28×17×4-cm (2 L)
2-quart rectangular baking pan	30×19×4.5-cm (3 L)
13×9×2-inch baking pan	34×22×4.5-cm (3.5 L)
15×10×1 inch jelly roll pan	40×25×2-cm
9×5×3-inch loaf pan	23×13×8-cm (2 L)
2-quart casserole	2 L

U.S. / Standard Metric Equivalents

⅛ teaspoon = 0.5 ml

¼ teaspoon = 1 ml

½ teaspoon = 2 ml

1 teaspoon = 5 ml

1 tablespoon = 15 ml

2 tablespoons = 25 ml

¼ cup = 2 fluid ounces = 50 ml

⅓ cup = 3 fluid ounces = 75 ml

½ cup = 4 fluid ounces = 125 ml

⅔ cup = 5 fluid ounces = 150 ml

¾ cup = 6 fluid ounces = 175 ml

1 cup = 8 fluid ounces = 250 ml

2 cups = 1 pint = 500 ml

1 quart = 1 litre